HITLER'S
SECOND ARMY

HITLER'S
SECOND ARMY
THE WAFFEN SS

Edmund L. Blandford

Motorbooks International
Publishers & Wholesalers ®

This edition first published in 1995 by Motorbooks International,
Publishers & Wholesalers, PO Box 2, 729 Prospect Avenue,
Osceola, WI 54020, USA.

© Edmund Blandford, 1994

Previously published by Airlife Publishing Ltd., Shrewsbury, England, 1994

Library of Congress Cataloging-in-Publication Data is available

ISBN 0-7603-0021-6

Printed and bound in England.

CONTENTS

INTRODUCTION

Perhaps no army in history has emerged with a reputation quite like that of the force known by the two letters 'SS'.

This work is an attempted objective account of the 'second army' formed by men whose goals were entirely military and experimental, soldiers with ideas very different to their political masters. Unlike most other works on this often controversial subject, this effort includes unique testimony by the men involved, both as organizers and combat soldiers who experienced in their youth some of the biggest and most intense battles of the Second World War. These collected post-war accounts have to be an essential ingredient in such a history; the quoting of copious 'Himmler documents' may appear academic but it is a sure way to obtain a distorted picture. Apart from which, in view of the well known accusations levelled at these élite troops it is quite unjust to ignore their version of events, they deserve a fair hearing if only for the sake of a factual history.

Edmund L. Blandford

'A small band of the best and most determined is far more valuable than a large mass of camp followers.'

Adolf Hitler in 1926

'First, there is loyalty, God be praised, we have never had a single case of treason in our ranks.'

'Every man who joins the SS must know, that at any moment, he may be mortally wounded.'

Heinrich Himmler, speaking to SS generals at Poznan 4 October 1943

'Men like Steiner and later Eicke . . . These were the people I most identified with and we often discussed how we could organize a soldierly force, an army along very different lines who would be superbly trained in a new way.'

Sepp Dietrich post-war

CHAPTER ONE

Both the SA brownshirt army and the later-established élite guard SS owe their origins to the large communist organization which burgeoned in Germany after World War One. The armies of the right and left were born in times of economic and political ferment when that nation's affairs were in a state of great flux and when violence was rife. The multiplicity of political parties, but above all that of the Reds resulted in the emergence of counter forces, most notably the Nazi brownshirts who were used by Adolf Hitler as a stepping stone to political power.

It has not been sufficiently recognized outside Germany how powerful the communists had become in the post-war period; it was the future Chancellor of a later era, Konrad Adenauer, who said in 1919:

> 'Germany is in grave danger of falling to Bolshevism.'

The communists were a large, well organized party who commanded considerable support among the lower classes. Their propaganda was powerful, based on the teachings of Marx and Lenin, but to most Germans it seemed to aim at bloody revolution, with the elimination of the middle, upper classes and intelligentsia as the first aim. Whatever support the Reds received from the hopeful, less privileged, there were very many Germans who lived in fear of a Bolshevik takeover. Worst fears seemed realized when in some places the Bolsheviks actually gained power and set up the first 'soviets; their success was short lived, a combination of army and right-wing factions ousted them in bloody clashes which put paid, temporarily to the Red menace in those areas. It was in this atmosphere that the leader of the new National Socialist German Workers Party (the NSDAP) felt obliged to form a small troop to act as a personal protection squad and *Stabswache*, or headquarters guard in Munich.

Josef 'Sepp' Dietrich was one of Hitler's earliest supporters, one of those men so impressed with him that he offered his services. Dietrich has been variously described as an 'ex-butcher', a 'chucker-out', an 'uneducated bully', 'Hitler's chauffeur' and 'private detective', while the eminent American Berlin correspondent William Shirer, referred to him as one of the most brutal men in the Nazi Third Reich.

Born in Bavaria, Dietrich emerged as a small, tough character with a forceful, outgoing personality, and while totally different in one respect to his contemporary Ernst Roehm, whom he later shot, there is no doubt that both men were typical NCO types. Both had seen army service during the war, and although Roehm achieved officer status he remained an NCO at heart; Dietrich ended his war as a sergeant in the new tank troops. But, apart from his sexual perversion, Roehm was a danger to Hitler and probably Germany, so according to Nazi realities had to be eliminated. Thereafter his name and face were expunged from all publications, even the friendly, comradely inscriptions on the 'honour daggers' presented by him were removed.

Dietrich has told how he came to join up with Hitler:

'I joined the Nazi movement because it seemed to be the best way to counter the Reds and to try and effect some radical improvement in our country's situation. I had been a Sergeant in the tank arm at the end of the Great War and had seen enough horrors to know that we should try to avoid such a conflict in future. I met Hitler in Munich and saw at once that he was far and away the best speaker we had ever heard; wherever he spoke he captivated his audiences, not all saw eye to eye with his ideas and statements, I did not myself. But there was something about the man and his ability which laid hold on me. So I offered him my small services, such as they were. He was rather short of real followers, though this was to change later of course. We had a heart to heart talk and he told me that I could be of most use to him by way of protecting him from those of the far left who would likely try to kill him. This was a very real threat at the time for the communists, or Bolsheviks as we called them, were by far the largest political party with real strength; they were uniformed and armed. By that I mean they usually carried cudgels or arms of some sort and were not slow to use them.

'I agreed to become Hitler's personal bodyguard, but very soon we organized a Stabswache of some six men who had the muscle to intervene if any brutality threatened. Later on we increased the number to a round dozen or so as some of the men had homes and families to go to. In my case I had forsaken my own family to become a full-time companion to Hitler, so inevitably I got to know him very well with all his quirks — and there were some. But he had an iron determination such as I had never seen before, and I could see that properly directed this would take him far in politics.'

Dietrich did not become Hitler's chauffeur at this time, that post was occupied by Julius Schreck, another close confidant and friend of the leader. And there came others, of course, in increasing numbers who tied themselves to Hitler.

Dietrich:

'Unfortunately, there were others who saw him as a man they could manipulate. I refer to Roehm and his clique, and these had to be guarded against. Hitler had thrown in with the brownshirts I believe for one reason only — he needed the numbers to offset the Red menace. It was no use at all having a political party in those days unless you could march the streets waving flags and holding *bigger meetings, no one would take the slightest notice of you. So Hitler saw, quite rightly, that have to columns of brown uniformed men marching with him and waving a particular banner would be the answer. This is why he threw in with Roehm's crowd, but I don't believe it was anything more than a temporary arrangement.*

'In my case, I was never a member of that band, even though the uniform I and my comrades were obliged to wear was all too similar. But we soon made our own changes and since we wanted something distinctive we chose the skull and crossbones. Various interpretations can be put on this, but I do not recall anything of special or sinister significance being attached to it at all. I cannot recall how we half-dozen arrived at this decision, but I know various symbols were put forward, but the skull and crossbones seemed to be the most distinctive. It did not, I am sure, act as a warning to others of what they might expect, I can reiterate that. It had no sinister connotations and of course had been used by various military formations before.

'Since we were in fact Hitler's protection squad the word 'schutz' seemed right for us, and 'staffel' or the other word was added. I know at one time we were called the Sturmstaffel, *but this did not last long.*

'Hitler was of course a little woolly-headed, his will was that strong that it overrode his ability to plan carefully. He did not, despite other great abilities, have a planner's mind, he worked on raw emotions and enormous will-power to force through his ideas via others.'

The Stabswache of 1923 evolved into a larger unit, but at the time of the ill-planned and abortive putsch of November the small unit was known as the *Stosstrupp Adolf Hitler*. As such its members, clad in a motley garb of kepis, odd tunics, greatcoats and raincoats, some wearing steel helmets, with the Reich's war flag and NSDAP banners, attempted to take over the administration in Munich. As Dietrich remarked:

'So the Munich putsch failed simply because he had not planned any detail, he had no idea what to do, so that was that.'

The failed Nazi uprising cost Hitler a surprisingly short time in jail and the banning of his organization, but he made use of his time in Landsberg to consult with followers and write his political testament, the notoriously turgid *Mein Kampf*, or *My Struggle*, a book which would bring him some royalties later but remain read by only a comparative few. The ban on his activities was soon lifted so he started to work again to rebuild his organization, and here testimony diverges as to just who helped to re-start the SS squad; Julius Schreck is alleged to have been responsible for the assembling of three dozen, utterly reliable, hand-picked men.
Dietrich:

'When Hitler came out of jail I met him again and we started afresh. I could see that he was determined as ever, and I agreed with others to reform his HQ

guard. But once again he threw in with that rascal Roehm and his gang, so my ideas of trying along different lines were frustrated. We gathered pace however, Hitler found supporters and began opening up offices all over Germany. This led to the forming of more and more SS squads, and we insisted that no matter how many brownshirts there were our people would remain a very, very select bunch and not mere roughnecks.'

Naturally, Hitler became known beyond his own stamping ground of Munich once he expanded his activities, and one of the first SS squads to be formed outside Bavaria was in Berlin. As Dietrich has mentioned, the opening up of political offices across Germany meant the forming of more and more protection squads, especially in those areas where the Reds were already well entrenched. Roehm's brownshirts had long been established beyond the confines of Bavaria, some units setting up as early as 1921 in places such as Hannover in Westfalia.

The organizers of the SS squads, men like Dietrich, Schreck and Berchtold etc, had introduced elements of black into their rigout, the black kepi with its silver skull and bones, a black necktie over the old *braunhemd* shirt, black breeches tucked into black high boots to replace the outmoded puttees. Soon their all-black uniforms would become symbolic of the SS, enlivened by the red-white and black on the swastika armbands.

By the second anniversary of the failed putsch in Munich, the force had officially become known simply by the term 'SS', and had adopted the double runic symbol, the solar emblem of victory, the double lightning flash, both as its collar emblem and henceforth in all written and published literature; even the typewriters were to have this sign fitted to their keyboards. Its course was now set to gain an unsavoury reputation, even though there were motives unconnected with the terror later attributed to it:

'I realize that the SS in their black uniform gained a very bad reputation (Dietrich has said), and were looked upon as thugs, but this was very far from the case. Certainly, because of the situation at the time they had to know how to look after themselves physically and eventually how to shoot a pistol, though initially they were unarmed. Because of this some men paid with their lives — shot by the opposition. It was no democracy, but a case of the toughest winning.

'As for the fledgling democratic parties, they were all very well, but they failed to solve Germany's problems, and in any case in that era we needed a strong central leadership. A bunch of willing but weak democratic politicians could not combat the Reds who had actually taken over everything in some districts in Germany. It is worth mentioning that the Bolsheviks modelled their ideas on the Soviet system which began with not only the murdering of the royal family but thousands of intellectuals and middle-class people who had contributed so much to Russian society. We were honour bound to prevent any such catastrophe happening in Germany. It was despicable that fellow Germans could lend themselves to such an ideology.'

It is perfectly clear from talking to Germans who were around at the time that one view above all became paramount in this period: despite what happened subsequently, Hitler and his Nazis had indeed saved Germany from the horrors of Bolshevism and the Soviet system.

If Julius Schreck did command the SS then he soon relinquished the job to Josef Berchtold who had been off duty, having been wounded in the 1923 uprising. This change took place in 1926, by which time the SS numbered some 1,000 men. In July of that year some of the first signs of Nazi liturgy emerged when Hitler handed over the now sacred *Blutfahne* or 'blood banner' to the care of the SS, this being the swastika flag carried by the plotters in their march in Munich on 9 November 1923.

Sepp Dietrich has said that the funds resulting from Hitler's gains in the late 1920s enabled him to set up his SS organization on a national scale. There is no reason to doubt that whoever ran the office in this period, it was Dietrich who did most of the legwork in expanding the SS. Which is perhaps why it is said he was disappointed and irritated later when Paul Hausser was elected to head an SS Inspectorate and oversee the leadership schools. But while Dietrich was running around Germany doing the donkey work, others — or one man in particular — stepped in as Hitler's favourite, so gaining Hitler's ear with his schemes and theories that the Fuehrer appointed him 'Reichsfuehrer SS'.

'Unfortunately' Dietrich says, 'it came to be headed by Himmler, a rather feeble type of man who did however have a great organizing ability insofar as he was able to envisage things and set them down on paper. More importantly, he had Hitler's ear with a great deal of racial nonsense concerning the Jews which was music to Hitler, which was why he got along so well with 'treue Heini'. Otherwise, Himmler was a very weak type of fellow, almost effeminate in some ways, despite the fact that he had done a spell of military service which he liked to exaggerate as if he had fought at the front which was untrue. Frankly, I despised him, but I was stuck with him and he came to lean on me heavily for the real organizing. It is all very well to set out theories on paper, but the legwork has to be done by men with energy and determination. In other words, Himmler was a clerk of rather grand proportions. It was unfortunate that he became my political master, and though we of the military tried to distance ourselves from his kind we never fully succeeded until it was too late.'

The first rumblings of discontent between the old brownshirt leadership and Hitler now began. Ernst Roehm had temporarily lost control of his army to Captain Franz von Pfeffer who strongly objected to the exclusivity of the new SS. In the wrangle that followed Lieutenant Berchtold resigned, to be replaced by another veteran of the Strosstrupp days, Erhard Heiden, not to be confused with Konrad Heiden, a man who had opposed Hitler from the start and later fled to the United States where he wrote a notable work on these early days.

The SS now became even more restricted, its numbers fell to a mere 280 and it adopted the motto:

'Nobility is seen, not heard.'

This somewhat pretentious view of themselves as some kind of new upper caste and a breed apart was evident long before Himmler climbed into the saddle. While the SA men kept order at political meetings with their fists or anything else that came to hand if necessary, the small SS squads stood in front of the speaker's podium, their only task his protection. The SS man did not carry arms, he was not permitted to argue or brawl in public, his bearing and behaviour had to be exemplary. Unlike the SA revolutionaries, they were not asked to go out into the streets and among the working class, attempting to explain National Socialism, or win recruits or collect funds. Yet, the SS man was expected to carry out the most humdrum tasks, and any small infringement of the rules of his order brought instant dismissal. It is said that in three years (before Himmler came to power) only a further 30 men were allowed into the SS, but this hardly jells with Dietrich's account of an expanding organization across Germany.

All this undoubted exclusiveness was carried through by Erhard Heiden, who according to his prejudiced namesake was a 'stool pigeon of the worst sort' — ie, an informer, not to be trusted. It was the former who saw the SS as 'the New Guard of Germany', likening them to the élite guards of both ancient and more recent times, from the Persians to Frederick the Great whose 'lange Kerls' were allegedly seven feet tall. Here we have the first signs of a very different direction being taken, the germ of a new Praetorian Guard along military lines, the forerunner of the coming *Verfuegungs Truppen* and Waffen-SS, and, as we shall see the old *Schutzstaffel* squads were to be split into two completely different camps. On the one hand would develop the repressive political policemen and murder squads under the obsessive grand clerk and inquisitor-in-chief, Heinrich Himmler; in the other camp a small group of ex-soldiers whose only interest lay in setting up a rather special kind of army.

Hitler had indeed turned to 'treue Heini' for, whatever his notions, Erhard Heiden lacked the flair for large organizing. Dietrich was good in this role, but in Himmler the Fuehrer found a man who could not only confirm all his own pet theories and prejudices picked up from his hungry days in Vienna, but join with him in the grand design for the East. He could also help to set up a nationwide network of political reliables, men anxious for whatever reason to side with the new master.

Himmler had undergone some military training during the war, including a machine-gun course, but to his chagrin had arrived at the Western Front just as the cease-fire took place, so saw no action. He was thus robbed of the chance to become a war veteran in fact, even though his claims were to be otherwise.

Himmler came from a respectable, middle-class family, rural Bavarian stock, though his father had worked as a private tutor and had once taught a prince of the local aristocracy. With the war ending so badly for Germany, Himmler junior had, like so many other ex-soldiers, taken up with one of the right wing veterans' organizations, become embroiled with the National Socialists, and in his spare time indulged in a little chicken farming. As a political helper, he was employed by the Strasser brothers, Otto and Gregor, touring the countryside on a motorcycle combination, drumming up support among the folk he loved. But when the Strassers left Bavaria to begin organizing in North Germany, Himmler turned to Hitler and soon gave him his servile loyalty. He took part in the abortive putsch in Munich, and can be seen in one photograph clutching a Reich war flag beside a street barricade. Somehow he managed to impress people, including one girl friend who saw him in his role as flag bearer as heroic. Like Hitler, he had quirks, some of his diary extracts revealing a scornful, dispassionate view of female weakness during lovemaking, for during such moments he took care not to abandon himself to passion, but instead retained sufficient control in order to observe and later record the girl's reaction.

Himmler's interest in military affairs, despite his claims to be a veteran of war, was minimal; he really sought no glory in combat, no fulfilment in the building and commanding of armies, his true leanings soon became apparent as soon as he gained Hitler's confidence. At one point the Fuehrer was listening to some of his circle deriding the published works of the Jewish Marxist, Leon Trotsky, but Hitler upbraided them, for he alleged that he too had read the work and referred to it as brilliant, for he admired the methods advocated to gain power over the people. Whereupon Himmler, who was also present, intervened, asserting that he was familiar with the writings also, but more: he had also studied the organization of the Russian Secret Police forces, the dreaded Cheka, Ogpu etc and he boasted that he could do better. This resulted in 1933 in his being allowed by Hitler to take over the Gestapo from Goering, though in 1929 he had only just been appointed head of the SS, and the Gestapo as such had yet to be born, its kernel being only the political department of the Prussian State Police in Berlin and beyond his reach.

It may seem odd that in a so-called 'democratic' state as Germany weakly was at that time, that 'national' organizations comprised of uniformed men, some bearing arms, should ever have been permitted. But that was the reality of it at the time, weak laws and a government and army which saw the Nazis as an additional bulwark against further encroachment of Bolshevism enabled the setting up of huge paramilitary organizations which most other states would have banned at the outset as a threat to lawful government.

Each Nazi Party office was permitted its small squad of SS men, these units variously reported as six, eight or ten men who, although classed as part-timers, had to be on call evenings and weekends and even between those times if needed. The men were usually recruited from among the better type of unemployed, of which there were millions, and whatever care had been taken during the 'years of struggle', by 1932 the SS had risen greatly in strength, largely due to the increasing fortunes of Hitler and his followers. Their numbers are recorded as high as 52,000, and these black-suited men attended every public meeting, large or small, every Party Day rally which were mammoth affairs staged with great care to impress both themselves and the public. Whatever the Reichswehr generals thought of these great shows which were almost exclusively military in character, they must have smiled cynically, for it was the SA brownshirt members not the regular soldiers of their own units who ended up on mortuary slabs or being visited by Hitler in hospital after fighting with the Reds in the towns and cities across Germany.

CHAPTER TWO

The huge expansion of SS numbers which took place after Hitler assumed power in January 1933 was due to the rush of opportunists who sought to jump on the victorious Nazi bandwagon, and these included some of the former communists who merely changed uniforms and slogans. The exclusiveness of the SS vanished almost overnight, and it was alleged that even half the Prussian aristocracy enlisted, certainly some well-known figures including a prince were to be seen garbed in their new, black rigouts complete with SS honour daggers. This was all very fine for some, including Hitler who was crafty enough to cultivate such people and the wealthy industrialists into his camp.

But Himmler became alarmed by this turn of events, and began a purge. As he later said:

'Between the years 1933-35 I swept out all those who were of no value to me, excluding some 60,000 members . . . the actual number of the SS in 1937 was 210,000.'

This figure included 180,000 part-timers of the Allgemeine or General SS. Dietrich:

'After Hitler founded a government of sorts, which really consisted of himself manipulating his friends who had helped him to win, the power of Himmler grew enormously, for with Hitler's connivance he took over the Gestapo and police forces and turned the SS into something neither I nor my closest friends had ever envisaged — a political force of repression. It is a fact that the SS and the power associated with it were split down the middle — the political and the military, and it was difficult to reconcile the two. On the one hand there were men like Steiner and later Eicke, who despite his association with the concentration camps for a time, was a very good soldier and organizer. These were the people I most identified with and we often discussed how we could organize a soldierly force, an army along very different lines who would be superbly trained in a new way.'

These notions would, like seeds, ripen in time into the armed SS; Dietrich and the rest of his ex-army friends would gain their way, attempting to dissociate themselves from Himmler as the new Reichsfuehrer SS sought to build his own crazy empire on repression and force.

Himmler stated that in time of war Germany would face four fronts: air, sea, land and the home front, by which he referred to the threat of internal disorder within the Reich borders, which is the normal indication of insecurity in any dictatorship. This is why such a huge force of police of one kind or another was maintained throughout the short life of the National Socialist State. The Nazi government would never permit any second revolution, by either subversives — or its own brownshirt army; there would be no 'stab in the back', as in 1918.

From the protection squads emerged the General Service SS which was enlarged to the status of an auxiliary police force, and as such were liable to be called out at any time to maintain order. This was usually during public speech days and rallies by the Nazis, parades and all manner of 'festivities' being frequent and turned by the authorities into massive displays of Nazi power, the predominant facets being colour and music, coupled with vociferous speeches and calls for adulatory support for the new messiah — Adolf Hitler. The SS man was also required to attend political indoctrination lectures, one evening a week being set aside for this purpose.

The SS were also called on to assist their SA brownshirt colleagues in rounding up known and suspected Reds, Jews and all manner of suspects believed to be hostile to or working against the new regime. This kind of work had already been taken in hand before Hitler took power, the brownshirts setting up the first concentration camps to hold these unusual prisoners. The Nazis would later take pleasure in pointing out that 'concentration camps' had been set up by the British during the Boer War, which was true; it had unfortunate results then and did under the Nazis.

It can be said that since the 'Bolsheviks' did indeed intend taking over the state and probably carrying out measures even harsher than the Nazis then those guilty of plotting such things were best removed to places where they could do no harm. At times the Nazi authorities pointed out the comparatively mild regimes that existed in the camps at that time, the aim being 're-education', with numbers of reformed prisoners being released from time to time, such as goodwill measures at Christmas.

All this had a connection with the SS, for that force inherited responsibility for the camps and under Himmler's direction reorganized and enlarged them greatly. This side of the SS has been well and accurately documented elsewhere, it is only mentioned here insofar as some of the guards and organizers of the original camps went on into the armed SS. The principal example is Theodore Eicke, who because of his connection with them has been singled out in some books as one of the 'SS killers' and thugs responsible for torture and murder. Eicke was made inspector of concentration camps later in 1933, and at once set about cleaning up the organization, apparently finding the recruited guards like oafs clad in oddments of uniform. These were dismissed and new men recruited on a properly organized, terms-of-service and contract basis. The comments of one such man will be given later.

After 1933 the history of the SS began to assume a more complex nature, for the group of military men within its ranks attempted by some stealth to set up a cadre for their own ends, while on the other side of the fence sat Himmler, intent only on constructing an all-powerful police apparatus designed to hold the German people in a strait-jacket.

When Eicke formed the first SS *Wachverbaende* camp guard units he had as indicated found himself saddled with a collection of mostly 'rural blockheads', clad in ragged denims. These were soon combed out and replaced by better quality personnel who were provided with improved uniforms, pay and contracts, the units later re-designated *Totenkopfbanner* and then *Totenkopfverbaende*, Death's Head units, which in view of the comparative mildness of the regimes claimed by some Germans (for that period) seems rather inappropriate. Their title plus the skull and bones insignia on their uniforms was, from the point of view of their propaganda unfortunate to say the least, though by the later programme the guards were well inscribed.

But, to an unemployed man in Germany in the earlier 1930s there seemed nothing reprehensible in applying for a job in the SS camp guard troops who seemed, after all, no different to prison warders. Gustav Doren was one such applicant:

'The job was quite arduous, but the pay reasonable. Our uniform, food and quarters were provided free, we had warm huts with cots and good stoves. We were at Oranienburg, one of the camps formerly run by the SA. I was taken on as a guard, but we had no arms at that time except for a short rubber cudgel. Although we lived on the camp we were allowed out in free time at weekends, with one week's leave every six months. I signed a contract for twelve years service, this I later saw as foolish, but at the time when I was out of work and with no particular trade it seemed a very good opportunity.

'The regime in the camp was not really harsh, we were told that all the inmates in the camp were there for a good reason, they were simply enemies of the Reich, which meant Jews, Freemasons, Reds etc, though at that time there were no common criminals in the camp, that came later.

'The prisoners were raised from their bunks at 5.30 am by us, we entered their huts shouting "Raus! Raus!" and banging on the ends of their bunks with our cudgels. They paraded in two lines outside, their uniforms inadequate, but most had overcoats. Once counted they were marched to breakfast which consisted of porridge, bread and coffee, and in those days it was real. They were then taken to ablutions for washing and shaving, and after more counting were allocated work. This consisted of road construction, the clearing of building sites or making gardens. At no time were they ill treated, but watching them was very, very tedious, though later there were more staff and the shifts were shorter.'

This regime continued more or less unchanged until 1940, with some prisoners deciding after interrogation that they were supporters of Hitler after all, and periodic releases were made which was good propaganda, for criticisms had appeared in the foreign press.

Doren continues:

'To my certain knowledge up to this time there were no beatings in such camps, I am fairly certain of that. Neither were there executions or torture of any kind. However, I am quite certain that ill treatment was meted out elsewhere such as at the Gestapo HQ, but this was outside my personal experience. I believe in those days before the war the Nazi government was doing all it could to export the Jews and other factions who could either not see eye to eye with the new government or were 'the wrong colour' in some way.'

These opinions have been amply verified elsewhere, and Doren's testimony on the camp guard aspect is included in part because he was one of those later transferred willy-nilly into the Waffen-SS.

By 1937 only a comparatively small number of inmates were held in the camps: 8,600 men were detained and guarded by no less than 3,500 'watch troops', for Himmler had decreed that:

'No service is as devastating and tiresome as the guarding of criminals.'

As indicated, the guards recruited into these particular units were SS men in name only; they had not undergone the usual rigid selection process, being simply unemployed men put into black uniforms. They were not even members of the General SS, nor ex-SA brownshirts, and at that time had no apparent destiny in the future armed SS — the *Verfuegungstruppe*. The coming of the war brought no great change for these SS guards, but then common criminals began to arrive in the camps in increasing numbers, these included homosexuals, thieves and later black marketeers, plus of course the usual crop of 'unreliables' and 'unsafe elements'.

Judging by Doren's account and some other references, the assertion that camp guards had first completed two years military service would appear to be untrue. It is also unlikely that these men were selected to provide cadres for the 25,000 'political readiness troops', the *Bereitschafttruppen* organized into *Hundertschaften* or 'centuries, the SS policemen with whom, as Himmler put it: ' . . . we can guarantee security at home'; for Hitler and Himmler were yet nervous of a poisonous residue of Bolshevism-Judaism-Freemasonry in the heart of the German people which had to be guarded against, this plus of course the old fear of a 'stab in the back', created the myth of an undefeated army at the front betrayed by the people back home. A new anti-insurrection force was to be formed which would be stationed at key points across the Reich, highly mobile and able to stamp on the slightest sign of revolt, should it occur.

But whether this notion had already entered Himmler's crafty and able mind is debatable, for other testimony points to the possibility of his merely trying to hijack such units which had already come into being through the efforts of more soldierly elements within the SS — Sepp Dietrich and his cronies. But before their hopes and plans could be realized certain other events took place which helped to establish both the military wing of the SS and finally divorce them from their SA brownshirt 'comrades' forever.

Soon after Hitler came to power in January 1933 he desired a new *Stabswache*, this to take post at his new Chancellery and replace the old guard provided by the Reichswehr. The task of organizing this was given to Dietrich who picked 120 men and formed them into Hitler's special guard on 17 March, and by September the unit had been designated the *Leibstandarte SS Adolf Hitler* (LAH), the SS Bodyguard Adolf Hitler. On the putsch anniversary date of 9 November the LAH swore an oath of allegiance to Hitler, and thereafter the unit, rigidly disciplined and smartly turned out in their black uniforms, helmets and white gloves, provided an honour guard on all important occasions, as well as providing sentries for the Fuehrer's Chancellery.

The Leibstandarte were placed under Hitler's jurisdiction, not Himmler's, and was soon set up as a body of men independent of both the Nazi Party and State laws.

The 'special commando' units which Himmler had just set up were called into action on the night of 30/31 June 1934, the so-called 'Night of the Long Knives' when Hitler was finally persuaded by his close advisers (notably Himmler and Goering) to act against the huge SA brownshirt army of four million men which had outlived its usefulness and posed a threat to the newly established legal Nazi state. For Roehm was a firebrand, a conspirator and a man of action who like many of his men saw the fruits of their hard-won revolution slipping away from them. Roehm also saw his men as a new kind of 'people's army' who were more truly representative of National Socialism, so from his point of view he was a real threat to the old established Reichswehr whose generals knew it. To Hitler it was a matter to be dealt with by his SS, as Dietrich explains:

'Ernst Roehm was a very great danger to Germany and to Hitler. There certainly was an amount of plotting and skullduggery that went on against this man, and it is probable that some faked documents were produced. But the fact is that Roehm's bunch were becoming notorious across Germany for their excesses and there was no way that we could get rid of them easily. You cannot politely hand a man like Roehm his written notice! He is likely to take out a pistol and shoot you.

'Hitler and Himmler called me and alerted the Leibstandarte plus a number of special SS units which had been held in readiness for any eventuality. You have to realize that Roehm and his gang had several million men behind them and were armed, so we had cause to fear them as they far outnumbered us. Hitler was also of course under pressure from the army to do something.

'On the evening in question I rode with Hitler, Himmler and other leaders in

a fast column of SS men, all of us armed. We found Roehm in bed with a youth and shot them both dead. Heines (Roehm's close friend and a pimp who allegedly drew Roehm into his homosexual circle) was also found in bed with some other fellow and they too were shot on the spot. Hitler did not do any shooting, neither did he give Roehm a gun (to shoot himself with as some have suggested).

'This ended the matter as far as I was concerned, but Himmler and others ordered a general round up and hundreds were arrested and quite a lot done away with, innocent or otherwise. This was a very traumatic event in Germany. As for my own part in it, I was disgusted and incensed with Roehm and his gang and felt at the time and later that we had no other course than to get rid of them. I suppose if we'd had a different sort of government they would have been tried, as it was we were not that kind of people so that was that.'

In July, Hitler, in view of its 'meritorious service', declared the SS as a whole an independent organization, and of the work carried out on 30 June Himmler said:

'It appalled everyone, yet everyone was certain it was absolutely necessary.'

So effectively did the SA lose its head that it never again posed a threat to Hitler or the conservative Reichswehr. The brownshirts became disinherited of Germany, for having marched, fought and in many cases died for so many years in the hope of becoming the cream of a society which would provide them with just rewards they now found themselves relegated to a backseat role, assigned mundane tasks such as their usual, old task of street fund collecting, and the instruction of youth prior to conscription into the new 'Wehrmacht'. Many were ex-servicemen who had believed in Hitler as a leader of a social revolution who would see them right once they hoisted him into power. Even so, their first allegiance had been to Roehm; the army of four million brownshirts shrank in size, especially after war came.

But for the SS it was a different story, yet the oath of allegiance they gave to the Fuehrer would, after 1935, also bind the men in the Wehrmacht and bring a dilemma and disgrace to some. Having established themselves in Hitler's eyes as truly worthy of his trust, the Fuehrer now lent a sympathetic ear to those who were intent on forming a 'new model army'.

On the day that Hitler and Goering shocked their neighbours outside Germany by announcing conscription and the existence of a new 'Luftwaffe' the Fuehrer issued an order establishing the SS-Verfuegungstruppe. This at once offended the German Army chiefs, and it was the generals' opposition that delayed the forming and equipping of the first full SS division until 1940. The actual strength of the new 'VT' force two months after Hitler's decree was 8,459 men, of which 2,660 belonged to the Leibstandarte, 759 in the so-called 'Fuehrer Schools', the remainder organized into six battalions of the 1st and 2nd SS Regiments. Added to these were 1,338 garrison troops and 2,241 guards in the concentration camps.

How the militarized SS came into existence at all is best described by some of its original inspirers, the ex-regular soldiers who moved to further their own dreams of an élite force.

Dietrich:

'I had behind me some sort of military experience and I must admit that I did not fit into civilian life, no more than did Roehm, Eicke or Steiner and the rest. But while Roehm was an out and out political revolutionary, apart from being a pervert, we were wholly military types and always had in mind a certain goal which was to try and organize a new type of army.'

Obviously, such ambitions had only begun to emerge at a later stage, after Hitler had secured his mandate, and then Dietrich and his fellow conspirators began to see the possibilities in the select body of men under them. Dietrich had long teamed up in a sense with other ex-army men who had joined the Nazis in the hope of rescuing their country from chaos in the 1920s.

But to Dietrich and his friends, one man proved a constant obstacle:

'Himmler saw the SS in a very different light. They had begun in politics and that was where he wanted them to remain, which was why he organized such a large number of Allgemeine SS as auxiliary policemen. To us this was nonsense once the Reds had been smashed. Then he tried to have a motorized SS standing by in case there was a revolution in Germany. This was nonsense too. It was men like Steiner and to a degree myself who eventually managed to organize the V-SS and later Waffen-SS. But again, Himmler got his fingers into this too which resulted in a great deal of nonsense about race etc. I will say however that his fanatical insistence on physical standards did give us the best men available, so that was some advantage. However, a lot of claptrap and time wasting went on with regard to the mystical side of things which to us was absurd. Fortunately, it was prevented from ever taking over completely and interfering with our military programme.'

Dietrich asserts that he and his cohorts were able to manipulate Himmler to some extent in these matters, as well as persuade Hitler that a military force of loyal troops apart from the Army would be a good thing, and:-

'The concentration camps were run entirely by Himmler's Special SS police and guards and took a very different line to our own development. I met my like-minded colleagues and we did our best to further our ends in organizing a new model army. This came about very gradually and despite Himmler's desire to reserve them as political troops. Even after they were fully organized into

*regiments and began to receive military training Himmler still tried to usurp
them for his own ends.'*

Once Hitler had been won over and the V-SS began to take shape as a
military reality it became necessary to implement proper training which
had been lacking. To this end an Inspectorate was set up on 1 October
1936 under Paul Hausser, who had resigned from the German Army in
1932; Hausser would now become a key figure in this second army:

*'I left the Army as a Lieutenant-Colonel in 1932 because I was very frustrated
by all I saw. Although I had achieved a certain rank in the hierarchy the
German Army at that time was terribly hidebound and I could see no future.
Apart from this, being a military tradesman I had certain ideas of my own but
no chance whatever of pursuing them. Then too there was the chaotic state of
our country. True, certain experiments in democracy had been tried, but at that
time it was not what our country needed. What was needed was a firm,
inspired hand at the tiller, democracy could come later. That was why some of
us Army men threw in with Hitler. Despite his faults he seemed to be the only
man for the job, apart from which he was virulently anti-Red and would
certainly do his upmost to rid his country of these people who were bent on
ruining society by violent means.*

*'After Hitler came to power I and certain other army comrades evinced the
desire to form a new kind of army, but we had problems because of the
enormous political power wielded by the man in the best position to help us,
and I mean Himmler. He was no more than a political policeman who did his
upmost to convert all we saw as the best material into a force for political
repression. This was a complete nullification of all we had in mind.*

*'I myself was not in the best position to forward my own views or those of
my group, but Sepp Dietrich had the ear of both Himmler and Hitler, and it
was through him that we were eventually able to make a start in getting
together a select group of men who we thought could be formed into the kind of
national army we had in mind. But we did not see this force as usurping the
role of the regular army. This must sound very strange, but at the time we were
at loggerheads with the old Prussian, conservative leadership of the German
Army, and being military men with ambitions we did our best to further them.*

*'I was in a sense a junior member of our group trying to further these aims;
it therefore came as a great surprise to me when I was elected to start up an
Inspectorate of the V-SS and officer training schools. It was a great
opportunity to lay the foundations of a new officer corps based first and
foremost on comradeship throughout all ranks. We had a very firm belief that
the fighting spirit of the troops as a whole depended a great deal on the quality
of leadership from top to bottom, so it was this aspect which took precedence.
We agreed that the officer candidates should be inculcated above all with a
desire to know the men of every rank below them, as well as those above. We
desired to produce a homogeneous whole that would work together as a team as
no other army had done before.'*

Mention has been made of Steiner, who like Hausser had resigned from the German Army, for as he said later: 'In the 1920s everything was quite stagnant, with prospects very bleak'. In view of the fact that his country had just been defeated in a major war this was an understatement and understandable. But like others, Felix Steiner thought he saw a chance to further himself so after Hitler assumed power he left the Army with the rank of Colonel and transferred to the SS:

'At that time there was no thought of forming a large army of SS troops, but a very small start had been made. There was a small number of ex-army men who saw a chance to further their careers in the military, in fact they were presented with a unique opportunity, for Hitler was of a mind with Himmler to set up armed SS formations in case they were needed as 'political troops' to counter any serious internal unrest. But those of us who had been in the Army had very different ideas. I was among those who frequently plotted to set up a field force of a rather different nature. In doing this we felt we could thereby contribute to Germany's security in the international sense. I must admit that we were a little aggressive in our desire to prove our theories in the military field and further our own ambitions.

'It seemed to us that if only the Nazi government could be persuaded to part with the necessary funds then our desires might come true. In all this we were contravening the mad schemes of Himmler, who despite his small military background was an out-and-out policeman of the repressive kind and had no real idea at all of military matters. Yet he it was who had the power to put paid to our dreams, so for this reason we were obliged to tread very cautiously.

'To advance our cause we enlisted the help of Sepp Dietrich and one or two others who had Hitler's ear, as ex-soldiers we knew they would always be sympathetic to our ideas. Sepp's position was a difficult one as in a sense he had two masters, both Hitler and Himmler, though owing a long-time allegiance to the Fuehrer. He was certainly never afraid of Himmler who I believe he looked down on.

'Gradually, we began to see a way how we could set up our first SS cadres, and this came about via the original LAH bodyguard, but was soon followed by the forming of three regiments which we convinced Himmler would serve well as political troops, and this idea caught on. We emphasized the need for mobility, so they were soon motorized. So, to our great joy we had our first SS field troops, and they were completely mobile.

'The idea that they could become useful as combat soldiers was of course not Himmler's, but was put to him as usual in a roundabout fashion, and obtained his approval, though he believed that he would retain full control. It was only later that he conceived the idea that "his SS" would need to be bloodied in battle, and thus earn their spurs, so to speak. By the mid-thirties we had managed to install ourselves as commanders of these cadres, the embryo SS combat units who were at that time little more than novices, very keen but without any military training at all. Of course, they carried arms and could put on a good show on parade, but little more. This was when Lt-Colonel

Hausser was approached.

'Like myself he had resigned from the Army and joined the Nazis because he saw them as the best chance of restoring order and perhaps self respect in a new Germany. Naturally, being a career soldier he also hoped for an opportunity to use his experience, but until we enlisted his help he had not been able to do very much because the SA millions were under the firm control of Ernst Roehm and his clique of perverts. Our obvious need was for a set programme of training so that our pet regiments could at least be brought up to Army standards, and hopefully beyond that. So Hausser was put forward by us as a candidate to set up training colleges in the best possible locations. He would of course have all the help we could provide.*

'But nothing could be achieved in this direction without Himmler's sanction and adequate funds of which we had none of our own. As a resigned Army officer I had forsaken my pension rights, I had nothing but a relatively small income from the SS. We had hopes of good careers with rapid promotion, but above all we had the idea of creating a new military force from scratch along new lines.*

'With the help of Dietrich and Hausser, Himmler was persuaded that these SS troops were of little use without proper military training, which they had never had. He agreed that they needed to become 'Spartans', and saw a great chance I believe to show the conservative diehards of the Army that anything they could do his SS could do better. I think that was paramount in his thinking.*

'So Hausser was voted the best man to act as Inspector of our V-SS troops, and we set about finding the right place for our colleges. But in the event we were forced by Himmler to accept policemen into the courses which was unfortunate but could not be helped. The two principal academies, or Junkerschulen as they were to be called, were at Braunschweig and Bad Tolz. But once again we were not allowed to set up an entirely military calculus, for Himmler and a few other crackpots insisted on interfering, so that the teaching included political tenets and racial themes which had no place in our thinking. However, none of this was allowed to interfere with the military side of the programme; the young officers were there for one purpose — to learn the trade of leading men in war.*

'I believe we succeeded in producing a very fine type of young leader who was above all inculcated with the team spirit in a way never taught in the German Army. Everyone in the SS units joined in activities together, the greater emphasis was always on team spirit and comradeship. If this was focused on the letters 'SS' then very well, it was, but this was only a symbol of the unit. We intended to instil an unparalleled esprit de corps in our force that would mark it out as one of the finest ever assembled. In the main I believe we achieved this objective, despite what some said about us and at times not without reason.'*

Obviously, as career soldiers, Hausser and his colleagues had engineered an opportunity very few military men ever receive.

'The amount of enthusiasm surprised me,' Hausser said later. 'I had expected an uphill struggle, but this never happened. The schools were set up and I was well satisfied with our beginning. The only problem was the interference of Himmler and his staff who had politicisation in mind from the beginning, coupled with racial theories and dreams of eastern conquest which were not in the least anything to do with our way of thinking. But, unfortunately Himmler held the purse strings and we were forced to accept some of his curriculum. But when he tried to have political officers attached to every unit just like the Soviet commissars we demurred and insisted that the officers in charge of field training take precedence. Even so, it was impossible for us to prevent a certain amount of political indoctrination creeping into the school lessons. But overall the emphasis in those courses was the simple integration of all ranks which would provide the backbone of leadership through comradeship — but without loss of discipline, this was very important.'

The great problem for Hausser and his colleagues was the acute shortage of suitable candidates, preferably men with military experience to take command at all levels in the newly militarized SS units. Himmler and his staff made efforts to lure men from the Army, and to some extent they succeeded, for there were soldiers who were tired and frustrated by the conservative rigidity of the old style military life. The SS seemed to provide something new and dynamic, and held out above all excellent chances for promotion.

As for the rank and file, it is said that in the early days Himmler himself inspected every recruit, and that he even pored over photographs of his applicants for hours, looking for visible (racial) defects. In those times newcomers had to provide photographs of themselves, and of girl friends if marriage was contemplated, for no SS man was permitted nuptials without consent and after providing a rigid c.v. of self and prospective bride. The physical standards demanded were very rigid. An applicant for the Leibstandarte needed to be five feet eleven inches tall, though the other SS units admitted men half an inch shorter. This requirement marked only the beginning of the tests. For a start, only those youths who had come up through the Hitler Youth were eligible, but by the mid-30s this included most fit German boys, and later on every applicant would have completed at least six months toughening up and discipline in the *Reichs Arbeits Dienst* (RAD) or Labour Corps.

The SS *Bewerber* (Applicant) needed to be not only of minimum height, his bodily proportions had to be correct, while defects of eyesight or even a filled tooth ensured instant rejection, as did prominent cheekbones, for they reminded the Reichsfuehrer (so he said) of the Reds who formed the Soldier's Councils in the dark days of 1918. Such types, Himmler believed, would eventually go over to the enemy. His own looks were not exactly Nordic and ironically, the only SS man allowed to carry the sacred Blood Banner displayed distinctly, non-Aryan, almost Eastern-type features.

In keeping with his theories and belief in racial purity and the superiority of Nordic man, Himmler introduced stringent tests concerning the applicant's blood line. Every man had to show proof of ancestry back to 1800, for officers the date was set fifty years before that.

'Only good blood brings out the best performance', Himmler said. 'I know that people above a certain number of centimetres must somehow contain the desirable blood.'

Himmler had set down his ideas on this matter as early as 31 December 1931,

'The SS is an association of German men, defined according to their Nordic blood and specially selected.'

He conceded, however, that it did not do to be too one-sided about the matter. It was possible that applicants below the set height could contain the right blood, he just worked on probabilities. To restrict the number of applicants even further, Himmler had even as early as 1929, and despite the hard times of the depression just beginning, insisted on every SS man buying his own uniform at a cost of 40 Reichmarks, this on top of the fact that the applicant already needed to pay higher membership dues than in the SA.

'If he did not do this.' Himmler explained later, 'or declared, "I cannot do it", then we told him, "Please leave us, as you have not grasped this thing, you are not ready for the last sacrifice, we cannot use you'. Thus we gradually arrived at the kind of blood we desired.'

Those who passed all these tests received their SS membership book, plus the *Ahnenpass*, or Book of Ancestry.

Yet the most stringent requirements began to be eased slightly when the V-SS began its life and expansion in 1936, and so attractive did it seem as an élite force to many young Germans that it was never short of applicants. Recruiting was carried on through SS enlistment centres which spread throughout Germany, and as indicated, Hausser and his colleagues had no reason to be dissatisfied with the men they received. At this time the pay rates were fixed and paid through the SS Hauptamt HQ in Berlin, the money of course having come from the State Treasury, but from 1938 SS troops were paid according to Wehrmacht scales.

Among rites and appurtenances which would *not* be included in the curriculum of the armed SS was the presentation of an SS dagger, an item of dress wear basically identical to that already worn by every SA brownshirt but with black wood grip, bearing the SS runes, standard eagle and swastika and the new motto etched into its blade, *Meine Ehre Heisst Treue* — 'My Honour is Loyalty', which was actually a revamped phrase used by Hitler to his SS earlier. Considerable complications attended the dagger since Himmler instilled the item with the same rites and 'holiness' afforded all else in his organization, and this is amply confirmed by the various edicts issued by his office over these years. This aspect of the SS uniform of pre-war days was however much in keeping with existing traditions not solely confined to the Germans but certainly greatly amplified by the political and to lesser extent the military organizations of the Nazi period. The subject of Nazi political and military, daggers and bayonets has filled books and a few points are worth mentioning where they touch on Himmler's SS of the 1930s.

Several thousand daggers were issued to SS men who had joined the organization prior to 31 December 1931 and served continuously afterwards. More were awarded by the disgraced and executed Ernst Roehm both to his own men and those who had gone over to the SS; all so personally given were inscribed *Im Herzliche Freundschaft Ernst Röhm,* and as mentioned following his demise all such inscriptions were ordered to be removed by a local grinder, the blade could then be re-polished and worn again.

Daggers which had been issued and not bought were not considered personal property, so when an SS man was expelled or had to leave for any reason the daggers were to be handed back; those bought could be retained by such men but the insignia removed.

Under a Himmler order of 1935 it became a criminal offence to ridicule or make fun of the SS dagger, this being taken as an offence against the SS. In that year Himmler also decreed that a recruit could only be classed an 'SSMann' after three years service, prior to that he must remain a mere 'Applicant'.

The awarding of honour daggers could only take place on 9 November, the putsch anniversary date, and the formal presentation parades marked the entry and acceptance of recruits into the SS.

None of this counted one iota however for recruits joining the V-SS, where the only rituals that mattered were marked on the barrack square and the manoeuvring grounds. But before circumstances forced Himmler to tone down some of his rituals he remained in his element, forever devoting time to the dreaming up of new liturgies and rites on a par with the very organizations he was sworn to eliminate — the Freemasons for example.

The pre-war SS man was required to swear an oath that he and his family would live by the code and principles of the SS, and once admitted to the order he was cosseted in terms of welfare, especially if married with an expectant wife. No army anywhere provided facilities as did the SS of the 1930s for all its mothers-to-be and those with babes, whether child was conceived in or out of wedlock. In all respects the SS took very good care of its own.

CHAPTER THREE

By late 1937 the V-SS had grown to three regiments: the Leibstandarte, the 1st SS Regiment *Deutschland*, with four battalions based in Munich, and the 2nd SS Regiment *Germania*, with three battalions in the Hamburg areas of Rodolszell and Arolsen. There were also small ancillary units of engineers and signals. But of these units only the Deutschland was considered combat-ready, the rest could only field one battalion.

The training schedules set up by Hausser and the others were paying dividends: according to one leading historian the armed SS developed the most efficient of all military training systems in World War II. In their training the units were drilled to present not only an immaculate turn-out but their own brand of battle tactics, and in due course became what one writer has referred to as a 'cross between the Spartan Hellites and the Guards depot at Caterham'.

Werner Ostendorff was yet another officer who went over to the SS from the Reichswehr, recruited by old friends who told him there was a great opportunity to break free of the old ways into new thinking and a good career with far better prospects:

'We had a body of men with which I hoped we could achieve much and by this I mean the forming of a formidable army, though of smaller and very select scale. That is the way of the military officer, he always seeks to pursue his chosen career and for most in the hierarchy it was an unavoidable destiny.'

Ostendorff saw the great weakness in the early V-SS — its lack of leaders. They had weeded out many applicants, many unemployed, but had managed to find some of good intelligence and class, all volunteers and very keen. Ostendorff and the other leaders thought that given the right curriculum they could make excellent officers.

'The funds for setting up the Junkerschulen came from the Party, which is to say the Treasury, and these enabled us to take over existing buildings in legal fashion, which after much hard work were turned into suitable quarters and comprised both lecture rooms, accommodation and places for relaxing off duty. We had many conferences to agree on the agenda, and decided that above all this new force should be based on mutual respect between upper and lower ranks, the old way of ruling by fear would be avoided. We felt it was possible to bridge the divide between officers and men and still retain discipline, we

believed that if the men respected their officers enough then they would obey them. And so it turned out.'

Ostendorff had studied the methods of other armies and thought he could do better:

'While it is true that men do train soldiers to kill, it is also true that other, commendable qualities can be fostered. It was always our aim to bring out the best in all our personnel; there would never be any question of looking on them as mere ciphers, which is why the commanders of the schools taught the instructors that they must get to know every man under them, while the men themselves had to look up to their leaders as both commanders and friends. Naturally, the divide would remain; to an extent this was essential. But a private soldier who respects his officers will follow orders to the letter if the man above him is seen as a caring individual who has his welfare at heart, and I am aware that in this death is often the end result. However, there would be no leading from behind in our field force, every officer had to be prepared to lead in the field, even at risk to his own life. There was no other way. I myself led men in certain actions, though obviously as a practice it was not advisable, for top commanders were few, and an army without leaders is rudderless.

'We were able to circumvent the more absurd ideas and strictures of Herr Himmler and concentrate on the more military side of things, and I believe we succeeded, despite difficulties, in producing a new type of soldier rarely equalled in the history of warfare. Naturally, this 'new model army' was comparatively small in size until the mid-war years, and this was all to the good since we were able to concentrate on giving each unit the great amount of instruction needed to achieve our ends.

'We had certain difficulties with the Army though who resented us as upstarts, especially in the matter of equipment, but I can say that once they saw us in action and got to know us in combat a very different atmosphere prevailed, especially at the higher levels. I never had any difficulty in my relations with the Army, and of course the fact that I was an old soldier from within their own ranks helped.'

Georg Keppler had been a Colonel in the post-war Reichswehr, the German Army of 100,000 men permitted by the Treaty of Versailles, but resigned in 1929 while temporarily off sick, though as with the others it was the sense of no future which drove him to give up his career. He later admitted that if he had stayed he might have made headway, but doubted it on account of the Army's structure and lack of ideas.

A year or two later he was introduced to others of like mind, and despite some reservations all agreed that Adolf Hitler was the man most likely to succeed in pulling Germany out of its troubles, and above all of defeating Bolshevism:

'. . . which understandably had a certain appeal among many of the lower

workers because it promised them much, though perhaps they did not realize what would become of our country if they succeed in their aims. We enrolled in the Nazi Party, though not in the SA, and became in a sense supernumerary, though Dietrich told us he felt sure that the time would come when we could be very useful in some way or another, though he seemed a little vague. I believed it pleased Hitler that he had 'captured' some Army officers over to his side. But we took very little part in any of the Nazi proceedings.

'Then after Hitler gained power we saw that a great number were about to join him, and about this time we conceived the idea of trying to form some kind of military force from these volunteers who came flooding into the SS. This was helped in a way by Hitler's own decision to form a sizeable bodyguard, and in due course we prevailed on him and Himmler through the good offices of Dietrich to form a military wing of the SS.'

The *Verfuegungstruppe* ('Stand-by Force') continued however to be seen by Himmler as a force of picked men he could rely on for anything. Keppler helped to form the battalions of the three regiments mentioned, and eventually became a commander of one of them.

'We set to work to have them motorized, for Himmler believed they would be able to fly all over Germany to put down any unrest.'

Yet despite its supposed independence the SS was forbidden to train more than a certain number of officers, this due to Army pressure on Hitler, and this resulted in a continuous shortage, especially when the big expansion came in 1940, and even though the schools contrived to exceed their set limits. The problem was aggravated by the academies being called upon to train police officers, and when war came the drain of casualties added to existing difficulties.

It is odd that a nation already in possession of a regular army, beginning to swell enormously through conscription should suddenly produce a second field force, apparently quite independent of it. But this was possible in the odd world created by Hitler who allowed his cronies rope to do their own thing while maintaining overall control and always playing one off against the other. This resulted also in two intelligence services and Goering's own Luftwaffe field divisions, which were in no way comparable in role to the British RAF Regiment; then there was the multiplicity of police and surveillance agencies. It all added up to competition for resources which was wasteful.

For a start the Army delayed supplies of heavier weapons, for despite its degree of independence the V-SS was wholly dependent on the older service for equipment at this time. Some of the SS procurement staff, irritated by the delay, attempted to 'go private' and ordered supplies direct from the manufacturers, but the Army soon learned of this and protested to Hitler who was obliged to order the SS to be more patient. However much he owed to his loyal SS, by comparison to the German

1st Company SS Leibstandarte Adolf Hitler, Koenigsplatz, Munich, 9 November 1935.

An SS Unterscharführer (Corporal): the 'Second Army' retained its own rank system. (Squadron Signal)

Young recruits of the SS-VT engaged in a pre-war 'pack march'. (Munin Verlag)

Dutch soldiers captured by SS troops, May 1940. (Munin Verlag)

*SS troops in a Dutch city. Outdated
puttees contrast with pioneering use
of camouflage clothing.*

*An SS company commander, 1940,
suitably armed with Schmeisser and
stick grenade. (Munin Verlag)*

Troops of the Germania regiment await the order to advance. Note MP28 machine-carbine.

An SS trooper in the West, May 1940, laden with grenades and boxes of machine-gun ammunition.

'The brave lads of the Adolf Hitler Division have reached the Gulf of Corinth'; so ran the original German caption (April 1941).

An SS motorcycle team advance through a Russian village, summer 1941.

SS troops manhandle a 50mm anti-tank gun(pak) in Russia. Note machine-gun protection.
(Squadron Signal)

The NCO – backbone of all armies, especially the Waffen-SS.
(Munin Verlag)

An ideal of SS propaganda: a 'Richtschutze' mans a 2cm flak gun. (Munin Verlag)

Tales of ill treatment against SS prisoners were not usually substantiated. Here a wounded man is treated by Soviet nurses. (Ullstein)

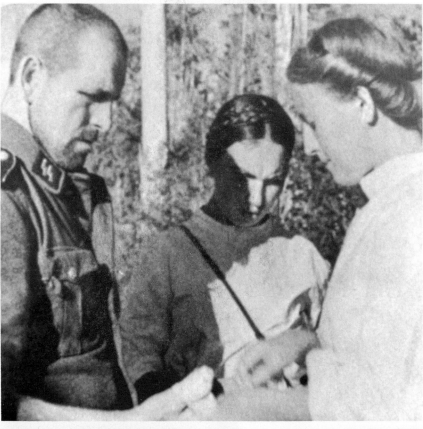

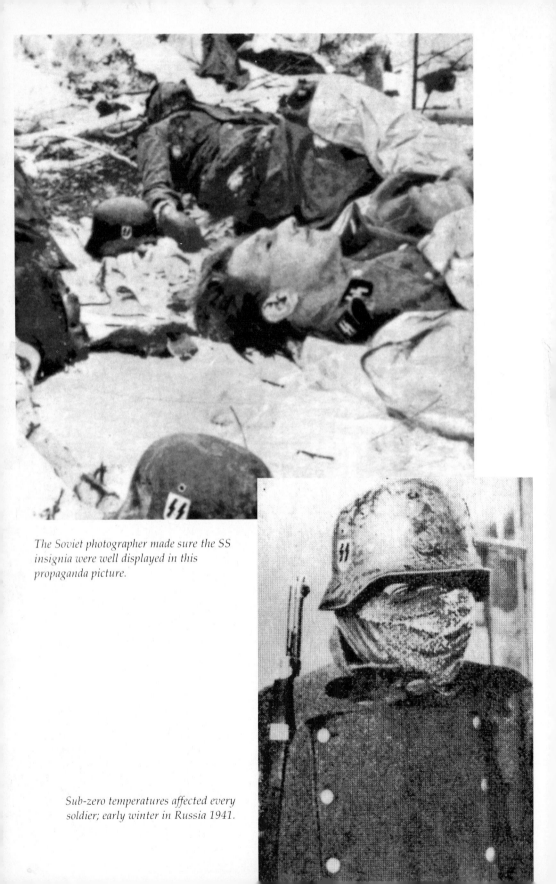

The Soviet photographer made sure the SS insignia were well displayed in this propaganda picture.

Sub-zero temperatures affected every soldier; early winter in Russia 1941.

Army they were insignificant in military terms. The situation was to change later, and as many historians have noted, the SS troops were always the best equipped both in numbers and equipment.

Increasing international tension and German involvement in Franco's civil war in Spain added greater impetus to the preparation of the V-SS units. Great emphasis was laid on physical fitness; like the SA, the SS practised its *Wehrsport* or military sports in which the men undertook all manner of gruelling contests, and on forced 'pack marches' with a heavy load of equipment including weapons. Some of these activities such as the military obstacle races became standard as 'assault courses' among the Allied armies later.

The youth of Germany grew fitter as never before under the marching and sport activity of the Hitler Youth, Labour Corps, SS and other organized fitness tests. It was usual to aim for the awards offered which ranged from the common military sports award badge of the SA to shooting proficiency badges in the Hitler Youth. Hitler's regime geared itself to war through the production of large numbers of super-fit, athletic young men who in those terms put to shame the specimens abroad.

The SS battalions competed with each other in the gruelling marches, the officers of course also participating in them, as well as in the leisure activities which included culture, with the forming of bands and orchestras and above all choirs. The great *kameradschaft* and *esprit de corps* aimed for by the tutors became a reality and would stand them in good stead when war came.

The instructors, helped by the small size of this new army, were able to concentrate their teaching down to company and even lower level. There was nothing basically new in what they imbued, only in its application. There were officers in other armies who held similar views on the handling of men, though these were usually frowned on by those above them as injurious to discipline and good order, especially in the British Army which was class-ridden and where strict barriers between officers and men were maintained for the sake of battlefield discipline. It is a fine point, and experiments in this direction did not always come off. Outside of Germany and the SS troops, perhaps the best example of a similar approach was seen among parachute troops where 'bull' and the rigid demarcation line was slackened considerably, with excellent results. Too many private soldiers in the British infantry had little respect or confidence in their officers, and contact with those above their immediate superiors was usually almost completely lacking. In the US Army the spirit of 'democratic rights' meant that men would argue with their commanders in a battle over the sense or suitability of orders.

The tenets drummed into the Junkerschulen instructors by Hausser and his colleagues were undoubtedly correct, and even though they may not have been new, it was the V-SS who vigorously put them into practice. Yet beyond this basic need, the SS field training was based on that of the light infantryman who relies above all else on speed, this is amply borne out by the testimony to be given by SS soldiers who trained in that fashion. Speed and aggressive attack which it was believed would lead to swift penetration of an enemy front, cunning outflanking movements and less casualties. They were the precursors of the lightning war.

The troops spent day after day in mock company and battalion manoeuvres, until at last all they needed was something on a grander scale involving the whole force available. They received this 'finishing' by permission of the Fuehrer, using the German Army's own practice grounds at Munsterlager. Anxious as ever to prove his SS troops superiority, Himmler arranged for the usual safety precautions to be waived so that the SS regiments demonstrated their battlefield skills before the Reichsfuehrer and Hitler under fire from live ammunition and a real artillery barrage. The SS soldiers went into the attack with bullets whining over their heads and shells bursting not far away. Inevitably, there were casualties which led to Army criticism, but the conservative generals benefited in the coming war when they were only too glad to call in the 'fire brigade' SS formations to restore difficult situations. In addition, this realistic combat training also ensured a sizeable cadre of NCOs and potential officers from the pre-war V-SS which had grown to 15,000 men.

It is now time to look at the experiences of some 'rankers' who joined the force before September 1939.

Peter Zahnfeld was born in Berlin of middle-class parents and enjoyed a stable home life, though inevitably they had been affected by the economic troubles of World War I and afterwards. Both Peter and his younger brother Karl were influenced to a degree by the tensions and generally unsettling atmosphere of the period, attending school with pupils from different home backgrounds and distinctly leftist parents who had tried to instil their own beliefs into them, which often resulted in fights. Like many, the family Zahnfeld were relieved when Hitler took over Germany:

> 'We were like most families, we wanted a better start for our country and an end to the Bolshevik threat.'

Peter went into the Hitler Youth when he was twelve or thirteen; it soon became compulsory for all young people:

> 'We enjoyed it very much. We were boys and liked to hike across the country-side and sing songs, and when we were able to shoot rifles it was good fun. We did not think of the songs we sang as political, they were just tunes to learn, the words were not all that important at first, though later on of course we began to learn better and saw it all in a new light.
>
> 'Hitler really saved Germany, and even though he was a little coarse at times, as were his followers, their message was clear. "Germany is now rising to its feet again and deserves a rightful place in Europe and the world."

'This all seemed very reasonable to us lads, we knew enough to feel ashamed that our great country had lost the war and suffered greatly as a result. I know my parents felt that way and were delighted when order was restored.'

At eighteen Peter went out to work, being quite good at figures which enabled him to find a job in a tailor's shop where he looked after the accounts. It was a start, and he recalls how happy he was to run home to his mother with his first wage packet. But he was then conscripted for labour service and went off by train and truck to a work camp:

'We lived virtually as soldiers, with a lot of marching, singing, and hard physical labour. We were taken out as battalions to work on various projects which was very hard, but of course it made us very fit. We dug drainage ditches in the countryside and town around Berlin and were taken to a new location every few days, a variety of venues you might say, although the work was all very much the same.

'After a month I was allowed home on leave as were most of the lads and my parents were amazed at the change in me. My young brother was in the Hitler Youth and then he too went into the labour corps, so we were both wearing the same uniform and living the same hard life.'

After one year of this Peter was released, but as conscription for the new Wehrmacht had begun he at once became eligible for military service proper:

'I had some choice, I could go into the army, navy, air force — or the SS. The last I had heard was very hard to get into, they had all sorts of funny restrictions. But I had been told by some of the lads that they were a very special bunch of men, a kind of new army where you learnt not only discipline and politics, but had a special kind of relationship with the staff. I did not quite understand all this, but being young I decided to give them a try.

' I must mention that the kind of SS I had in mind were not the policemen we saw about the streets in their black uniforms. I had no interest in that kind of thing at all. I must also say that if I had had a choice I would not have joined any of the forces at all, it was only conscription which forced me into it.'

Having to report to one of the service recruiting offices by a certain date Peter went along to the SS where an NCO told him that he could only be accepted as an Aspirant under very strict conditions, which for a start were concerned with physical condition, mental ability and attitude and family background:

'Well, this was all right with me as I was very fit after all the hard labour I had done in the RAD, and I thought I had enough intelligence. My parents were good Germans and we had a family tree of sorts, though I had little knowledge of it then. I had a first medical check-up the same day, but had to return a few

days later for a much stricter one which took two hours. This I passed with no problems. I was then given forms to fill in and told to return with them in a day or two, so I went home to study them and my parents helped me to fill them in.'

Peter had met several more would-be recruits at the SS recruiting centre and one in particular who lived near his home, so they agreed to meet and return with their completed application forms together. This they did, being told that they would receive notifications within a week. During this time, as he learnt later, his family background and other details given were checked into, and when he was called back to the SS office he was given an interview by an officer who tried to obtain some idea of his mental make-up, what he thought of the Fuehrer, of Germany, world affairs, and why he wanted to join the SS.

'All these difficulties were there, even though these people were advertising for recruits. There were big posters in their window, but being admitted was a rather different matter.'

Having satisfied the officer by his verbal responses, Peter was told to wait outside with other applicants, noting that two of them had come in from the countryside and were very keen.

'We were then shown into a larger office, except for one lad who was taken away by an NCO, I believe he was refused entry and we did not see him again. The officer then addressed us and told us we had been accepted as SS Aspirants and that we were to go home to settle our affairs and return at eight o'clock next morning to be entered into the SS proper and sent away for training. This was all very exciting and I left in a daze with my new friend. We walked home in good spirits, talking of our coming adventure. We had only handled spades in the RAD of course, but had some knowledge of rifle shooting from our days in the Hitler Youth.'

Peter points out that various written tests had already taken place in the youth movement and if passed satisfactorily eligibility in the SS was assured though not guaranteed. But if such preliminary tests had been a failure then 'you stood no chance'. The papers were always checked by the SS.

Karl Lempke was the only child of loving parents in Leipzig and two years older than Peter Zahnfeld; he attended high school and entered the Hitler Youth before going to college where he studied to be a teacher. Then came service in the labour corps:

'It was a hard life, especially for those of us not used to physical labour. But it made me very fit, and then I went straight into the SS.'

Karl had no great desire either to become a soldier, but conscription and some glowing reports from a fellow ex-student who had already entered the SS convinced him what a great bunch of lads they were, though it was hard to get in. Yet, previously he had decided that if forced to join up he would make it easy for himself by trying to get some sort of office job.

'But my friend persuaded me otherwise. He seemed very keen that we should be together and like a fool I was soon led to the SS office with my sponsor. After the tests and questioning I wondered what I had got myself into, but I was accepted as an SS Aspirant and later saw my friend in the training squad. I'm not sure how much political interest there was among those lads, but I doubt if they were particularly 'Nazi'. They believed in their country which seemed to be coming together wonderfully under Hitler. They certainly had no thoughts of going to war or anything like that.'

That comment surely typifies the young men who were called to the colours by the hundred thousand in Germany from 1935 and marks them as no different to the youth of other countries who also faced conscription later on. Like their parents, most German youths saw Hitler as having pulled their country out of chaos and disrespect, they certainly felt patriotism, but this hardly labels them as fanatical Nazis, either then or later. The SS soldier imbued with hatred was a rarity, even during the war.

Interestingly, one would-be applicant encountered a problem in trying to enter the SS in this pre-war period. Karl Hummelkeier lived in Hamburg and went through the usual processing including Hitler Youth training which his parents thought 'too regimental', followed by a stint in the labour service. Like the previous case, he too had a chum who persuaded him to opt for the V-SS when conscription time came. But Karl notes that even though the other lad's father was a Party member it was no help to him when he applied to join the SS.

But in Karl Hummelkeier's case he was surprised to find he was classed as 'of suspect origin', i.e. — slightly 'non-Aryan', and was baffled as to the cause until his mother confessed to having a Jewish uncle. Karl could not understand how this had come about or why it should make any difference to his application, but to his relief he was admitted as an SS Aspirant.

Unlike those recruits mentioned so far, Lothar Vogel began his service in the General SS in 1936, but transferred to the military branch by application and suffered the usual delays. Like the others, he had simply volunteered for the armed SS and had no idea to which regiment he would be sent after training.

Peter Zahnfeld recalls that he and the new men he was with were greeted by a rather jovial NCO when they arrived at the camp and barracks outside Berlin and were at once shown to their rooms:

'We were quite pleased to find that there were only four men to each room, with

adequate facilities nearby. The NCO told us to get sorted out, there were cupboards for our belongings, but we would soon be taken to the equipment store to receive our uniforms etc.'

When they returned to their room later, heavily laden with gear, another junior NCO showed them how to fit it all into the proper places in their wardrobes and how to dress themselves.

'We had no weapons, but were very soon paraded as a new squad and marched to the armoury where we received Mauser rifles of an old kind. Then we were taken to the mess where we found two battalions having their evening meal. So we joined them, the food was good and plentiful and we ate well. When we returned to our barrack room an NCO began instructing us in the daily routine to come. We would join others to form a training squad before moving into one of the battalions. We had much to learn although the RAD had been a good grounding, but we knew nothing about soldiering.

'We had been issued with three uniforms: one was a denim work suit, the second was the new field-grey tunic with all the necessary equipment and new-style helmet; the third uniform was a black type for formal occasions and more or less identical with that worn by the General SS. That evening we returned to our rooms early after a visit to the kasino where many other lads already in training were singing songs and drinking beer.

'Next morning we were roused rather noisily at six a.m. to get washed and shaved (if we needed to), and then marched to breakfast. Then we were ordered into full equipment and marched to the barrack square to meet the rest of the training squad. There were two NCOs who then proceeded to teach us the rudiments of drill which went on all morning. After a break for lunch we went for a short lecture, a kind of indoctrination before being taken out for more drill and a run round the camp in PT kit and then into the countryside. By evening we were very tired, but content with our progress.

'The fact that we were only SS Aspirants meant that we were on probation. I knew from some older members of the squad that they had had to provide details of ancestry back to the last century, but our own lot were never asked for this. I believe that by then such requirements had been waived. I do know however that my own family were investigated and our details looked into. I was considered racially pure, otherwise I would never have been allowed to stay in the SS.

'Our work now began in earnest with field training and manoeuvres with live ammunition which was quite frightening as the bullets were directed over us as we crawled over the ground, firing as we went. We had to fire and run, fire and run, all the time. Then we joined up with the battalions on exercises which included more live firing and lectures, both in the classrooms and in the open about fieldcraft, fortifications, and how to use various weapons to best advantage. We were shown mortars and machine-guns and in a few days were learning how to use them, so the training was very comprehensive and went on at a rapid pace for week after week.

'We became tough and hardened after being out in all weathers, and before long began to feel like veterans. Of course, in fact we were not, we were still only candidates for the SS. But this situation changed quite suddenly when in a big parade many names were called, including my own and we were declared 'SS Sturmmen' and no longer Aspirants. So we had passed our first hurdle and were now admitted to the SS proper, which at that time was known as the 'V-SS'.

At the time we were without transport, but as soon as our field training finished we were provided with trucks and shown how to move rapidly from place to place; in other words, we became motorized infantry. Then, following another big parade we were split up and sent to various units. I went with twelve others to the Deutschland regiment where we were addressed by an officer who told us that we must uphold the honour of the SS at all times, that we must be obedient and loyal to the Fuehrer. We had already been sworn in when we first arrived so we now felt we had been admitted to the armed forces of the new Reich, but much more so as the NCOs and officers told us all the time that they were stirring times for Germany, and that we in the SS had a very special responsibility and were of course far above all other soldiers and were the élite troops of Germany.

'I must say that when we were allowed out into the city we walked about in very proud fashion in our black uniforms and felt that we were indeed the very best. We ignored the men of the General SS as nobodies, they were untrained, part-time policemen and of no consequence. We had only to look at them to see how weak and unfit many of them were by comparison. We felt even the Wehrmacht people were not impressive, for we had been instilled with that special kind of SS arrogance which all so-called élite soldiers acquire in every country. We felt sure we were the best, but we were under a very strict code of behaviour, and at no time were we allowed to behave in an overbearing or inflammatory manner.

'When I saw my parents I believe they were proud of me, I know my brother saw me as something heroic, though I did not yet see myself in that light. I had a lady friend who was very impressed with me in my uniform, so of course this all helped to boost my confidence and self esteem.'

Karl Lempke found the training hard 'but enjoyable at times', and although he had no great desire to become a soldier, he found compensations:

'Such as the girls who flocked to us when we were allowed into town on leave. I cannot say I had been much of a ladies' man in the past, but I was obliged to join in the general fun, though we were always under strict discipline and forbidden to let ourselves go at any time when on or off duty. At this time I saw myself as a temporary soldier who would do his term of duty then return to finish his studies and become a teacher, but in due course this ambition fell away from me and I felt uncertain of my future.'

Karl Hummelkeier had been sent to Arolsen with a batch of recruits as Aspirant for the Germania Regiment:

'The training was hard but quite fun at times, and when at last I went home I felt proud of myself and hoped my parents would agree I had made the right choice. In fact, my father was a little dubious but made no complaint. At least I was a soldier and not one of those strutting policemen of the General SS who we proper soldiers soon learned to look down on.

'I was sent off with the training battalion on hard combat courses and learnt to make war. In all these efforts the NCOs and officers constantly taught us the great value of two things — speed and comradeship. They also taught us to believe in ourselves, the SS and the Fuehrer. They said we were the world's élite troops and the world would know it. Well, we had no desire to be killed in battle I'm sure, whatever our patriotism; I know I didn't. But we knew the international situation was bad, and if war came we would be in it without doubt.'

On completing his training Lothar Vogel was surprised to find himself sent to the prestigious Leibstandarte:

'I saw this as a very great honour as they were the premier unit of the V-SS and accepted very few men in their ranks. I believe even later they remained one of the most exclusive and smallest of the SS divisions. My new comrades made me very welcome and I was made to feel one of them. It was a great honour and this was brought home to me on various occasions, such as when I was seen by Sepp Dietrich himself who told me that if I pursued my duties diligently I could go far. On other occasions officers impressed on us the absolute need to uphold the honour of the SS at all times and to behave correctly on or off duty.'

How these men reacted and indeed the armed SS as a whole to the stresses of battle will be seen later; this is obviously of interest in view of this constant reference by their officers to the 'honour' of the force, and also of course in view of the long term belief later of this army as ruthless and capable of murder.

Lothar mentioned in passing that he came from a respectable Berlin family, and that he had a brother who entered the Luftwaffe a year earlier, became a sergeant pilot and was finally killed in Russia.

Karl-Heinz Anold volunteered for the V-SS on receiving his call-up papers in 1938, and after completion of training was posted to the Germania regiment, commenting that by then the force was an 'élite motorized infantry'.

Peter Krollman was one man who, having joined the V-SS in 1937 and completed infantry training was recommended for an officer course at Braunschweig. This he successfully completed and was seconded to the Deutschland regiment, but his combat career would be a short one.

An account of conditions in one of the Junkerschulen has been given by Peter Zahnfeld, who somewhat to his surprise discovered that he was rated 'officer material':

'By that time the world situation had deteriorated, so any idea of only having to spend a year or two in the SS forces was illusory. We were stuck under arms for as long as the situation lasted, and of course began to realize as young soldiers that we might have to fight for our country.

'We heard lectures on the dangers of Bolshevism and the rottenness of the capitalistic, plutocratic democracies, and how they wished to keep Germany down. But we were never told that we might be used as political troops against internal dissension. We took part in some big parades in Berlin which were quite impressive affairs, and saw Hitler and the other Nazi leaders including Himmler who inspected us. We also saw our own higher leaders of the V-SS, Dietrich and others. At that time I was in some doubt as to the meaning of having such another army, though this did not particularly bother me. I felt we were the army of the new Germany, and although I did not see myself as a Nazi, we were obviously something unusual and rather special.

'Soon after that, following one of our bigger exercises with several SS regiments taking part I was invited to an interview by our CO, who suggested I might try to become an officer, but I told him that I was only a comparative newcomer and did not have the qualifications. He told me that like all the rest I had been watched and assessed and that with my kind of background I seemed to be the kind of man they needed. I was very surprised by all this as I had no idea we had been assessed, but I learnt that this was the way of the SS, they had their eyes on you all the time.

'I had already been pleasantly surprised by the easy-going, friendly attitude of the NCOs and officers, there was none of the Prussian bellowing on the barrack square type of thing. They were strict on discipline, but it was of the comradely kind. The officers really went out of their way to be helpful, they spent a great deal of time trying to help every man, and this kind of treatment helped to inspire confidence in them, and when war came it proved a very big asset in the field.'

This kind of testimony proves how much better trained were these SS soldiers than their counterparts in other armies who would have to meet them in the field. Anyone who served in the British forces will recognize the stark differences, especially in the army, where even the so-called professional officers were often little more than gentlemen amateurs and before the war at least only taken from the 'right caste'.

'I felt so impressed and I suppose flattered by the officer's remarks in this interview that I accepted his offer and agreed to become an officer candidate. This meant an immediate promotion through what in the Army would have been Corporal and then to Sergeant. It so happened that a drive to produce more officer cadets for the schools was under way, so I received my first

promotion at once and became a Sergeant a week later of the junior grade. And not long after that I was sent away to Bad Tolz with some more lads to be trained and assessed as an officer.

'We were extremely impressed with all we found at the leaders school. It was spotlessly clean and a kind of castle-cum-barracks, the accommodation excellent, the instructors friendly, and we enjoyed it immensely. Most of our time was spent in lectures, but with field problems also. There was a certain amount of political indoctrination too, but this did not bother me especially, I was only interested in the military side of it and the talks on how to handle men and in this we met 'Papa' Hausser who occasionally visited the colleges he had done so much to organize. He was very friendly, unusually so it seemed to us for a high ranking officer. I believe he had been as army general and held the equivalent rank in the SS*.

'The whole course was conducted on an almost non-military level, by which I mean we were not regimented in any way. The object was to produce efficient military commanders, but even so it was very informal, and I think this helped us absorb much more of the instruction. I think all the teachers were ex-army men who had gone over to the SS; they knew what they were talking about. I believe there was talk later in other countries of the fearlessness and recklessness of SS troops and of their absolute disregard for casualties. I can say that the whole object of our training was to reduce casualties to a minimum, this because of our speed in action, the need to overwhelm the enemy by speed and aggressiveness in a manner not previously attempted in the old army. Of course, if you are trained as an élite infantry then you must expect losses and these can be high, but the same applies to all armies. I do not believe the SS losses in action were greatly higher if at all than say by the élite Allied regiments including the US Marines.'

This is certainly true. Critics of the SS troops have always taken pains to point out the heavy losses the units suffered in battle. As one other writer has said, this was primarily due to the fact that the best soldiers are inevitably in most demand and therefore tend to become 'used up' more rapidly. Allied losses in some areas and certain actions were horrendous.

'But we were always inculcated with this great emphasis on speed-speed-speed, much more so than the army I believe. Added to this was the constant emphasis on our superiority in every way, of our certainty of success, and above all the rightness of our cause which was Germany's.

'When I finished the course I was promoted to Lieutenant or the SS equivalent (Untersturmfuehrer), and went home on leave a very proud man. My parents were delighted with their son and I had no problem in proposing to my young lady. I was then sent to command a company in the Deutschland regiment and felt a good deal of responsibility. The fact of this only then began

---

* As an army Lt-Colonel in 1932 Paul Hausser took the rank of Obersturmbannfuehrer in the SS, was promoted to SS Brigadefuehrer or Maj-General at the time in question, ending the war as an Obergruppenfuehrer or Colonel-General.

to dawn on me, but I had little time to ponder as we were plunged into more and more training which as usual was very realistic.'

The last pre-war recruit in this account was an unusual one and in a sense does not qualify since he did not immediately join the V-SS. Karl-Heinz Roberts joined the SS just before the outbreak of war in 1939, and apparently had no special kind of service in mind:

'I was at once offered a post as an officer interpreter and did not go into the V-SS until later. Because of my university education in Berlin and my knowledge of English and French they told me that I would be more useful as a translator in various duties. So in my case I was not sent away on an infantry course as I was not actually a recruit of the V-SS. I had a week in which to clear up my affairs and this I did, and when I reported back to the SS office an NCO drove me to the main RHSA HQ (SS Reichssicherheitshauptamt) where I met an officer who also spoke English and he tested me as to my knowledge of the language. Apparently satisfied, he told me that I would be given certain security duties when I had been sworn in and obtained my uniform. For this I was given a certain amount as an allowance but told I would have to put some towards it myself. So I went along to the tailoring section where they fitted me up with a smart black outfit and took the money I had towards the cost. There was a certain amount of form filling before I returned to the same officer who then swore me in as a loyal member of the SS with a special oath to them and the Fuehrer, as well as to Himmler.

'I was then taken to a department dealing in codes and ciphers, in part run by the SD I believe as an intelligence section. I had no knowledge of codes but this proved unnecessary as all I had to do was translate messages from French and English into German. These I understood from their contents were the results of espionage and phone tapping by the SD and Gestapo of all French and English diplomatic and other calls as well as meetings when our own observers and spies had been present.

'I must say it was an extraordinary start to my military service as I was able to go home every evening as if I was in a civilian job. I was not the only person in that department engaged in that kind of work, there were others including a woman I got to know rather well later on. I believe she had been partly educated in France and England and was rather a clever girl.'

We shall return to the rather interesting career of Karl-Heinz Roberts later.

CHAPTER FOUR

The strength of the armed SS at the beginning of the war was 28,000, and, as mentioned, Reichsfuehrer Himmler conceived the idea that 'his' troops should be bloodied in battle. But it would be foolish to imagine that military tradesmen do not wish to try out the tools they have forged in war, as Dietrich said:

'I suppose it is inevitable that military men desire to see their creations in action, so we were not averse to having the SS troops enter the Polish conflict.'

There is no need here to recount the Hitler-inspired, contrived attack on Poland which began at dawn on 1 September 1939 and involved a small number of SS units as follows (but under army control):

SS Regiment Deutschland, SS Regiment Germania, SS Engineer Battalion, SS Regiment Leibstandarte, SS Artillery Regiment, plus some signals and flak troops.

The Poles could field a very considerable army, so much so that the adjutant of the SS *Aufklarungs* (Recon) column gave it as his opinion that it would take up to two years to crush them, and that the enemy would fight to the last. In the event the first of the so-called Blitz campaigns was to last barely a month, and it did cost the attackers quite heavily.

The SS went to war, inevitably to the great interest of its commanders, including Paul Hauser, though they probably felt some frustration that their troops were under army control. The Deutschland regiment, with its artillery, motorcycle, signals and reconnaissance details were seconded to the Army's Kampfgruppe Kempf on the left flank; Germania was given to the 14th Army in the centre, the rest of the SS-VT being attached to the 3rd Army on the right flank, and these units included the Leibstandarte which according to one source had acquired a few Mk 4 tanks.

Himmler too was to follow the campaign with special interest, and it has been suggested that he envisaged his SS troops returning to Germany as bloodied heroes, but hardened in battle and even more ready to take on any tasks on the home front.

So far, all that has appeared here in direct testimony appears to contradict the common belief which grew up, largely outside Germany and based on propaganda, of fanatical young Nazis who were utterly ruthless in war and ever ready to commit unsoldierly acts. The witnesses quoted seem very ordinary young men from decent homes, forced into some kind of uniform by the state. Obviously, it is impossible to tell from such a small sample just how much these impressionable youths were affected by political indoctrination and hate propaganda. But this aspect is of little consequence in a war, though some will contradict this. The élite troops of all armies are hardened by the kind of training given and will fight accordingly in battle. The case of paratroops is a good example, whether German or Allied. No matter how much they believe in their country, the chief cause of their élite status lies in their training and morale, and none came higher than in the paras, simply because they had done something that most others had not which placed them at once beyond all soldiers of the 'common' infantry and of course the soft civilians. It was this tremendous self-belief and comradeship and *esprit de corps* which made them the best soldiers, it had nothing to do with political motivation. As one writer has observed, and it is relevant, if soldiers are trained as an élite and to kill (as all soldiers are) then in certain situations they will react accordingly. This has been amply demonstrated in many wars since World War II.

We have heard that the SS recruits were exhorted over and over again to uphold the honour of the SS, and that they were under strict orders to obey and behave at all times. Although not much open to the mystic rituals of Himmler, the V-SS had however taken part in huge military displays and in a real sense seemed to exude the Nazi ethos of 'might is right', and like all armies had trained for war. It may surprise some to learn that the SS was not an atheistic organization, the tenets expounded from the top were only 'anti-Juda', though whether actually anti-Christ is debateable. It is not the intention to enter fully into these matters here, but only to bring them into the question of motivation in the V-SS force.

The SS were not anti-God, the Creator or Creative Force they envisaged (or at least Himmler did and tried to foster), was in some ways more of a realistic view and perhaps pagan in outlook, certainly in its ceremonials. It rejected the old style religion based on the Christianity which had emanated in the Jewish land, it would have been too much to expect otherwise in an anti-Jewish state. The 'religion' of Himmler was based on the old land worship, perhaps due to his background, it extolled Nature in its manifestations; there is nothing bad in that. Yet no SS man was prevented from thinking as he chose in such matters, there was no censorship in that way; men married in church in the normal way and were free to bring up their children by 'Godly' principles and the norms of society, though naturally the Fuehrer and his Reich would figure in it too.

Religion never figured greatly among the Allied armies, certainly as far as the British forces were concerned church parades if compulsory were an infringement. The subject simply did not have importance in a battle, which is not to say soldiers did not believe in a higher power. They were in truth more concerned with their own immediate survival and their comrades; it was no different in the SS army. Comradeship in stark adversity becomes the order of the day, an even greater *esprit de corps* can be forged under fire, and everything points to the fact of the SS army having this in plenty and certainly more so than most with the exception again of the paratroops. The word 'fanatical' is most often used in describing the SS troops in battle, but surely this word implies a degree of unbalance; these young soldiers were so imbued with self-belief that in action — just like other élite troops — they proved very hard to crack. It is possible to see the code of the top class soldier as 'religion'.

It has been said more than once by military writers and historians that these early SS soldiers were indeed an élite, with the former 'asphalt soldiers' of the Leibstandarte SS at the pinnacle of the superb SS warrior caste. They had been moulded by men who held a dream of super soldiers, the like of which did not exist elsewhere, who in fact fitted in very nicely with the warrior 'tribe' seen by Himmler as to prove worthy of the rewards he would give them later.

It has been said that at this point — as soon as the SS went to war that is — they became victims of an ideology and at once showed this by the committing of atrocities. It is impossible and improper to avoid this question, not only because it has bedevilled and tarnished the SS army ever since the 1940s, but also because it would in no way be a balanced account otherwise. Even so, this narrative will not be broken by it, the whole question of SS culpability on the field of battle will be looked at later.

The young SS soldiers entered the shock of battle, and whatever hard training they had received, nothing could equal the first hours of real combat.

Peter Zahnfeld:

'Then came the great crisis with Poland. We moved into East Prussia to carry out manoeuvres with the Army. I will never forget my first time in combat.

'We advanced into Poland under a barrage of noise which was very great. We rode in trucks and in time reached some ruined villages and were obliged to proceed on foot across fields and under fire. Several men went down as we rushed forward in a great dash to capture some ruined homes where a number of Poles had set up a strongpoint. We had fired all our weapons and when we reached the ruins we discovered several corpses. These were the first dead we had seen and we were quite sickened by them, but soon pulled ourselves together.

'After a brief pause we moved on again and came under fire and were forced to deploy across the fields. By that time I had lost about six men killed and wounded. The next objective was another village where the Stukas had already done their work, but the Poles had simply moved back into the rubble to set up their machine-guns. So we were under fire the whole way but still rushed forward. I had a Schmeisser, a pistol and some grenades. There were bullets flying around us and in some cases they found their mark. Then we were among the ruins and threw our grenades among the suspected Polish positions, and by the time we had surrounded the village all the Poles were dead or giving

up. They were a rather sorry looking crowd and we waved them back to the rear.

'We had a few more sharp battles before we ended our first day of the campaign and could take stock, sit down and have a meal. We had lost twelve men killed and wounded which was not too bad, but it was a week before replacements came.'

Since most Germans were obliged to rely on Dr Goebbel's version of current events, this coupled with lectures gave the SS soldiers enough motivation for attacking the Poles. Karl Lempke recalls that he had attended lectures on Germany's rights and the greatness of the Fuehrer's decision:

'We could not really understand why other countries were adopting a hostile attitude. After all, they had won the Great War and had many colonies, yet seemed intent on putting Germany down. Of course, some of our leaders were very bellicose and made inflammatory statements which did not help. But overall we felt we had a right to be heard and live our lives as we saw fit. We took part in some big parades before the war began, and by then we had come to see that we were considered by our leaders as something very special.

'I remember that when we went into Poland I had a terrible feeling that I had made a wrong decision that would cost me dear. I don't know why I thought this, it was just a feeling that I had made a mistake.'

Lempke fought with a Totenkopf unit put together as part of the reinforced infantry battalion *Heimwehr Danzig*, and like the other SS units was under Army control in these operations:

'We went into our first attack and I was hit by a bullet at once. That was a moment I will never forget. I had gone forward with my comrades under fire from an enemy we could not see at all. They were concealed behind a high embankment with rifles and machine-guns. Our aim of course was to outflank them, but to do this we had to cross their line of fire.

'I was hit twice, once in the left calf, and also in the upper chest. It felt as if someone had kicked me in two places at once. I fell to the ground in pain and knew I was in trouble as the blood was welling out of my chest and soaking my uniform. Then the pain eased and I fainted, but seemed to wake up now and then before going under again. Then I felt a medic turning me over and applying bandages, and it all went grey and black and I was happy to pass out again.'

It had been a very short war for Sturmmann Lempke.

Karl Hummelkeier, like most Germans, imagined that when the British Prime Minister Neville Chamberlain went to see Hitler that some compromise would be reached, but this did not happen:

'So when war came we were thrown in at the deep end. We went into Poland

with the Army and received our 'feuertaufe' (baptism of fire). You have heard how we were taught to attack, so we did our best to put the teachings into practice. The noise however was far greater than expected and took some time to get used to.

'In my first action I saw some dead Poles already killed by the units in front of us and this was very disturbing. But we had been warned that we would see some unpleasant sights in battle and not to take too much notice. This was hard to do, for no matter how long you train the real thing is rather different and we were very young and had never seen dead bodies before.

'We ran on and fired our weapons, not often seeing the enemy before us, yet when we reached our objectives there they were lying dead or wounded. Some of our own lads paid the price too, but these were soon removed from the scene. I remember the first time I saw a Polish soldier and killed him. He had a long rifle and was partly hidden behind a ruined wall. He was shooting at us and I knelt down and took careful aim before pulling the trigger of my rifle. He fell over sideways and I rushed forward in some excitement, but felt strangely unhappy when I found him with a hole in his head. My NCO pushed me on with the rest of the squad. This was the first victim of my trusty Mauser rifle, and not the last, though as I said, on most occasions the enemy were invisible to the attackers.'

Peter Zahnfeld wondered how he had fared in his first action:

'Fortunately, I had some first-rate NCOs with me who knew their stuff, though one had been killed who I thought highly of. As to my first attempt to take life, I can honestly say I had no idea if I had killed anyone or not. When we fired at suspected enemy positions it was all very much guesswork, so when we found corpses we could not say who had done the actual killing. Not that it mattered to us, for in that kind of situation a soldier does as he is trained to do, it all becomes rather automatic and a case of 'them or us.'

'Just the same, to see the first mangled dead man is upsetting for anyone. I thought of my family and of what their reactions would be if they saw their son standing over bloody corpses. But as an officer I had to set an example so did my best to hide my feelings.

'We ate a cold meal as hot food did not reach us until later that night, then we slept fitfully in the ruined cottages. But at dawn we were roused by heavy artillery fire from our own guns and planes flying over us. Then an officer arrived on a motorcycle to give us our new objective, and after a quick wash from water out of our bottles we ate some food and soon moved off along a cratered road until we reached a ruined bridge and were obliged to ford a small river, emerging soaked on the far side. We came under fire at once from a wood which was soon obliterated by our Stukas and this saved us quite a fight.

'We were allowed no rest. Some trucks came at last, having driven through the river, they took us on a mile or so until we again came under fire and we deployed to try and locate the opposition. We could not see the enemy but could hear the rattle of their machine-guns. Fortunately, they were firing too high so

we rushed forward and then saw the Poles scurrying away on a horses, so our m.g. gunner took aim and brought them all down. It was hard to see those horses killed. We then moved on rapidly until reaching a wrecked town where our bombers had done their work. The rubble made progress difficult, so we tried to infiltrate round the flanks but came under fire and lost men. In the end I crept forward with a small assault group to within grenade range and was able to deal with the opposition.

'I ran forward with my men firing our weapons and suddenly the Poles threw up their hands around their machine-gun, but we were still firing and all of them were killed. We climbed over their dug-outs and holes where the bodies lay. There were six Poles, only one of them still alive and wounded and he was taken away.

'These small actions went on day after day, by which time I could not see why I had not been killed as many of comrades had vanished and I had seen much of the ugliness of war. However, such had been our hard training and indoctrination into self-belief that I had no intention of throwing up my hands in horror and shouting "enough!" I was a trained soldier for the job and firmly believed that it had to be done. The Poles had been committing atrocities against our minorities in the border areas so the fighting was inevitable. The fact of Nazi lies and propaganda was not then known to us.

'After another week my company had lost nearly half its strength but received only a dozen replacements. These new lads had of course to learn all we knew, but much had to come to them by experience. It was impossible to inculcate the real thing. Fortunately for these newcomers the campaign soon ended and the cease-fire came. If it had continued I would have ended the battle with an entirely new complement.'

Karl Hummelkeier survived several engagements and after the battle ceased was detailed to guard captured Poles, great numbers of them. His unit was then inspected by higher SS commanders before returning to Germany:

'Everyone was in celebratory mood and expecting peace to come again. We were all very disappointed when the war continued, but I recall one rather arrogant NCO telling us that the Western Allies would be 'dealt with'.'

Peter Zahnfeld went home in 'great thankfulness' to his family and girl friend,

'who were terribly relieved to find me in one piece. Naturally, we had been shocked by the outbreak of a general war with France and England, but could not see why it should continue now that Poland was finished. We all hoped it would end in peace. But this was not to be.'

It is a fact that this was the attitude of most Germans, though of course in the case of Hitler himself there were more complex motives.

Georg Keppler:

'We were quite satisfied with the performance of our troops in Poland, though at the time the Army were quite hostile to us, wondering as to our true motives and apt to criticize just for the sake of it. We did not suffer any undue casualties in that campaign, proportionately no more than the Army.'

Some writers on the SS have stated that the force suffered heavy losses in Poland, but no exact figures for them alone are available, only those for the Army including SS units as a whole, and these can hardly be seen as light:

Killed 10,572   Missing believed killed 3,400   Wounded 30,322

While the SS commanders may have been satisfied with their troop's performance they certainly thought that the units would have done even better outside Army control. However, there is no doubt that the SS-VT did all that was asked of it in Poland.

CHAPTER FIVE

Following its successful participation in the Polish campaign Himmler saw ample justification in expecting his SS to be expanded into properly organized divisions, though as always the Leibstandarte would remain a separate case.

Keppler:

'When Himmler inspected the men after the Polish campaign he told them that the Fuehrer would undoubtedly be glad to give them a much larger part to play. But Himmler was wrong as Hitler disagreed. He was far too circumspect in this and would not allow any general expansion of the V-SS by recruitment.'

Hausser:

'When the war came we were able to a small extent to prove our theories; by and large we were well pleased by the performance of our men in battle, though once again Himmler began to see this new force as his own and never ceased to have ideas as to their employment. I was given an example of this right after the Polish campaign.

'Without consulting us, he, through his recruiting officer, Gottlob Berger, had two whole new divisions formed by calling on camp guards and policemen who were in the first place unselected by our process and secondly, totally without military experience or training. This was their solution to the recruiting problem because the German Army was beginning to have serious doubts about this new army and had made certain difficulties already in recruiting and the supply of weapons.'

Himmler authorized his recruiting staffs to get busy, but obviously with a great new campaign in the offing in the West time was of the essence, for Hitler planned to attack the Allies before Christmas 1939, though in the event for various reasons mostly connected with the terrible winter weather this date had to be postponed. It needs to be made clear: Hitler's refusal to allow a general large recruiting campaign for the V-SS stemmed largely from his respect for the army's objections. The generals saw no possible reason for an enlargement of the SS field army simply on the grounds that it had made some contribution to the victory in Poland, their arguments really based on deep suspicion of its true motives. Whether

Hitler 'tipped the wink' to Himmler is unknown, but it seems inconceivable that he would have allowed the large expansion which did take place if he really disagreed with it. The way Himmler and Berger got over their problem is extraordinary to say the least, though the same method used later in the war would have been seen as normal. Men from the camp guard units and civil police were simply transferred *en bloc* and pronounced the new Totenkopf and Polizei divisions, the policemen retaining their usual large insignia on their upper left arm of their tunics and were actually in the front line in the West before the great attack took place.

Hausser:

'Himmler and his staff thought they had pulled a master stroke and indeed there was not a thing the Army could do about it. Thousands of men were thrown at us who had not been selected and would certainly never have been in normal circumstances, by which I mean if we had been left to our own devices. This infusion of inferior material (as it was in many cases) gave us problems later, as did the fact that Himmler reserved the right to use certain SS units for 'special purposes', and in no case were such men of the regular combat units even though they wore the same uniform, which as things turned out later was very unfortunate for us.'

There are interesting sidelights on this period, apart from the above. The generals of the German Army refused to accept the new SS intake as combat soldiers at all, or to put it another way — they could not agree to calling camp guards and policemen soldiers, and they were right. Secondly, a further dilution of SS standards was brought about by Himmler when he allowed all SS units bar the Leibstandarte to take men of five feet seven and a half inches. The new expansion of the V-SS was also opposed by the Army by denying it heavy artillery, so for the time being the SS gunners were forced to take over captured Czech weapons. The relationship between the German Army and V-SS at this time was strained.

By April 1940 the SS-VT had been redesignated the SS Verfuegungs Division, but by curious arrangements then existing the Leibstandarte, Totenkopf and Polizei divisions were counted as separate entities. In the same month the Wehrmacht invaded Denmark and Norway, then on 10 May began the offensive in the West proper by attacking Holland, Belgium and France.

Like thousands of other German servicemen, Peter Zahnfeld had heard rumour of an impending attack in the West, but had been through the bad winter with no action. But then his unit was moved into north-west Germany where they were told they would have a small but important part to play in an assault on Holland:

'This was a big surprise to us as the country was neutral, but we had our

orders and were bound to carry them out. The plan was for us to break the country and then move on into Belgium, and if the situation developed favourably to go onward into France. Our commanders told us that the intention was to knock France and England out of the war. It all seemed a very big gamble to us and we had fears that a repeat of the earlier war might come about so that we were reduced to positional warfare. But our leaders assured us that the French would not be able to stand up to modern warfare, and the English army was too small to act decisively.

'My memory of that first day of the attack is vivid. We were lined up in column on our side of the frontier waiting for the command and moment to move. Everything was very still in the early dawn and I'm sure the men's nerves were stretched as the Dutch had been watching us assemble and knew perfectly well what was going on. It seemed a bad moment to me, to be invading a small neighbouring country. We had been told that the British had been infiltrating Holland, but we had no way of knowing the truth of the matter.

'At long last the whistle blew and our leading armoured car crashed through the frontier barrier with all the vehicles moving up behind it as fast as possible. I was with a group of my men in a radio truck with orders to keep moving as rapidly as possible. We heard a few shots fired but nothing very much, all we could really hear was the noise of our vehicles and behind us our column stretched for miles.

'There was hardly anyone in the streets at this early hour, but very soon we heard the sounds of more concentrated battle and the whole column came to a halt. We were obliged to jump down and take cover beside the houses as machine-gun bullets began to fly. We advanced at once, along the pavements on each side of the road. Our leading armoured cars had passed a Dutch strongpoint without noticing it and the wily Hollanders had allowed them to go by without firing a shot. But as soon as our softer vehicles came along they let fly. Two of our trucks were hit and put out of action.

'We were obliged to lie flat as a stream of bullets struck the houses around us. Creeping forward we soon reached the Dutch post with at least one machine-gun. They could not hold us off; some of the men went through the houses and gardens and outflanked the Dutchmen. There was a series of grenade explosions and the post fell silent. We then ran on until some of our trucks reached us and we were able to climb aboard again. So far it had been fairly easy, we had lost only one man wounded.

'But then it became more difficult as we came under heavy fire from all arms.'

Karl Hummelkeier had suffered in the terrible winter, with training curtailed by the big freeze-up which affected Germans and Allies alike. But once the thaw came manoeuvres started with expectations of a big offensive:

'I grew very apprehensive as I felt this would be a very difficult campaign

53

against a better organized enemy. When the big day came and we went into Holland I had already made out a will, such was my pessimism. The idea came from a friend who said that although SS troops were very good and probably the best, many would die as we would always be in the forefront of the attack. So I allowed him to talk me into making out a will which I placed in my wallet. Not that I had much to leave at all, in fact, looking back it seems to have been a futile gesture.

'The campaign in Holland was marked by sudden, rapid advances and short sharp battles, especially when we came up against the flooded countryside which was a problem. The Dutch fought bravely but were no match for our forces and it was soon over.'

Karl-Heinz Anold took part in the campaign but saw little action in the few days it took to subjugate Holland as he was stationed in the rear of the columns.

Lieutenant Krollman also entered Holland on that May day, but was wounded in the knee and returned to Germany in a hospital train. Meanwhile, what of the other pre-war recruits?

Lothar Vogel had become well ensconced into the ceremonials of the Leibstandarte and was obliged to turn out on many occasions in his best rigout as part of the Berlin honour guard:

'I saw many foreign dignitaries including the British Prime Minister Mr Chamberlain during 1938-9, as well as the French leader M. Daladier and the Italian Duce, Mussolini. But then we had a great increase in purely military training and when war came I thought we would be caught up in it, but to my great surprise a squad, of whom I was one, remained to guard Hitler's Chancellery and other places. In this capacity I often saw Hitler and was inspected by him as one of the honour guard. Of course, I was very young and did not understand much beyond my duties and the honour of belonging to an élite guard. I enjoyed frequent leave to my home and believe I was looked upon by my family and neighbours with respect.

'The war did not greatly affect my life as things went on much as usual. There was the great victory over Poland and then the triumph in the West followed by celebrations, but we of the LAH guard felt out of this in a sense for we had not earned our laurels in battle. Other units returned from the war with honours and medals and we wondered what would become of us. In fact, we were referred to as the 'asphalt soldiers' I believe.'

Karl-Heinz Roberts had continued in his danger-free occupation of translating French and British messages, but:

'This work changed as soon as the war came, for all the enemy staffs left the country. But there was still work because there were neutrals who often spoke to each other in English or French and much of their conversation was spied upon by the Gestapo who used all kinds of people in that work (including the

domestic staffs supplied to the embassies, even the Italian — author). *But for me the end was near, for the work was that much less that I found myself increasingly under-employed. I was therefore taken out of that office and became a kind of liaison officer between Berlin and various other headquarters throughout the Reich.'*

This would lead Roberts to an even more interesting post in due course.

The short campaign in Holland was at times dangerous for Peter Zahnfeld. When his unit came up against heavier opposition they were forced to go to ground as shells and bullets flew about them:

'We had good air support, but the fighting became more confused, with Dutch positions in little streets and fields in front of us. Our companies had to deploy on a wider front and put in a number of attacks. In one of these I led my men across a flooded field, up to my knees in rising water, with bullets flying and shells passing overhead. We lost a few men, but considering the circumstances casualties were light. A few prisoners appeared and moving on we found some guns abandoned among the trees.

'Then we entered a fight with a larger force of Dutch infantry whom we had to outflank through more flooded fields. This took several hours as the Hollanders were well prepared and the floods were an obstacle to us. But by late that afternoon we had almost surrounded the enemy who began to give up in numbers. We were exhausted, hungry and thirsty and rested a while to await further orders. Some of my men had gone missing during an assault through the watery fields, some killed and wounded, but all in all we were still fairly intact. But we were obliged to move on to consolidate our position before dark, so we ran through the streets until we had reached a dominating position from which we could cover all approaches with our machine-guns. It was sometime before food reached us and we were able to relax and eat our first meal of the day.

'We entered some deserted houses and made ourselves comfortable but were careful not to create damage and I advised the men to do no looting. While some slept others took post at the windows in the upper storey. But we were allowed little rest as the battalion commander arrived and ordered us to resume the advance for the rest of the evening. It was very warm and we were exhausted but formed up and boarded our transport. At the head of our column we had armoured cars and they led us out of the built-up area of the small town and across the countryside. We saw a number of abandoned Dutch posts but encountered no enemy fire until nearing Arnhem when we were forced to deploy again in the gloom of the evening.

'The flashes of the enemy weapons gave away their positions and we rushed towards them in great style, shooting with everything we had. The Dutchmen were very brave, but we soon penetrated their defences, brought up mortars and machine-guns and gave them a real pasting. They were then outflanked and forced to give up. By then it was quite dark, but our CO again told us to board trucks and move on for another hour before finally halting in a village for the night. When I assembled my men at the end of this day I found twelve missing, but one or two turned up later, having become separated during the battle.

'Once more we tried to get some rest in the houses which were pretty and contained some food to supplement our meagre rations. We had a 'cannon kitchen' (goulasch kanone) in our column and received a hot meal, and I found some milk and cheese in the house we occupied which made a decent late night supper. Then I took my boots off and fell asleep on the sofa, my men were stretched out on the carpets, but three were on sentry outside. So far the campaign had been fairly easy and we were told that the attack was going according to plan and that the Army was heavily engaged with Allied forces in France and Belgium. Our paratroops had dropped in some places and gained great success.

'I was roused by our battalion CO in the very early hours for an officer's conference and the line of advance shown to us. So before sunrise we had mounted up, and this time we had two infantry guns with us. Other columns were already moving off on our flanks and we began our advance again behind a probing pair of armoured cars but soon came under very heavy fire from Dutch artillery which plastered the houses and the road. So we were forced into the fields alongside but then came under machine-gun and rifle fire. We advanced behind our armoured cars which gave the enemy posts a pasting before we rushed them.

'I saw a neat little house with some Dutch soldiers firing from it, so shouted to some of my men to cover us while we tried to outflank it from the left. The enemy fire was very rapid as we ran across the wet grass and dropped down behind some small trees. We were now to one side of the house and saw some Dutch soldiers moving along a road. We let them go, then rushed the house as firing went on from the ground and top floors. We hurled grenades through the windows and some of us rushed inside through the front door, firing our weapons and shouting. The din was terrific and I heard yells and screams and some Dutchmen came rushing out of the upstairs rooms with their hands up. One was badly wounded and collapsed. The rest ran downstairs and were searched before being sent away. On the ground floor we found three dead Dutch soldiers with a machine-gun.

'The rest of my company advanced and we resumed our attack across some flat fields until reaching some abandoned artillery positions. The guns had been put out of action and there was no sign of the enemy. Our vehicles then reached us and we rode along a highway until once more we came under infantry fire and were forced to leap for cover. Two of my men were hit. As usual we let our mortars and machine-guns give covering fire while we tried to outflank the Dutchmen which we did successfully and the enemy were all captured. We found an officer who spoke German, he was very civil and congratulated us on our dash. But he said the Allies would soon halt us!

'That afternoon we made a big advance and by dusk had covered a very considerable distance. We waited for a hot meal and were congratulated by our CO. It had been another hard day and we were further depleted in numbers.

After a meal we moved off again and at once entered more fighting with losses on both sides. The Dutch defence was organized in depth and we could see it would be a bigger battle. We had some Army tanks on our flanks and a set-piece battle was organized with all the trimmings of artillery and Stuka attack. The noise was very great and the Dutch fought hard, and in this battle I received a slight wound to my right arm, but carried on. We managed to reach the cover of some houses and waited while the tanks put paid to some enemy guns and machine-gun posts before we rushed on.

'In an hour it was all over and the locality was cleaned up. I saw many dead and wounded Dutchmen and a few of our own. Then the tanks moved on and we followed in our vehicles across flooded fields to enter a village where to our great surprise we found some civilians still in occupation. These Dutch people had not panicked or fled as we approached though they must have seen the big battle not far away. They watched us in silence as we dismounted for a break while the tanks went on to probe for more enemy forces.

'I must say the Dutch were not unfriendly considering that we were invaders, but when I tried to speak civilly to some of them they ignored me, so I did not press myself on them. In any case we were then ordered to move on rapidly. By then the campaign was in its final stages and we were nearing the Belgian border. I was not sure of our route, but our CO told us to rush on with all speed to penetrate the Allied defences over the border, and this is what happened.'

By 20 May the Leibstandarte with the other V-SS units which had conquered Holland had entered Belgium and France. On this day some 40 Allied divisions comprising a million men were cut off in the northern half of the front, having been split from the French armies in the south by the German spearheads in the Ardennes and Arras-Abbeville areas. The Germans reached the Channel coast and the Belgian army was in the process of collapse; the British were faced with disaster, the possible loss of the entire expeditionary Corps — or perhaps the escape of some by sea, the evacuation of an entire army seemed impossible. But this is what it came to, the operation went ahead without consultation with the French, the general most concerned astonished to find the evacuation in progress, when he had planned to turn Dunkirk into a base for a counter offensive. This apparent perfidy by the British was to have lasting consequences and be fully exploited by German propaganda.

Karl Hummelkeier also crossed into France where he found the battles fiercer and more costly:

'The Allies were no walk-over. At one village the English had erected a road-block and held us up for a while, and when we tried to encircle them we came up against artillery fire and lost more men. But our Stukas were called up and really flattened the place and the resistance melted away.

'Then we had a battle against the French forces who soon gave up when our panzers got among them. There were very many prisoners, and we had soon

penetrated far into France and their front collapsed, every time they tried to form a line we outflanked them. In one battle we fought against some cadets who were very brave and caused us casualties, but we bested them and raced on in our transport at a good pace. This kind of action was repeated daily until we were deep into France.

Karl-Heinz Anold was not however involved in any action and found himself guarding large numbers of French prisoners:

'They were very demoralized but I believe thankful to be alive and out of the war.'

Peter Zahnfeld crossed into Belgium:

'We soon came up against Allied forces who were already in trouble through the deep penetrations of our panzer spearheads. The battles we now entered were not greatly different, it was a war of movement. We advanced under cover of our heavier weapons, attempting to outflank the enemy positions, and soon saw our first dead Frenchman and some prisoners. The fighting varied from short, sharp battles to other engagements which tested us to the upmost. In these we inevitably lost men. My arm wound was of no consequence, but I felt I had been lucky to survive so far.

'Then we came up against British forces for the first time and had some heavy engagements. The Tommies fired fast and pinned us down again and again. Then we were ordered south and came up against the French again who in some cases were simply not fighting at all. There were crowds of these troops sitting by the roadside waiting to be captured, and we began to realize that the forecasts of our commanders had been correct. However, in some places we had hard fights when the enemy gave us battle and I will describe one such encounter.

'We had tried to enter a village in our vehicles but were ambushed and found ourselves fighting for our lives quite desperately, with bullets flying at us from all directions. The enemy were in the houses and round about and took a great deal of winkling out. We had to wait for tank support and these blasted the buildings one by one. Then we were able to go in and clean up. It was quite a bloody business and we found many French corpses which were ugly sights. We were also obliged to scour the grounds round the houses to winkle out snipers and stragglers before we could regroup and advance again. But that was an isolated battle, in most cases the French front was collapsing and we were able to move on rapidly. In fact I believe our commanders were amazed that things were going so well, and when that night came they hurried to us to make sure we really were where we claimed to be!

'The number of prisoners was staggering and caused us problems as we had no means of feeding them at all so we were obliged to direct them to the rear. Our own ration trucks were hard put to keep up with us and we often spent whole days with very little to eat. It was necessary for us to halt each night so we could be found and fed.

'Eventually, after days and days of advancing we were ordered to halt. It seemed amazing, but the whole French army seemed on the point of collapse. This we never expected at all. The limits to our advance were no longer there, and as we went on and on to the south we wondered where we would end up. There were a few skirmishes and small encounters, but overall our battle seemed to be over and we were very relieved. In due course we were ordered to move far south to the Spanish border where some of our V-SS units had already arrived. This was staggering news and had come about because the French had quit and called for a cease-fire.

'We went on in good order through the very attractive French countryside, day after day until we reached the southernmost tip of the south-west coast near Spain and gazed upon the sea at the Bay of Biscay. It was an amazing sight and we were overjoyed. None of us had expected such a triumph.'

Indeed, the SS Verfuegungs Division had more or less motored its way in a grand, triumphant tour through France where at last the leading troops were able to exchange greetings with the Spanish frontier guards.

Karl Hummelkeier records that they took so many prisoners that they had no idea what to do with them, so simply told them to march east:

'We were ordered into a long drive south and eventually reached the Atlantic where we had a grand holiday, mixing with some of the Spaniards who treated us like friends.'

Karl-Heinz Anold:

'Then we motored down to the Spanish coast which was very enjoyable but it ended soon.'

The SS Verfuegungs Division was finished with the campaign in the West, enjoying the fruits of victory, bathing in the Atlantic at the fashionable spots of Biarritz and San Sebastian and generally savouring a brief touch of the good life before being ordered north again. But elsewhere, in northern France, the Leibstandarte and Totenkopf had some hard fighting to do against the British which involved both formations in not only their most severe test in battle to date but atrocities; these incidents to be explored in a later chapter.

CHAPTER SIX

The troops of the SS Verfuegungs Division reluctantly left their seaside location and new Spanish friends, driving north-east through France and then back into Holland where they took up occupation duties before being included in the preparations to invade England. And on 22 August the V-SS forces were awarded their first Knight's Crosses:

SS-Hauptscharfuehrer (Sergeant-Major) Ludwig Kepplinger of the largely Austrian *Der Fuehrer* Regiment was cited for bravery and leadership in action with only two of his men against some ninety Dutch soldiers near Arnhem.

SS Oberfuehrer* Georg Keppler, cited for leadership of his Der Fuehrer Regiment during the campaign in Holland.

SS-Oberfuehrer Feliz Steiner, cited for leadership of the Deutschland Regiment in action against French troops in Belgium.

On 4 September two further awards of the Knight's Cross were announced:

SS-Obersturmfuehrer (1st Lieutenant) Fritz Vogt of the 2nd Reconnaissance Company had already won both the 2nd and 1st Class Iron Cross for his actions in Poland. He was now cited for leadership and bravery in an action by the Maas-Waal canal line.

SS-Sturmbannfuehrer (Major) Fritz Witt, commander of the 1st Battalion of the Deutschland Regiment, had won the Iron Cross 1st Class in Poland and was further cited for his action against 20 British tanks on the evening of 27 May 1940.

In Holland the Deutschland Regiment spawned a singing star, one SS-Schutze (Rifleman) Rolf Schroth of the 15th Company, who had been a music teacher in the Reich Student League before the war. Under the leadership of Oberscharfuehrer Schletz the company choir (featuring Schroth as soloist) performed over the Dutch Radio Hilversum, later being presented with a recording of their performance.

Paul Kretzler successfully completed an officer course in the agreeable surroundings of Bad Tolz and was then posted to the reserve pool, but then sent on his first assignment with two other men to help train personnel of the new Totenkopf Division; this task took place after the unit's battles in France. Although composed largely of ex-concentration camp guards and policemen, the division had of course to be led by experienced SS NCOs and Officers.

---

* A rank between Colonel and Brigadier-General later abolished.

'We found a lot of men who had no military training whatever. They were not very fit and knew nothing of infantry tactics or anything else. In fact, many of them had not even fired a rifle. We therefore had a very long programme of work to put them through their paces, and for this we were provided with some NCOs of experience from established units. I think it must have been at least four months before we could call ourselves a reasonably trained unit, and even then we were not satisfied that we were up to the standard required by the SS. This was made clear to our superiors, so they allowed us an extra month in which to complete the training. These new units included replacements and additions to the existing division which had fought in the West.'

This reorganization of the Totenkopf Division went on over the last months of 1940 and into 1941 and directly involved Gustav Doren, who it will be remembered had until then carried on a comparatively quiet and certainly safe existence as a camp guard:

'A very sudden and totally unexpected change occurred. We were engaged in our routine duties at the camp when we were told to report at once to the CO's office, and paraded outside where he told us that as a result of the great success of the SS in the Western campaign the Fuehrer had been pleased to sanction the expansion of the V-SS. As a result we would be transferred at once as soldiers. Just like that. We were amazed and wondered what would happen to the camp if there were no guards. This was soon resolved, as even while we packed our things a truck arrived with some policemen who were to act as temporary guards at the camp.

'Within a few hours we had been taken by truck to a location outside Berlin where we found a large camp with hundreds of other SS men who were to form the new division which we later learned was to be called the 'Totenkopf'. I am aware that certain things have been written about this unit with regard to war crimes, but I can only speak of what I myself experienced on the Russian front.'

Doren spent over two months in training as an infantryman, receiving the usual lectures on the élite status of the SS and the need to preserve its honour before moving into Poland for manoeuvres with other SS formations.

Whatever opposition the German Army generals had shown to the SS army, it began to wilt or was lessened following its performance in the West, and an indication of the attempts to make the SS divisions larger and stronger than their Army counterparts can be given.

At the close of the six-week campaign in the West (in June 1940), the Totenkopf Division numbered 20,000 men, but no less than 13,246 of these were over-age reservists, ex-camp guards and policemen. The big reorganization which took place was partly to weed out these less suitable troops and replace them with younger men, even though judging by some testimony these too included camp guards who never passed through the old, well-established rigid, SS selection procedures. One year later, just before the start of the Russian campaign, Totenkopf is said to have reached the astonishing strength of 40,000 men, but in fact this figure included occupation troops comprising older men, the younger, fitter soldiers were allocated to the 'front units'. Yet, the fighting part of this division still numbered over 18,700 men, which put them on a par with British infantry divisions which were invariably stronger in personnel than either the German or American and certainly the Soviet divisions.

In July 1940 Paul Kretzler was sent to SS General Eike's Totenkopf Division HQ in France, his mission to deliver a table of replacements he had helped to train:

'As it happened I had a brother already in that division and I was able to go and visit him for a short while. There was a great deal in progress in the unit as they had large numbers of prisoners to contend with and this was proving very difficult and a diverting problem.

'A few days later I returned to Bonn where the replacement HQ was situated and made my report, after which several detachments were sent to the division in France as replacements and I was given command of one of these. However, the fighting had of course finished and by the time we caught up with them they were on their way to the demarcation line (i.e. the border between Occupied and Unoccupied France), and then down to the south-west. So although we had seen no combat we enjoyed something of a holiday until finally moving north again.'

Meanwhile, with the German occupation of Paris, Karl-Heinz Roberts found a new opportunity to display his linguistic talents:

'I was sent to Paris as an interpreter which was a very interesting time for me as there were lots of French officials to deal with and I found I was in great demand. Some of these officials were from Vichy and very ingratiating towards the Germans, hoping I believe to keep us out of southern France. Others were industrialists who saw a chance to do business with the occupying forces. This lasted some months and I was allowed regular leave and was able to take home presents for my family, including French perfumes for my sister.

'Then I received another change of duty as I was sent to Brussels, put into a grey uniform and told I must work on intelligence matters with the SD. I had new people to meet of these staffs, some of whom were rather coarse, but they were policemen and I had no problem with them. Their task of course was to prevent any upsurge of terrorist activity, and at the time things were fairly quiet and there was little for me to do. Occasionally a suspect was brought in for me to question in French, but it was all very mild compared to what came later. I was not of course a policeman and knew nothing of such work and in due course I was returned to Paris where there seemed to be an increasing anxiety concerning resistance activity.

'I was now used as a sort of mobile interpreter and I suppose interrogator, though I never did anything brutal at all, I simply translated the questions put

to me by the police and passed on the replies. However, in some cases these prisoners were obviously in a state of shock and had been beaten. This I felt was inexcusable, but there was nothing I could do. It became obvious that I was being drawn into this police work which became more and more brutal, so in the end I had had enough and wrote to the right department in Berlin requesting a transfer to that city, or else the Waffen-SS.

'They probably thought I was mad to ask for a transfer from a place like Paris, but it became obvious that my life which had been reasonable was being changed completely. I never knew when I would be called out to interrogate some unfortunate Frenchman or woman. So in a couple of weeks I received a summons from the head of the security police in Paris, and he told me to pack my bags and go at once as they no longer had use for my services. He was cold and unfriendly so I packed my bags and left for Berlin the next day.'

For the Wehrmacht and SS forces the stunning victory in the West brought its rewards, especially in France where much of the population was not unfriendly. It is accurate to say, judging by most accounts, that many in the occupied lands got along very well with the conquerors, especially the middle and upper classes. And there were always farmers in the countryside willing to barter their produce — eggs, butter, cheese and milk in exchange for German beer and cigarettes and perhaps even scarcer items such as cans of petrol. Then too, inevitably, there were girls and women who liked to flirt and even engage in affairs with the Germans, for stylish uniforms and the age-old fascination of the foreign male worked wonders.

Peter Zahnfeld refers to the 'dreamlike days' in the south-west of France where a good time was had by all, the Spaniards on the border calling 'Arriba Allemania!' to obtain the response 'Arriba España!' The men swam in the warm sea, ate well and began to indulge in foolish notions of sitting out the rest of the war in luxury. This was of course nothing but daydream, for the British decreed that the war had to go on, and Hitler would see to it anyway since he now began actively pursuing his old dream of Eastern conquest.

In his speech to the mock Nazi 'parliament' — the Reichstag — in July he vaguely let it be known to Britain that he was satisfied, happy to let bygones be bygones so to speak, observing that he saw no reason for the war to go on. What the Fuehrer really wanted was for Great Britain to remain a quiescent observer, the island people content to retain its Empire (guaranteed by Hitler), while he moved East.

But to the German people and Wehrmacht, Hitler had proved yet again to be the most amazing prophet and war-lord, so surely his magnanimous, unmistakeable offer of peace would be taken up by the obstinate English?

'The war in France was over,' recalls Peter Zahnfeld, 'we believed the

stubborn British would now give up their senseless struggle. We were ordered north again, and after a long journey carried out in stages we again entered Holland as an occupation force. Some of us moved on to set up defences on the coast while others were set up as garrison troops. Then the word came that we might have to take part in the invasion of England.'

This was the case, for Hitler's overtures had been brusquely rejected, first by the impudent BBC, and then by more official comments from the government in London. Hitler sincerely wanted an accord with Britain, and like other Germans believed that there were those in British circles who saw Germany as an excellent bulwark against communism, which was true.

But for the Wehrmacht and SS troops the thought of a sea crossing was daunting:

'It seemed an amazing undertaking to us,' Zahnfeld recalls, 'and there followed a certain amount of half-hearted preparation as barges were readied and landings practised. It was all very experimental. We were in no way ready for such an operation over the sea. For myself I was very relieved when it all fizzled out.'

Karl Hummelkeier also spent some time as an occupier in Holland, like his comrades amazed that the supposed most powerful army in Europe had collapsed like a pack of cards:

'Then we returned to Germany, by which time our losses had been made good (in the Germania regiment), promotions had come and I was hoisted two rungs up the ladder to Corporal, which meant more pay and responsibility. We also had inquests into our campaign and performance. When I went home to my family they were most relieved and during this period I found a nice girl friend who promised to write to me. Her name was Ann and I'm sorry to say she did not survive the air raids.'

Although the decision had been taken months before, it was not until his speech in July 1940 that the term 'Waffen-SS' became official and widely known. It also marked the start of a new era, for the German Army generals agreed to this 'second army' becoming a 'fourth branch' of the Wehrmacht, even though this curious arrangement continued to bring problems. One of these has been mentioned; the Army's refusal to recognize camp guards and policemen as 'proper soldiers', or to supply them with heavy weapons, so once again the SS were forced to use captured Czech, Polish and even French equipment.

On the other hand, some of the Army's anti-SS prejudices had been worn away, such as on the occasion when one Army corps commander inspected Eicke's Totenkopf units on parade, apparently being much impressed by their turnout. The division would go on to become one of the best on the Eastern front, though some of its lesser units of the same name would fare far worse in terms of performance.

Lieutenant Kretzler spent the rest of 1940 helping to integrate and train replacements into this division, which included trying to pick up tips from the combat veterans, even though none of the formation's units had seen any action until late May. In Kretzler's case he was, perhaps to his satisfaction, taken off routine duties and used as a liaison officer.

The coming attack on Russia was one of if not the worst kept secrets of the war, a campaign which would as in such drawn-out struggles claim most of the old guard of the Waffen-SS in killed, wounded and missing. It was not too long after Hitler first advised his top generals of his intentions, certainly by early Autumn of 1940, that the first rumours began to circulate through the German divisions, finally percolating through to the lower ranks. Paul Kretzler:

> 'Early in 1941 I heard something of a great assault pending in the East, this rumour was rife for several months, but it was not until May that we were sent into Poland and concentrated in the eastern province near the border with the Soviet forces.'

The SS divisions stationed in the West had missed the huge celebrations and parades in Berlin following the victory over the Allies, and it was some time before the units left Holland. This occurred after the proposed landing in England was finally shelved in late September, though those troops billeted on the coast were frequently alerted against British air attacks and the landing of agents and saboteurs.

Karl-Heinz Anold

> 'I enjoyed a wonderful leave in Bremen with my family, and my lady friend seemed to look on me as a returned war hero, which I certainly was not. Then, in the New Year one of our Corporals told me that he had heard that we were going to the Eastern zone. I remember he looked at me for my reaction, but I had no idea what it could mean, so he laughed and said no more, yet within a few days he told me that a war with Russia was likely. This was a great shock to all of us and we could not understand why it should be. However, we heard no more until the battles opened in the Balkans when we began moving with the Army into East Prussia.'

Peter Krollman, because of his knee wound had spent six months recovering, but when he returned to duty he was re-classified as 'non-combatant' because his knee was no longer reliable:

> 'As a result I was posted to a depot in Berlin as a lecturer and spent a year on that job before requesting a re-assessment in the hope of returning to normal duties. This was only partially successful, the doctor told me that although my leg had healed it would give out again in combat. I told him that I would take

65

that chance, so I was regraded and sent to join the Leibstandarte Division (as it had become). The unit had taken part in the Balkans campaign and I joined it at the close.'

German involvement in the area was perhaps inevitable, but specifically brought about by the mess the Italian dictator had involved his forces in when they invaded Greece after usurping Albania; second, by the unexpected defection of Yugoslavia whose pro-German government had just signed a pact with Hitler, only to have it declared null and void by the Slav King and his followers, ably provoked by British influence. Yugoslavia was one of those artificial creations which sprang up following the earlier war, largely through American intervention; the results are still reverberating today in the '90s, with Serb and Croat at each others' throats, the latter establishing a German link which has survived.

No sooner had the Nazi Foreign Minister Joachim von Ribbentrop signed his much trumpeted pact in Belgrade and returned home in triumph than the British-inspired monarchist forces struck and overthrew the existing government. This event threw Hitler into a rage and within hours German ground and air forces were in action to reverse the proceedings. Hitler was already in considerable irritation at the distractions brought about by his Fascist partner the Duce, both in Greece and the longer standing fiasco in North Africa which had begun to divert German forces under General Rommel.

The German 12th Army comprising fifteen divisions including the Leibstandarte plus paratroops was launched on 6 April, and although these operations were not costly for the attackers in terms of casualties the wear and tear on the vehicles and the great cost in fuel offset this. Apart from this as well recorded in the histories since, the unexpected operations upset Hitler's schedule for the build-up and launch of Operation Barbarossa.

Lothar Vogel remarks that in his exalted position as one of the Fuehrer's Chancellery bodyguards he first heard of the impending attack in the East as early as the tail-end of the 'Kanalkampf', the Battle of Britain, and by early 1941 had been transferred to the field troops for training:

'We had received camouflage jackets and more equipment and went on exercises, but had no real idea of what lay ahead. Then came the unexpected bombshell of the Balkans war which included us. Everything came on in a rush. We were put into columns and drove off heavily-laden with all our equipment and rations, through Austria and then into Yugoslavia where we had our first battles. The Slavs were not at all good troops, poorly organized and equipped. We had one or two casualties but overall it was an easy victory. It was the bad road system and the many prisoners that caused us problems.

'We advanced right through the country and had only skirmishes on the way. Then we were obliged to enter Greece and came up against the British and Commonwealth troops who were tougher by far, but too weak in numbers and

not well positioned for large scale battles. Our first encounter with them came about this way:

'We were driving along in column on a rather precarious road leading to a plain when we came under machine-gun fire and were forced to take cover. We had air support and Messerschmitts were directed on to the opposition, but obviously had great difficulty in seeing them owing to the very rough nature of the terrain. So we were obliged to advance on foot in short rushes under covering fire of our armoured cars, eventually reaching level ground and deploying for a proper advance.*

'But the enemy machine-guns were still hampering our advance and movement, but then some of our squads managed to infiltrate the flanks of the opposition and forced them to withdraw. Then we were able to resume our general advance, but were soon held up again by rifle and machine-gun fire from ahead. It was not easy to outflank these enemy positions because of the terrain which became high again. There was so much cover for the enemy among the rocks and little hills it was hard to see them. This is where our fighters came in again. They raked the whole area with machine-guns and we advanced again.*

'In due course we forced an enemy withdrawal across the whole country and took many prisoners from units which had been cut off by the speed of our advance and had run out of supplies. But on occasion we had some sharp battles with rearguards who delayed us. The prisoners we took included British Tommies and South Africans who looked very fit and tough and in good heart. All were fairly treated and sent off as prisoners. In due course the whole country was occupied and we were relieved by more permanent garrisons. We did not envy them their task as there were already signs of guerilla activity both in Greece and Yugoslavia. It was then that we regrouped and were reinforced and learnt of the real war about to begin against the Soviet Union.'*

It is fair to say that the Leibstandarte would never have become involved in this Balkan adventure had it not been for Winston Churchill's decision to despatch troops and air forces to Greece which cost Britain dear in the short term but delayed Hitler's attack on Russia by only a crucial few weeks. As an aside, the memoirs of some soldiers who were captured by the Germans in Greece confirm Vogel's assertion of the fair treatment given to them. The short campaign produced the usual Nazi propaganda songs, for until the reverses began Hitler's club-footed genius Dr Goebbels continued to direct his songwriters to pen a stream of victory anthems. Then too, as soon as Yugoslavia was occupied the enemy put Radio Belgrade back on the air with the famous *Lili Marlene* sung by the Swedish-German girl Lala Anderson, a song wholly approved of by all British forces in the Mediterranean theatre of war.

The Balkan campaign also enabled one young SS officer to make his mark in no uncertain manner. Kurt Meyer can be seen as the archetypal product of the SS military schools; dashing, fearless, heroic, a born leader of men in battle. It was once said that the nerves of the SS soldiers in training were tested by the placing and exploding of small percussion grenades on their helmets. The tale is probably unfounded, but the extraordinary zeal of many SS troops in action is known, with officers expected to lead from the front, and not armed with a useless revolver but sub-machine guns and grenades. There are many examples of bravery and tenacity by these troops in World War II which if carried out by Allied soldiers would have been hailed as worthy of high awards. Naturally, in wartime exploits by enemy troops were hardly likely to be presented to the public at home in the same manner, at best the enemy were said to be 'fanatical' or perhaps 'suicidal'.

The kind of action the most determined Waffen-SS officer was capable of in the field is exampled by an incident involving Meyer, later dubbed 'Panzer' Meyer, who gained his first real laurels in Greece.

At the time Meyer commanded the Leibstandarte's reconnaissance battalion, in other words he was at the point of the attack and had been ordered to seize the Klisura Pass which was well defended by Greek troops lying behind mines, rocks and armed with machine-guns. The SS troops were pinned down by fire; Meyer and his men cringing behind boulders as the bullets whined and ricocheted about them. It seemed that no man dared step out from the cover to rush the Greek defenders; the advance was bogged down.

Meyer yelled at his NCO to get moving, but the man simply stared at him as if he was mad to suggest such a thing. Meyer wondered how he could force the NCO to take the first step. He soon solved the problem.

Taking an egg grenade from his belt he removed the pin and rolled it across the ground towards the amazed Sergeant and his men who were forced to leap out of the way and rush at the enemy before the grenade exploded. The Pass was taken and Meyer was awarded the Knight's Cross.

The Leibstandarte returned to Prague and thence on to eastern Poland and the invasion of the Soviet Union. Never one of the bigger SS divisions, the LAH was at this point 10,700 strong, fully motorized and complete with its own reconnaissance, signals, anti-tank, flak and other units.

Hitler's Directive No 21 dated 18 December 1940 had stated:

'The German Wehrmacht must be prepared, even before the conclusion of the war against Britain, to overthrow Soviet Russia by a rapid campaign (Case Barbarossa).'

To effect this defeat on Stalin's empire, which included Latvia, Estonia, Lithuania and half of Poland, the German forces were ordered to annihilate the bulk of the Soviet armies 'in bold operations by deeply penetrating panzer wedges' and preventing the escape of 'combat capable' Soviet units to the wide-open spaces in the east. It was not the intention of Hitler to occupy the whole of the USSR including Siberia, just enough of it to prevent the Soviet air force from remaining within range of

Reich territory. At the same time, the Luftwaffe would eliminate any remaining Russian industry east of the Urals.

To carry out this gigantic task Hitler had solicited a certain amount of military help from his allies: the Italians, Romanians and Hungarians would all contribute troops, as later would Spain with its so-called 'Blue Division'. Seven German armies were assembled, four Panzer groups, each commanded by an expert tank general, plus three air fleets, a grand total of 3 million men, 600,000 vehicles, 750,000 horses, 3,580 armoured vehicles, 7,184 guns and 1,830 aircraft. Clearly, the number of tanks and aircraft for such a mammoth operation were insufficient, but then Hitler was counting on a lightning campaign that would be over before the Russian winter set in. Of his allies, the Romanians contributed the largest force, their Third and Fourth Armies, perhaps due to the fact that fear and hatred of the Soviets was high in that country, for in its latest demands the Soviet government had demanded parts of Bessarabia be ceded to them, though it has to be mentioned that the Soviet 'expansions' and demands were in some cases only reflecting the return of territory which had once been theirs.

The performance of the SS troops in the Western campaign and their expansion into divisions ensured the German Army chief's agreement to their inclusion in Operation Barbarossa, as Paul Hausser confirms:

'When the campaign began in Russia the four SS divisions were an integral and essential part of the Army's attack plan. Even so, certain doubts continued to exist, though these were gradually eliminated as the campaign progressed and we never had any problems in our dealings with the Army thereafter. In fact, in certain periods they came to look on the Waffen-SS as their 'fire brigade', as is well known, for very often our men restored apparently impossible situations.'

By this time the Germania Regiment had been taken to serve as a nucleus for a forth SS division called Wiking, probably because many of its personnel were Scandinavian volunteers. The remainder of the Verfuegungs Division, reinforced by a battalion from the Totenkopf, was re-christened SS-Division Deutschland, but since there already existed an Army division called *Grossdeutschland*, this was changed to *SS-Reich* and then *Das Reich*. The man chosen to command this Wiking division was Felix Steiner and it took part in the invasion of the Soviet Union on 22 June 1941.

Against the great force assembled by the Germans the high command estimated Soviet strength in Western Russia as ten armies totalling four and a half million men.

The Nazi-Soviet Pact of friendship and economic co-operation had come as a bombshell to the Allies in 1939, especially to the British who had been making tentative moves towards Stalin themselves. The Germans had concluded secret protocols with the Soviets agreeing to the

Russian occupation of eastern Poland, and by 22 September 1939 the German and Soviet forces had met and agreed on a demarcation line. The Wehrmacht was to remain west of the river Bug, leaving the citadel of Brest in Soviet hands. After agreement was reached a joint parade was held, colours were exchanged and toasts drunk (in vodka to please the Soviets). But the Russian commander of the armoured brigade had proposed a toast to 'Eternal *fiend*ship' — and hurriedly corrected himself. Yet everyone present knew it was an unnatural alliance, for Hitler and his Nazis had been battling communism for two decades. Yet the economic exchanges had gone ahead, both sides gained, though in the final weeks the Germans had fallen behind in fulfilling their part of the shipments, but the Soviets had stuck to their part of it, the last trainload of raw materials actually rolling across the frontier shortly before zero hour on 22 June 1941.

In an order of the day read out by German commanders to all their troops before the great attack, Hitler for the first time mentioned the 'Eastern Front', the greatest in world history. The German troops he told them, stood 'shoulder to shoulder with allies', to join in a battle that would decide Germany's and indeed Europe's future as well as the world's destiny. The Fuehrer claimed that he had long been forced to remain silent in the face of Soviet provocations, machinations and a great military build-up in the western half of their country.

'May the Almighty help us all in this struggle', Hitler concluded.

Stalin, by his war on tiny Finland in 1939-40, had beaten that nation into surrendering valuable bases, and he had taken over three Baltic states and begun pressurizing Romania. Yet the huge Soviet forces in Western Russia were not concentrated for attack.

The world would indeed hold its breath as the great armies of Germany plunged into Mother Russia.

Peter Zahnfeld had seen the 'English bombers' flying over the Dutch coast during frequent alerts, with some planes being shot down.

'I remember seeing an RAF prisoner passing through under escort. He was only a boy and rather unhappy with the way things had turned out, but he was well treated I am sure.

'We had a tremendous shock when at the end of that momentous year we heard rumours of a big operation in the East. Then we moved back into Germany and I enjoyed some Christmas leave. After that changes took place, with the arrival of replacements and an assessment of our role in the Western campaign. But I said nothing to my parents or lady friend of the rumours I had heard, and I felt it was no longer such a good idea to get married, and my fiancée was happy to wait for my decision.

'We began moving through Poland in April and did a lot of training. As the Waffen-SS we had expanded greatly. Then the campaign in the Balkans began and we wondered if we would go to Greece. But everything remained quiet in Poland and we received no orders. Not until we moved into the Eastern zone *did our commanders tell us that the Soviet colossus was to be smashed before it could attack Germany in the rear. Since we had long heard rumours to this effect it came as no surprise. Yet the scale of such an undertaking was apparent and everyone was hushed in amazement of what it could mean. I myself had no love for the Soviet system, but it was so big that I doubted if we had the strength to break them. But our commanders sounded confident, and on the morning of the attack read out the Fuehrer's proclamation extolling us to get rid of the Russian menace, or words to that effect, of the huge scale of our attack and how patiently he had waited before making his great decision.*

'It was a grey dawn when hundreds of guns opened up and the noise was rather fantastic, we did not see how anything could survive such a bombardment. Then we moved off in columns and crossed the border into Eastern Poland and at first encountered no opposition, but then came under fire from isolated posts using machine-guns and deployed for our first battle.'

It is a fact that the Soviet outposts and border units were taken completely by surprise, and when some telephoned their headquarters to report they were under fire their claims were refuted, the response in at least one instance being 'Are you insane?'

If the Soviet forces in Western Russia were surprised by the German invasion, then the attackers too received many surprises, some of them distinctly unpleasant. One of the first was the greater scale of equipment in the cream of the Soviet armoured divisions, which however failed to offset their total lack of preparedness and the rigidity of their command system run from Moscow which denied commanders in the field all flexibility.

The Germans and their allies had opened Operation Barbarossa at 0315 hrs on 22 June, but not until over two hours later did Major-General Potaturchev (then aged forty-three and sporting a Stalin moustache), commander of the supposedly crack 4th Soviet Armoured Division receive his orders. Not to go into an immediate counter-attack, but move his division into the vast forest east of Bialystok, the last great virgin woodland in Europe. When the division was assembled, 500 of its 10,900-man establishment were missing, the medical company of 150 staff had only twenty-five men, and thirty per cent of its tanks were unserviceable, others being out of fuel or useless. And no sooner had Potaturchev, already angry and baffled by his orders, got his force moving than a fresh command arrived ordering him to split his division in two — armour and infantry. This was a classic and fatal error, for the fast moving German panzers at first raced past the Soviets and then moved round to encircle them. The Russians, split asunder by crazy orders and now the enemy assault, fled piecemeal into the great forest, many of the Russian units being caught and destroyed before the remnants reached cover among primeval undergrowth and trees. In fact, Russian infantry were superb fighters in such terrain, trained to conceal themselves totally in foxholes with weapons facing to the rear in order to shoot down the enemy when they had passed. The German infantry on the other hand were unfortunate since none had received such forest combat training, usually because the German Forestry Commission guarded its woodlands well. A German division was detailed to comb through the 'green hell' like armed beaters, while a second was positioned to catch any fleeing Soviets on the other side of the forest.

Meanwhile, Major-General Potaturchev and some of his staff slipped away, trying to escape towards Minsk, the capital of 'White Russia', and in due course the commander changed into a civilian outfit on a collective farm and hit the road again. But he was captured, along with thousands of other Russians, and marched off to a POW cage where, footsore and starving, he made haste to confess his true identity to his German captors. During interrogation he told all. His division, he informed his astonished listeners, comprised: 355 tanks, thirty armoured scout cars, an artillery regiment with heavy weapons, even a bridge-building battalion equipped with pontoons capable of carrying up to sixty-ton tanks.

The Germans were amazed, for even the panzer expert General Guderian's entire group of five tank divisions only comprised 850 tanks — ie, a German panzer division possessed only 170 tanks as against this Soviet unit's 355!

'I saw my first dead Russian soldier,' Zahnfeld continues, 'a fresh-faced boy with half his body mutilated. We pushed on, using our vehicles as much as possible but being forced to go on foot every so often as we encountered enemy fire. The Russians were very disorganized and we soon collected many prisoners who we sent off to the west. They were grubby but quite good natured, and perhaps glad to be out of it.'

Karl Hummelkeier recalls that they felt confident that the Russian bear would take such a beating that it would never rise again:

'In this we were to be disappointed, and although our fears of communism gave us the spur we did not realize that Himmler and others had plans for the long term colonisation of the East. I can tell you that very few of us had ever read Mein Kampf! So we had no idea that our beloved Fuehrer entertained ideas in that direction. At first the practice of ridding Germany of the Reds really did seem a good one, they were a bloody menace. My own view was that they should be deported to Russia which seemed to be their natural habitat, but as to taking it over, that was a very different matter.

'However, we had our orders and the army assembled by Hitler for this huge undertaking was a great one. Our attack began in the grey dawn of that June morning and by sunset we had advanced far, capturing all our objectives and meeting little resistance. We took a few prisoners but very soon had to cope with hordes of them and they became quite a problem.'

Unlike others, the ex-concentration guard Gustav Doren had no idea to what use he and his comrades would be put once they had been impressed into the new 3rd SS Division Totenkopf:

'It came as a bombshell to us when the CO read out the Fuehrer's proclamation that we were to invade Russia. We knew of the war in the Balkans of course, but had no idea that it was a prelude to a larger attack. Our officer told us that the Bolshevik enemy had to be laid low before they attacked us, that Stalin had been very cunning and had massed a large army on his western borders ready to attack us. He had taken over three small countries in the north as well as demanding lumps of Romania, and was putting pressure on others such as Hungary and Bulgaria. So we had to put a stop to him before he attacked us. That was the message.

'The attack was a very huge affair, yet when you are in a unit you see only the men around you, even a whole division can get so spread out over the landscape or along a road that most of it vanishes from sight. So you come to think only in terms of those nearest you. And that is how we saw the great conflict in Russia. I can honestly say that in my year and a half there the only army I saw in mass was the Russian, and that usually as prisoners. Our advance and attacks brought them in by the thousands and we simply told them to trek west.'

For Paul Kretzler, the great assault in the East was his first experience of war and, as he says, an extraordinary one:

'I was in a fully motorized unit of the Totenkopf and we raced across the frontier in our trucks and became involved in mopping up Russian stragglers who had not been inclined to fight and preferred surrender. These were sent west while we moved on through the wrecked villages. The heat and dust were terrible and we soon lost touch with our ration trucks. The vastness of the country surprised us, we had not expected it to be like that. We covered hundreds of miles during the next few weeks and had only a few short, sharp battles.

'We were fired on by some Russians in a ruined village who were supported by artillery so we deployed to outflank them. The Russians fought on until it was too late to retreat and they were all killed or captured. I saw my first corpses but these did not upset me as expected although a certain reaction did set in later. We were urged to push on and this we did, although we were very tired and hungry, but thirst was our greatest problem. Our losses had been light, but my own worst experiences were yet to come.'

Karl-Heinz Anold, now part of the new 4th SS Division Wiking had, on hearing the Fuehrer's proclamation, grown very apprehensive, but was assured by his NCOs and officers that the SS 'were the best troops in the world'. The Russians had been about to stab them in the back but they would get in first and smash them forever.

'All went very well. Our artillery and air force were magnificent and we rushed off into the Soviet zone, meeting very little organized opposition and seeing the first prisoners who looked terrible. We were very encouraged. After a week of riding in vehicles and marching we had very little idea of our location and then enjoyed our first real rest. We were always hot, tired and thirsty and had to wait for our ration trucks to catch us up. There was no danger of a Russian attack, their armies were completely destroyed, most of them simply encircled and sent west as prisoners.

'I remember lying under the stars in those summer nights, there were vast plains of wheat and grass and I wondered when we would reach Moscow. The chase continued, and then we helped the Army in a big encircling operation with a vast round-up of prisoners. They were a motley crowd, thousands and thousands of them, but remarkably cheerful, in fact some of them were calling out "Stalin nix! Stalin nix!" They seemed glad to be out of it. We sometimes saw disconsolate officers, once even a general. But in the main these thousands of Russkis were simply private soldiers. The Russian was a remarkable fellow in some ways, as when properly fed and in a good position he was a tough and enduring soldier. Otherwise he became useless.'

Having caught up with the Leibstandarte division after the Greek campaign Peter Krollman returned north to participate in the regrouping prior to Operation Barbarossa, his injured knee not having bothered him:

'But it was in Russia that the doctors were proved right. My leg collapsed under me in the middle of a battle and I was invalided back to Germany where I spent some weeks in hospital. This was a very unsatisfactory state of affairs for me, but even so I was glad to be out of the war, for no matter how loyal one feels to one's comrades and unit, it is always a relief to escape death. It is fair to say that as a result of my wound I survived the war, whereas very many of my comrades did not. It was also the reason why I was given the chance to serve in a different capacity.

'In due course I was interviewed by the CO of the hospital who told me that I could never return to combat. I was therefore sent to the general pool of officers awaiting posting and interviewed yet again with a view to my employment. I had no great aptitude, yet felt competent enough, but did not wish to return to the job of instructing. I was therefore offered a job on the HQ Intelligence staff in Berlin and I do not mean Himmler's but those of the Waffen-SS which maintained its own strictly military research and intelligence group. This I accepted as a new challenge. In effect my life was now to be comparatively easy, for I worked in an office all day and had my evenings and weekends free. In this way I was able to find a small apartment for myself and my wife who came to join me from Hamburg. This life of comparative ease would continue until the air raids became very bad.'

CHAPTER SEVEN

It is alleged that some half a million non-Germans served in the Waffen-SS during World War II, which represents an amazing turnabout considering the severe restrictions imposed on even native Germans in the 1930s.

Yet Heinrich Himmler authorized the acceptance of foreign volunteers into the then Verfuegungstruppe as early as 1938, using the term 'Germanen' (Germanic) to designate those of Nordic blood who were found in Holland, Norway, Denmark, Sweden, the Flemish areas of Belgium, Switzerland, Great Britain and the USA. It can be seen therefore that the Nazi foreign volunteer concept originated much before the German invasion of the Soviet Union in June 1941. Published figures quote the combat SS as having 20 such individuals in its ranks by the end of 1938; by the Spring of 1940 this number had grown to 100, including 44 from Switzerland, 5 from the USA and 3 from Sweden.

Himmler, and others like him who advocated strict racial selection had in fact an ally from a past era, Hitler's crony from the 'days of struggle' following World War I, the famous General Ludendorff, who stated:

> 'People of foreign race do not belong within the armed forces of a country; people of Jewish blood do not belong to the armed forces of Nordic peoples; coloured people do not belong to the armed forces of white peoples. Placed there, they would not share in the life and death struggle for their own people.'

Here, as in the earlier section dealing with the SS as a whole, distinction must be emphasized between the General (Allgemeine) SS and the Combat (Waffen-SS) when opening the question of foreign volunteers. For in all the areas they occupied, the Nazi authorities went about setting up auxiliary, state police forces along varying lines, according to circumstances. For example in Holland and despite initial opposition from Dutch National Socialists themselves, the Nazis pushed ahead with forming the 'Allgemeene SS in Nederland', which came into being in September 1940; by November 1942 this comparatively small force was re-titled Germaansche SS. Like the Allgemeine SS in Germany the Dutch SS men wore black outfits with special insignia, the function exactly the same as their German counterparts.

Apart from the later need to find more cannon-fodder, it was expedient for the Nazis to look for foreign participation in the military; it was the logical extension to their policy of *rapprochement* as first practised by the occupiers in Denmark and Norway. The kid glove approach was continued in Holland, Belgium, France and Luxembourg. This softly-softly method gradually gave way to a more persuasive one, the carrot followed by the stick, bribery and coercion. It began with anti-British propaganda, especially among the French, many of whom took little persuading that England had run out on them at Dunkirk. Then came the promise to return prisoners-of-war in exchange for volunteers to work in Germany, then calls for 'Europeans' to join Nazi Germany against Britain, world Jewry and later the Bolshevik menace. The final step was compulsion, edicts conscripting men in a wide range of age groups for labouring in the Reich, the alternative being service in one uniformed group or another, and this did not necessarily mean the Wehrmacht or Waffen-SS. The Nazis set up foreign equivalents of the Labour Corps, NSKK transport columns and Organization Todt construction battalions. In some cases foreign personnel from such units became directly involved in fighting: for example, in Russia a Dutch transport unit were attacked by Russian partisans and being armed defended themselves, and to such effect that several Iron Crosses were awarded by their foreign masters.

As part of their intention to completely penetrate the life of the conquered nation the Nazis instigated a wide variety of associations and unions such as those for writers, artists and other cultural activities; especially vigorous were German efforts to influence and re-educate the youth in these lands. It was inevitable therefore that a proportion of the population would be won over or simply pressurized into joining such movements, all of this activity bore some fruit in forming 'volunteer' combat units.

During the war years the fact of forced labour, deportations and harsher measures under Nazi occupation were frequently reported in the Allied press, but the question of our subjugated allies actually producing volunteers to fight for Hitler was a very different matter and rarely if ever touched upon. It can be imagined what effect such news would have had on the Allied forces and civilian population in Britain and the USA, for ever since the collapse of 1940 both politicians and media had been promising liberation for the enslaved nations of Europe. The notion of thousands from the supposed downtrodden peoples actually fighting for Hitler against their would-be liberators was not something permissible.

However, the difficulties and trials of nations trying to live and preserve their dignity and identity under the Nazis was well understood, as was the fact that inevitably a certain number would find it impossible to refuse the blandishments and threats of the occupiers. But there were always those in Britain who doubted the value of our continental allies, so it is hardly surprising that Nazi propaganda and indeed any information concerning Hitler's foreign legion was suppressed. Only tales concerning well-known, high profile traitors were given prominence. In reality of course, there is no reason to suppose the situation would have developed too differently in Britain, had it been occupied. It should not be forgotten that Oswald Moseley's Union movement which aped the Fascists in Germany and Italy could apparently boast up to 20,000 supporters. As on the continent, a proportion of such men sincerely believed that their leader's political ideas offered a way forward and out of the turgid stalemate of the democratic system. In America the 'Bund' movement was even more Nazified than in Britain; naturally, to some it was the lure of slick uniforms, banners, bands and parades rather than social progress that prompted them to join such organizations.

On the continent, the already existing Fascist and National Socialist parties acted as focal points for the German attempts to convert the populace to their way of thinking, though not necessarily for the recruitment of volunteers for the Wehrmacht, Waffen-SS and other para-military forces. The campaign began soon after the German occupation, and in October 1940 Dr Goebbels wrote in *Das Reich*:

'We place our hopes in the young people of Scandinavia and Holland . . . they will hear the call for their help as the foundation stone of the Grossdeutsches Reich; they are waiting for the day when they may honourably serve under the swastika with arms in their hands.'

Of course, so cynical was the Herr Propaganda Minister that he is unlikely to have believed such nonsense, but to Goebbels the lie was irrelevant unless it was successful. With Britain obdurate in its refusal to give up and reach an accommodation with Hitler, the Nazis turned on the full blast of anti-British propaganda directed at those under their heel, coupling it with assurances that some kind of union with Germany offered their best hope, a loose confederation of vassal states in fact under Nazi domination that would feed the Reich with cannon-fodder but above all workers. It is a fact that for much of the war the German Home Front and especially German housewifes were cushioned by foreign domestic and other labour to an astonishing degree. Goebbels' call and other Nazi pronouncements were of course only a hint of what was to come, and in fact the Waffen-SS itself had got off the mark rather smartly even before the Norwegian campaign finally ended in June by setting up a recruit centre in Alsace, specifically for the reception of foreign volunteers. This was the start of the Nordland unit, designed for the Scandinavians; the Westland regiment was intended for the Dutch and Flemish (Belgian) recruits.

The full account of foreigners serving the German occupiers, whether in military or para-military units is complex and need not be gone into in depth here. Suffice to say that only a proportion of recruits entered the Waffen-SS and these can be divided into men from west and eastern Europe. In terms of sheer numbers those from the latter areas were greatest, in terms of combat worthiness those from the west came top. Here we are chiefly concerned with these men, and a salient point to remember is the size of the native populations involved. The following figures relate to the 1937 census:

Holland 8,640,000   Belgium 8,361,000   Denmark 3,790,000
Norway 2,908,000   France 42,000,000.

This compares with a UK population of 47,721,000, and one historian has mentioned the number of foreign 'volunteers' in Germany's forces during World War II as 'staggering', inferring that if a similar proportion had worked for the enemy following a Nazi occupation of Britain then, for example, and taking the alleged Norwegian contribution as example (50,000 men), then Britain's 'Germanified' force could have numbered well over half a million.

Denmark, invaded on 9 April 1940, was the first West European land to feel the Nazi hand of 'co-operation' as always an iron fist in a velvet glove. The country had lost its southern province of Schleswig-Holstein to Prussian-Austrian invaders in 1864, but following World War I and at the urging of American President Wilson a plebiscite had split the region into Danish-German and German-Danish, people of both nations residing in each segment. Further American attempts to calm fears of war came when President Roosevelt prevailed on the Danes to sign a non-aggression pact with Nazi Germany in May 1939.

In a lightning operation the Wehrmacht drove through Denmark and invaded Norway, for the Dane's astonishment was followed by anti-climax as the Germans made their coming as painless as possible. By August 1940, 25,000 Danes had been recruited for work in Germany and the Waffen-SS opened up a recruiting office in Copenhagen to induce men aged from 17 to 40 to join the Nordland regiment, offering inducements such as joint Danish-German citizenship and farm land following two years of service. A draft of volunteers joined Norwegians and left for training in Austria, and by December this group had been incorporated into the new SS Wiking division.

The so-called 'Danish Free Corps' sprang to life following the German invasion of Russia, its first commander a Lt-Colonel Kryssing of the Danish Army, its forming received (eventually) government blessing, including the reluctant permission of the king. The unit fell under the aegis of the Waffen-SS from the start, and when some 480 men paraded the streets under a Danish banner marked *Frikorps Danmark* they were accompanied by Waffen-SS officers. Most of the Danes in this unit were regular army men, and still wore their own uniforms. Kryssing made a public appeal for a mass response, stating:

'Along the Eastern Front the fight against the world enemy is in full swing. Join this fight against our common enemy for the safety of our Fatherland which shall give our children security and peace.'

Two drafts of men numbering under one thousand in all reached Germany by end-August 1941, being buttressed by one hundred Danes from the Nordland regiment, so that by December this new Waffen-SS unit numbered about 1,164 men. At this point, as soon as the men arrived at their German training camps the friction began. A lack of liaison seems to have existed between Himmler's HQ and the camp staff who displayed indifference and a lack of sensitivity towards the Danes, breaking promises given earlier concerning a certain amount of autonomy to be allowed the Scandinavians and especially the rights of their officers. To the Waffen-SS training staffs they were merely new recruits destined for the Russian front who merited no special treatment. Dr Goebbels had made sure however that his propaganda machine played up the foreign volunteers as a shining example of the new anti-Bolshevik spirit permeating Western Europe, their faces appeared in the German media with lavish picture displays of the lads entering training.

For a start, the men were placed under German military law, their own NCOs and officers were deprived of jurisdiction and often treated as common soldiers. All the recruits were required to learn the German words of command and how to deliver the Nazi salute. The result of what the Danes saw as insulting treatment was a failure of the training programme. Colonel Kryssing's operations officer was taken away by the Germans for instruction at the Waffen-SS college at Bad Toltz, the Colonel effectively began a go-slow, so that after many weeks Reichsfuehrer Himmler was surprised to learn the Danes were not yet ready for action. His investigators revealed a sorry state of affairs, the Danish officers had turned out to be 'anti-Nazi' after all it seemed, Kryssing had done nothing to further their training or co-operate with the German staff, discipline was slack and dissension rife. Colonel Kryssing was dismissed by Himmler in February 1942, his place taken by a very different type of soldier.

Christian von Schalburg was a curious mix, a Baltic German born in the Ukraine, son of wealthy parents, a Count turned Lieutenant in the Danish Army following his family's return to that country after World War I. Schalburg was one of the first to volunteer for service in the Waffen-SS, saw service on the Russian front, and was recalled by Himmler in March 1942 to take charge of the recalcitrant Danes of the *Frikorps*. Schalburg succeeded where the Germans had failed, and by May the unit was declared ready for action and sent east to join the SS Totenkopf Division at Demjansk. The unit went into battle on 2 June and Colonel Schalburg was killed, being awarded a hero's funeral back in Denmark. A Danish General SS unit was formed and became known as the Schalburg Corps. His successor at the front was also killed barely a week later. By the following year the *Frikorps* was re-named SS Grenadier Regiment No 1 Danmark and taken into the new 11th SS Nordland Division; by May 1944 it had been re-designated SS Panzer-Grenadier Regiment 24 *Danmark*.

Amazingly, the Nazi occupiers permitted a general election to take place in March 1943, the results showed great support for the democratic parties, those National Socialists who entered the lists received few votes. But it was also a time of change in Denmark, unrest, disobedience and sabotage were followed by Nazi counter-measures. The occupiers were able to recruit various auxiliary units from the Danes to augment their own security forces.

When the war ended 15,724 Danes were arrested, charged with collaboration, most receiving prison sentences, 62 for life; 46 people were executed and nearly 3,000 permanently deprived of their civil rights.

It is difficult to be precise as to exactly how many Danes fought in the Waffen-SS, the so-called 'regiments' were often no more than battalion strength, 600 to 700 men. Most were killed or vanished in the Nordland Division's last stand in Berlin in 1945.

Whereas Denmark had been subjugated in an almost bloodless invasion on 9 April 1940, the battle for Norway became a far more protracted affair owing to British and French intervention whose expeditionary corps was en route at almost the same time as the Wehrmacht struck.

As indicated, the Waffen-SS were swift to start work on building a 'Nordland' unit for Scandinavian volunteers, and when Himmler appointed Felix Steiner to the task he was able to extract the Germania Regiment from the Reich Division as a cadre. In January 1941 the Norwegian traitor Vidkun Quisling made a public appeal for 3,000 volunteers to 'join in the war of freedom and independence against English world despotism'. Quisling had been awarded the CBE by the British in the 1920s for assistance in Bolshevik Russia; he was known as an intellectual but political fumbler. Rejected by the Norwegian communists following his return to that country he ranged himself with the new ideas of national socialism, becoming a great admirer of Hitler with whom he had several meetings before his country was invaded. Appointed head of a puppet government, he was replaced as ineffectual by Hitler within days, but, as the Fuehrer put it, was 'held in reserve'.

The first age limits for the new Norwegian unit was put at 25 to 40, this soon being lowered to 17. One of the first volunteers was Jonas Lie, a policeman who now formed the Norges SS and was posted to the Balkans in the Spring of 1941 to gain some military experience.

But it was, as in other occupied countries, the German invasion of Russia which provided the impetus for the foreign volunteer movement. One week after this momentous battle began the Germans announced the founding of the 'Norske Legion', the fact that it was a Waffen-SS organization was kept hidden. Those joining were mostly from the national socialist 'Hird' who were the equivalent of Hitler's brownshirts (so-called 'storm-troopers); others were from the Norges SS. The first group of volunteers numbering 300 men departed for Germany on 29 July 1941; a further 700 followed in mid-August, being joined in Hamburg by 62 Norwegians who had been resident in Berlin. By then Himmler had named the unit 'Volunteer Legion Norway'.

Following the raising of Norwegian police and labour companies by the Germans, two more units comprising such personnel were organized into Waffen-SS troops under the now-Major Lie and after training sent to join the Norwegian Legion outside Leningrad. The experiences of one Norwegian on that front will be related shortly.

The Norwegian Legion was withdrawn from Russia for rest and refurbishment in March 1943. Himmler planned to amalgamate the 600 to 700 men of the unit with the Nordland Regiment of SS Wiking to create a new division. By then his notions on SS purity were fast eroding, he was forced to make good the loss to Wiking by inserting an Estonian battalion, while to complete his new division he proposed using Dutchmen. Surprisingly, these volunteers from Holland objected to mixing in a Norwegian-Danish division, and so vociferous were their arguments that Hitler was obliged to intervene, allowing them to remain independent. This left Himmler in a dilemma, for his proposed division was short of one regiment, in truth only comprising two battalion-size units since dissolving of Legion-SS Grenadier Regiments Nr 1 Danmark and Nr 2 Norge. His solution was to fill up with a unit of racial Germans (Volksdeutsche), mostly from Hungary, and in common with current practice a suitable name for the new division was sought. Having versed himself in all aspects of Norse mythology and heroism, Himmler decided on the title 'Varagian', this referring to Nordic warriors who had penetrated east and south-eastern Europe in the 9th and 10th centuries. But once again Himmler was overruled by his Fuehrer and the new unit became simply 11th SS Panzer-Grenadier Division Nordland.

Norwegians had, in common with Danes and Swedes, volunteered to fight in the Russo-Finnish war of 1939; Norwegian ski troops joined the 6th SS Mountain Division on the Eastern Front in October 1942, this Norge unit remaining on the Finnish front until that country made peace with the USSR in September 1944, when the Norwegian skiers returned home.

The Nordland division with its Norwegian component was one of several SS divisions which tried to stem the Russian steam-roller in the Baltic states in 1944, twice being forced to evacuate by sea before ending its days in Berlin.

Following the German surrender the restored democratic government in Norway proceeded against its collaborators, 400 people being executed, 288,000 persons received prison sentences, while 448,000 were fined or deprived of civil rights. To the 50,000 Norwegians who entered the German armed forces can be added a few thousand more who served in the Nazi-run security forces and various political organizations.

It should surprise no one that in every land they conquered the Nazis found willing dupes or even patriots bent on following what they saw as their duty. In Denmark the then Prime Minister Stauning declared in December 1940 'Denmark is the happiest country in Europe'. Doubtless, had this quaint utterance been reported in the British media many eyebrows would have been raised. But such statements by collaborating politicians reflected (at the time) the notion of some of these occupied countries of Western Europe that an excellent rapport was not only possible but had been obtained with the Germans. A like attitude was declared by the leading Dutch Nazis in Holland, the best known being Anton Adriaan Mussert who said — 'Hitler is the liberator of Europe'.

The Dutch National Socialist movement was the largest outside Germany, having been formed as early as 1931. As in other countries, economic stress played its part in driving ordinary men into extremist parties. By the outbreak of war Mussert's NSB claimed 28,000 members, bearing in mind the size of the population compared to Britain this was large; by the end of 1942 the party strength had reached 100,000. Ties with Germany were maintained from before the war when over 50,000 Germans worked in Holland, though not all were Nazi supporters.

After the German occupation in May 1940 posters began to appear depicting a German soldier shouting 'To arms! for Europe's civilization!' In that summer the SS Westland regiment was formulated, 1,000 volunteers from Holland and the Flanders region of Belgium came forward. This success encouraged Himmler to order the raising of a second regiment, this called the SS Standarte (regiment) Nordwest, this too was filled with its quota of Dutch and Belgian volunteers (by Spring 1941). These developments had of course, nothing to do with the forming of the General SS in Holland, this force was started up by the Dutch Nazis themselves. The Westland regiment was absorbed into the SS Wiking Division, while only a battalion of Nordwest was retained, the rest of the regiment's personnel being posted into other volunteer units. The Nordwest battalion was sent back to Holland where its members served as guard units at concentration camps and other locations.

Naturally, the German invasion of Russia electrified the whole world, but none more than the Nazi movements. In Holland, Mussert appealed for volunteers to join a 'Netherlands Legion', calling on a confirmed Nazi to take command, a man who had been Chief-of-Staff in the Dutch Army until his retirement in 1934, 69-year-old Lt-General Seyffardt. By the end-August 1941 two groups of volunteers reached Germany, some 1,000 men who entered training outside Hamburg before being sent on to a Waffen-SS camp in Poland. In these days the Germans termed the unit 'Volunteer Legion Netherlands', omitting the use of 'SS', still fostering the notion among the volunteers that they were in some fashion a Dutch formation about to assist in the destruction of Stalin's USSR. Needless to say, the two drafts of men who had originally paraded at The Hague in a motley collection of Dutch Army, National Socialist and civilian clothing had been re-outfitted in standard Waffen-SS field-grey, being only allowed a Dutch tricolour shield and 'wolf hook' emblem on the left collar patch.

Friction arose with this volunteer unit also, as with the Danes the Dutchmen had naively believed they would retain some control; as a result their commander Colonel Stroink and five of his officers resigned. But by January 1942 considerable publicity was generated as the unit joined the Wehrmacht and SS divisions on the Eastern Front, allowed a comparatively quiet initiation on the Leningrad sector, that city being under siege by the Germans. The Dutch troops had their own Red Cross unit and a large party of journalists, the Nazis had made sure of a propaganda coup by sanctioning no less than fifty reporters and film cameramen to exploit the entry of Dutch 'brothers-in-arms' in the battle against Bolshevism.

The Dutchmen of this legion remained in Russia until May 1943 when they were at last withdrawn to form a cadre for Panzer-Grenadier Brigade 'Nederland'. As described earlier, the Hollanders objected strongly to losing their unit identity, Mussert himself leading the protests. Himmler was left with only 2,000 men of the legion plus 3,000 new volunteers, not enough by far for a division; as a result the 4th SS Panzer-Grenadier Brigade Nederland came into being consisting of two regiments, named after men considered worthy of commemoration by both Germans and Dutch Nazis. Lt-General Seyffardt was assassinated by the Resistance in February 1943, and it seemed appropriate his name should be awarded for one regiment, the other being titled after the famous Admiral Ruyter. The newly constituted brigade trained in Croatia, took part in anti-partisan operations and then returned to the old stamping ground around Leningrad.

The Dutch regiments' trials began when the Soviets drove their enemies back in great offensives; the Brigade was cut off in the Kurland area, evacuation by sea proved hazardous, one ship and its troops being lost. The remains of the unit fought around Stettin and eventually retreated westwards where they were trapped by and surrendered to the Americans at Furstenwald.

The Dutch made the largest contribution to the Waffen-SS; at the end of 1944 some 12,000 were on active service, with many more engaged in para-military and other units. The Dutch soldiers won far more decorations than the troops of the other volunteer units. There is no doubt that the proposed 'European Ideal' as put forward by the Waffen-SS had considerable appeal to the youth of Holland who preferred a smart uniform and pay to enlisting in the ranks of the Resistance, which became heavily penetrated by not only the German security forces but their fellow countrymen in the pay of the enemy. The reality of Soviet communism was known in Britain and only resulted in the Cold War after Hitler was defeated, for the Germans and the Waffen-SS in particular a 'crusade' against the menace of Red Russia was espoused as former members later claimed long before the forming of NATO, expedient as it was.

It is believed that about 3,700 Dutchmen lost their lives in action, only a proportion of these in the 17,000 who joined the Waffen-SS; the remainder lost their lives serving the NSKK transport corps, German Navy, German Army, police and security units. About 60,000 Dutch were deprived of citizenship after the war for various forms of collaboration, but 20,000 of this number were merely wives of accused males. Over 39,000 served in the German forces, and those surviving were hardly treated harshly, the Dutch authorities preferred to forgive and forget, periodic reviews and amnesties provided leniency in many cases. It may be that, as in France, the scale of collaboration was large enough to create a problem for post-war politicians and jurisdiction.

In the case of Belgium, the Germans were dealing with two nations bound by one religion, but it was to the people of Flanders that the occupiers turned for recruits into the volunteer formations, for to the Nazis the Flemings were much nearer the racial norm so to speak, almost akin to the Dutch who could safely be accepted as pure. The less than four and a half million Flemings however were looked down on by their fellow countrymen, the French-speaking Walloons; it is therefore ironic that the one man hailed most by the Nazis as representing their new concept of a 'European Ideal' should emerge from the less favoured half of Belgium.

Leon Degrelle left university without a degree to try his hand at religious publishing, but became mixed up with the rise of Fascism, founding the Christus Rex movement in 1935. The motif chosen by Degrelle as its symbol can be seen as significant, the Christian crown and cross over the word 'Rex' with a broom added. In a period of unrest the Rex movement achieved its rise gaining over 271,000 votes in 1936, thereafter slumping to a mere 103,600 by 1939. Degrelle became one of those continental politicians who though elected stayed outside the assembly, and since he and his followers' ways were alien to the church the Catholic Archbishop forbade his flock to vote for the Rexists. However, Degrelle did achieve a safe seat in the Belgian parliament by the Spring of 1939.

After the invasion Himmler at once set in train his programme for a Westland SS unit, the original idea to use such men in General SS to help keep the population inert. As shown, Westland became a combat unit and went into SS Wiking. The invasion of Russia enabled Flemings to join the Waffen-SS at once; not so the Walloons, who were only permitted to serve in the less selective Wehrmacht. Volunteers for the Flemish SS Legion were aged between 17 and 40, with ex-Belgian Army men given preference, especially NCOs and officers. Those below 23 were promised a twelve-month contract of service, for the rest it would be 'for the duration'. In August 1941, 405 Flemings joined the men of the Nordwest unit already training in Poland, and it at once became clear to the 875 volunteers that they had fallen into a not too agreeable situation. Like the Scandinavians, even for the ex-soldiers, German SS discipline and methods proved a rude shock. It is doubtful if the treatment meted out by the SS drillmasters was much different to that endured by recruits in the British forces, but some continental armies had different standards. Complaints through Brussels led to Himmler trying to alleviate matters, the SS command even ordered its camp staff to study up on Flemish customs and history, one can imagine the reaction of such men.

It was inept of the SS commanders not to unite this latest group of Flemings with the 700 already serving in SS Wiking in Russia. They joined the 2nd SS Motorized Brigade near Leningrad. Curiously, the SS maintained a pretence of a 'national Belgian Legion' combatting the Soviets, probably for propaganda reasons, these distinct from those Belgians in SS Wiking. This practice was abandoned later, and in any case all such foreigners were in and controlled exclusively by the German Waffen-SS. As with the other volunteer units, the Belgians wore German grey-green and allowed only some semblance of nationality by their arm badge, in the case of these Belgians a black lion on a yellow ground.

Like many other units on the Eastern Front, the Belgians were hard hit by the winter of 1941-42, especially when the Russians launched their counter-offensive. The Belgian Legion commander Lippert was fatally wounded in April 1942, and as related Count von Schalburg was also killed; his successor promised much, Hans-Albert von Lettow-Vorbeck knew the Flemings and made his pact with them, but his good intentions came to nothing when he too met his fate in Russia in June. His replacement was a Belgian officer from the Wiking Division, Conrad Schellong, but his men were withdrawn from the front before July, to go into action again the following month and remain in Russia until May 1943 when they were again taken out of the line, refurbished and given the title SS Volunteer Assault Brigade *Langemarck*.

To return to Leon Degrelle: without military experience but obviously a well-known politician albeit of little power, Degrelle volunteered his services to the Germans, this in April, well before the Germans attacked Russia. Not until after Operation Barbarossa began did the Germans accept him into their new Walloon Legion, 1,200 volunteers travelling to Poland in August 1941, the politician serving in the ranks. At this time the unit was simply Infantry Battalion No 373 in the German Army lists, but briefly known as the *Corps Franc Wallonie*, bearing the Belgian national colours and the word *Wallonie* on its uniforms.

The Legion Wallonie was employed in the southern sector of the Russian Front in various roles, including behind the lines operations, and by February 1942 Degrelle had reached the rank of Sergeant and won the Iron Cross 2nd Class, the 1st Class followed in May when he was raised to the rank of Lieutenant. In July the Walloons fought on the River Don front opposite Stalingrad, were switched to the Caucasus and suffered disastrous losses, over 850 men including Degrelle becoming casualties. One historian has referred to Degrelle as an outstanding soldier and leader of men, that the Germans took this view is proved by their awarding him first the Knight's Cross, followed by the Oak Leaves.

By the summer of 1943 the Germans, desperate to gain replacements for losses in the volunteer units, revised the age limits from 16 to 45, and before Autumn 1942 recruits were being sought among Belgian prisoners-of-war. By May 1943 the Belgian Walloon Legion had risen in strength from a mere 187 men to 1,600, and in the following month it was granted the right to transfer to the Waffen-SS, this largely as a result of pleading by Degrelle, becoming the SS Volunteer Assault Brigade *Wallonien*; by June it was transferred to the Ukraine and the Wiking Division, though it did not become integrated with the other Belgian unit.

Meanwhile, its counterpart, the newly-titled Langemarck, had been brought up to strength by drafts of fresh recruits from Belgium and even a battalion of Finns. As for Leon Degrelle, he had now become a celebrated figure, fêted and pushed forward on tour by his German masters, even giving talks in Germany itself and of course exhorting his fellow countrymen to join in the struggle against Soviet Russia. All this activity, including a bout of diphtheria, kept him away from the front for much of 1943, but by the winter he was in action again, being surrounded by the advancing Russian forces who trapped 56,000 German troops including the Wiking Division in the Ukraine. In this great battle Wiking troops including the Belgians helped 35,000 Germans to fight their way out of the cauldron, but of 2,000 Walloons some 1,368 became casualties, their commander Lippert was killed and Degrelle took his place. The remnants eventually returned to Belgium under their new leader and were awarded a hero's welcome by that section of the populace sympathetic to them. Degrelle served the Nazi cause to the upmost, among his public utterances:

> 'The emblem of the SS shows Europe where political and social truth is to be found.'

It is impossible to say how seriously men like Degrelle believed such things, though it is very unlikely that he or his men knew of the activities being undertaken by other branches of the SS, the non-combat formations who ran the concentration camps and extermination campaign which was a virtual state secret.

By July 1944 the last page had opened in the history of Belgian military collaboration when both legions were rushed to help stem the Russian onslaught in Estonia. Following their usual mauling, the units were withdrawn into Germany itself, Degrelle being called to Hitler to receive his Oak Leaves, the Fuehrer assuring him — 'If I had a son, I would wish him to be like you'.

Despite maintaining more recruiting offices in Belgium than the Wehrmacht (23 in all) Himmler's Waffen-SS staffs were unable to keep up the flow of replacements for the Belgian volunteer units which by September 1944 had been nominally upgraded to the size of divisions, for no practical reason for neither were anywhere near such strength. They now became the 27th Volunteer Panzer-Grenadier Division Wallonien (the Walloons being mixed with some armour). To reinforce the former unit Himmler 'persuaded' a few hundred Belgian parents who had accompanied their youngsters to Germany as part of a Flemish Hitler Youth programme of military training to allow them to sign up for the Waffen-SS. In this fashion was another battalion raised and whisked off to the Langemarck Division.

In January 1945 both Belgian divisions joined the French SS units in trying to halt the Soviet advance in Pomerania. By end-February the Walloons were reduced to 700 men, and in counter-attacking the Russians crossing the Oder nearly 650 more were lost. Most of the Flemings were captured by the Russians. Remnants of the Walloon division were evacuated and Degrelle went to Germany, hoping for guidance from Himmler who had none, only showing him his cyanide pill. Degrelle then went to Copenhagen, then on to Oslo, finding no hope in either city. He then used the plane provided by Reichs armaments minister Speer for Quisling to escape to Spain where the aircraft crashed on the beach at San Sebastian. The Spaniards refused Allied and United Nations requests to extradite him, but obliged Degrelle to move on to that other haven for ex-Nazis, South America. In due course however, he was allowed back into Spain to live under an assumed name, write his memoirs and occasionally dust down and don his old Waffen-SS uniform.

A number of Belgian collaborators had been assassinated before liberation, after this came in September 1944 about 100,000 people were arrested, 87,000 being brought to trial, 10,000 were acquitted, 230 executed; 16,000 people received long prison sentences. Degrelle's brother, a chemist, had been killed by patriots in June 1944, the SS leader was himself sentenced to death *in absentia* in December.

The confusing miasma of French politics had thrown up strong communist and fascist movements, with a heavy streak of anti-semitism; during the war it would be the French themselves who introduced the harshest measures against the Jews. Most of the French population settled down after the German occupation in the hope of continuing a reasonable life under the occupiers who at first behaved themselves impeccably.

As in the other occupied lands of Western Europe, the German invasion of Russia provided the spark that enabled those fascists most fired to put themselves up for service on the new war front. The LVF or 'Legion of Volunteers of France Against Bolshevism' sprang to life, wearing French uniforms until they were taken to Poland in two drafts numbering over 1,700 men in all, then donning German Army uniforms bearing the French tricolour on their sleeves. By November the Frenchmen had joined the front before Moscow and became caught up in the terrible winter, losing half their strength to action and the weather. About 1,400 reinforcements reached the unit in December, amazingly these included some 200 coloureds of the French colonial forces, mostly from Algeria; these men must have suffered greatly in the harshness of the Russian winter. By Spring 1942 the unit was withdrawn and its chief relieved of his command. When two battalions returned to action they mostly fought anti-partisan actions behind the front. By the summer of '44 less than a battalion were engaged in defensive fighting and in September the Germans peremptorily absorbed the remnants into the Waffen-SS. Himmler had again been forced to amend his own dictums and in July 1943 ordered the admission of Frenchmen into his forces.

Despite this, the recruiting office opened up in Paris for the new French SS Volunteer Grenadier Regiment insisted on applicants being 'Aryan' and only between the ages of 20 and 25. The drive brought 3,000 volunteers, most of fascist leaning, with the usual crop of malcontents, adventurers and members of the hated French Milice auxiliary police. When the first draft of 800 volunteers reached the Sennheim training camp in Alsace they were confronted by Dutch and Flemish instructors. Those men thought suitable as officers and NCOs were in due course despatched to the appropriate centres for further training. Not until July 1944 did the unit, now designated the French SS Volunteer Assault Brigade move to the Eastern Front, numbering 1,688 men dressed as usual in Waffen-SS outfits bearing the French tricolour. It sustained severe casualties as part of the 18th SS Division Horst Wessel, 806 volunteers being killed or wounded. After being withdrawn the unit received the remnants of the LVF force as reinforcements and became the Waffen-Grenadier Brigade *Charlemagne*. With the Allied invasion and eventual drive across France many fascists fled into Germany including refugees from the Milice, 2,500 of whom were hi-jacked by Himmler into the SS; 800 French volunteers with the German Navy were also inducted, but some who protested strongly enough were released back into civilian life; not so the recalcitrants of the LVF who likewise tried to evade service in the Waffen-SS, they were posted to a concentration camp. At the end of all this Himmler had, by transferring Frenchmen from other units such as the transport and labour corps, 7,340 men for the re-structured Charlemagne.

By February 1945 the unit had been thrown into battle against the Soviets on the Vistula front, being split into three segments in the fight that ensued. One group of survivors was evacuated from the Baltic coast by the German Navy; the second was virtually wiped out by Russian artillery while attempting to escape, while the third, chiefly formerly Milice men, were all killed or captured. Of 7,000 Charlemagne troops only 800 survived, these now being re-christened yet again 'Assault Regiment'; and of these, those with no further stomach for combat were absolved by their commander, SS Brigadefuehrer Krukenberg, a German who knew that some of those under him had been impressed against their will. Only 500 stayed to swear a binding oath to Hitler and fight in beleaguered Berlin with the Nordland Division, being reduced to 120 men in the process. Practically every one of the remaining foreign volunteers were killed or captured in this final battle, apart from those who surrendered to the Allies on the Western Front.

Considering the widespread nature of collaboration with the enemy in France during the German occupation, the number who actually fought in the German armed forces must be seen as small. Assistance given to the enemy on other levels was greater in all its forms, from the highest political levels down to the humble labourer on the Atlantic Wall. The main accounting began after the liberation; 5,000 collaborators having been killed off by the Resistance earlier. The French Premier, Marshal

Petain was sentenced to death, but died of pneumonia in 1951; his most disliked deputy Pierre Laval was shot by firing squad in October 1945. The reckoning went on for four years, and of course has been resurrected more recently; 4,400 people were given death sentences in their absence, those in court receiving the same judgement numbered 2,071, of which 768 were carried out. However, revenging members of the Resistance and others carried out most killings, a figure of 10,000 being quoted, though some sources state the true figure is up to ten times higher. Thousands of French officers were dishonourably discharged or sacked, as were mayors, civil servants, magistrates and other lesser officials. Those combatants of the Waffen-SS and others who dared return home were offered service in French Indo-China (Vietnam) as an alternative to prison.

German attempts to recruit a 'Legion of St. George' for the Waffen-SS among British prisoners-of-war were largely unsuccessful, a unit formed being reportedly of less than platoon size, and a photograph exists of Britishers allegedly of this unit and attached to the SS Totenkopf Division on the Oder front late in the war. Their Waffen-SS uniforms supposedly bore a three-lion emblem and Union Jack. One such volunteer returned to England under arrest in 1945, the fate of Thomas Halle Cooper is unknown.

The Germans had for very good reasons tried to maintain good relations with the Swedes, these not only economic. Sweden contained a number of Nazi sympathizers, including families of German origin. There were allies to be found in the Swedish Army's officer corps, and it was to these that the Nazis directed some hopes of volunteers for the Wehrmacht and Waffen-SS. But having given one such volunteer an 'unceremonious discharge' no more were forthcoming from that source.

Collaboration, whether willing or coerced, never did produce the large number of volunteers for combat the Germans hoped for in Western Europe. One year after their trumpeted 'great crusade against Bolshevism' they had only managed to enlist about 5,000 men into the four so-called 'legions'. There was not the widespread pro-German feeling and ineptness in handling the recruits gained plus a growing realization of the true situation contributed to German frustrations. Despite a small core of Nazified 'heroes' who returned on leave to throw their weight about, others reported the stark realities of the war on the Eastern Front, their disillusionment discouraged others. However, even though the foreign volunteer programme never achieved spectacular results, the units fought well enough, some outstandingly so.

The key issue was one of motivation, and in this connection none were more desirous of hitting back at the Soviets than the Finns who had provided volunteers for the Waffen-SS long before the west Europeans were ensnared. Himmler had urged Gottlob Berger to find more men for the Wiking Division, but difficulties had to be ironed out with the Finnish government. Even then, only 116 veterans of the war against Russia reached Germany in May 1941, but by the launch of Barbarossa about 400

Finns were included in Wiking; this number was to reach 1,000. Hatred of the Soviets ensured these men were the best fighters among the foreigners on that front; but by mid-1943 when the tide turned against Germany the Finnish contingent was withdrawn by their government. Naturally, the Finns already had their own national army in action against the Soviets. Yet again, it was reported that German promises to keep the Finns together under their own officers had not been kept.

Himmler boasted that the SS had never suffered a desertion, but when disillusionment set in among the Scandinavians some skipped away while on leave into Sweden where tales soon reached the press of their experiences and Nazi perfidy. Then two soldiers (one Dane and one Norwegian) deserted from the Nordland regiment of the Wiking Division 'in the face of the enemy', an event that jolted Himmler, especially as it followed reports of dissatisfaction and near revolt in some of the volunteer units. Himmler attempted to retrieve the situation by issuing an order that officers in command of such units must attend special orientation courses to ensure proper handling of their men in future. But the damage had been done, German hamfistedness ensured that only a trickle of volunteers came forward thereafter to replace losses on the Eastern Front. One particularly thorny problem was the replacement of officers, for once these 'trusties' were lost units tended to fall to pieces. These posers especially concerned Felix Steiner who, as one of the leading architects of the Waffen-SS field tactics became an exponent of the new anti-Soviet concept whereby the youth of Western Europe would smash the Red menace of Stalin's USSR.

Obviously, the numbers quoted as serving in these Western legions formed only a small part of the alleged half-million foreigners who put on Waffen-SS uniforms. The remainder were east and south-eastern recruits who either entered the legions directly or were later transferred from the Wehrmacht, including Ukrainians, Latvians, and others from the Baltic states, plus of course the considerable numbers from the Balkans and central Europe. If these are taken into account it could be understood why the SS paper *Das Schwarze Korps* could claim that —

'A great number of men are fighting with the German sword, having been prised from the English sphere of interest.'

In fact, the paper was at the time referring to Nordics, so the claim was false.

Himmler's theories concerning the *untermensch*, the 'sub-human races' in the East had to be subdued in view of his ever-growing need for new recruits to combat not only the Soviet armies but the intensifying guerilla war behind the German fronts. Hitler had never subscribed to the notion of foreign volunteers, his reaction to pictures of 'SS soldiers' clad in the Moslem fez can only be imagined, for this is what it had come to as the Reichsfuehrer-SS cast his net ever wider.

However, there were quite rich sources of a more acceptable nature at first, for some two and a quarter million Volksdeutsche resided in Hungary, Romania and Slovakia, these areas became fertile ground for Wehrmacht and SS recruiting, though many of these men fought in the national armies of those countries against the hated Soviets. In Slovakia, according to German propaganda, following an appeal by the local Volksgruppe or Nazi party which looked after the interests of racial Germans, all restrictions on recruitment into the Waffen-SS were lifted, leaving all males between the ages of 17 and 35 free to volunteer. It was reported that in Hungary alone, 27,000 Volksdeutsche volunteered for the SS, while an all-Romanian company was formed in the 10th SS Infantry Regiment. It must be mentioned that a large Romanian army had entered the combat against the Soviets from the start, a lesser one from Hungary.

In Yugoslavia, the existing religious and political schisms aided German plans, as indicated in *Der Angriff* 3 June 1942:

'Hardly had Croatia been freed when the people remembered their honourable duty to fall in for the fight against Bolshevism, the rush of volunteers surpassed all that had been foreseen and all facilities.'

But according to another source it was a threat by Gottlob Berger to burn down their homes that finally persuaded these men to sign up for the Waffen-SS.

Throughout eastern Europe and into northern Italy the Germans found or rounded up enough men to form anti-Bolshevik brigades and divisions, though in many cases the men involved were more interested in fighting over local issues and would be unsuitable material for all-out war on the Russian Front, though a few appeared in Normandy in 1944. Every single European country outside the Soviet Union contributed volunteers for the Wehrmacht and Waffen-SS, and, as shown, Himmler's original stipulations concerning 'SS purity' had to be waived, with consequences both bizarre and tragic; the inclusion of dubious and religious elements into Waffen-SS ranks produced men in field-grey hauling out their prayer mats and bowing to Mecca at appropriate times of the day, while on duty atrocities were a certainty, though both sides were prone to this. Many of these eastern volunteers were of use only against their fellow countrymen as counter-partisan forces, in strict military terms their value was poor.

Post-war research produced interesting evidence as to why west Europeans became involved with the German forces. Not all Nazis were foolish enough to believe such men did it for national socialism or to form a common front against communism, the recruiting officers however were hardly caring. And realistic reasons often prevailed that ranged from social problems to a need to escape forced labour in Germany, though in the event most must have realized this later as the wiser option. Some men according to Steiner, turned to the Germans after years of economic despair in the '30s, which hardly seems plausible. Certainly, the early volunteers were Nazi sympathizers in the main and fancied themselves strutting around in German uniforms, but later it was the various facets of pressure brought by the occupying Germans that prevailed on many.

Jutte Olafsen was born in Oslo in 1918, had one sister and a normal upbringing. The German invasion shocked them; times became very difficult, especially as the enemy were so friendly. Jutte worked as a part-time teacher in college on various subjects:

'I often worked at the school I had attended as a boy helping to teach boys and girls all I had learned at college. In our school we tried to carry on as usual, but the Germans sent in new teachers and then parties of Hitler Youth boys and girls who were very nice to us. They brought us presents from Germany and told us that they were going to organize some Norwegian Hitler Youth.

'Then the Germans announced that they were looking for volunteers to join a great crusade against Bolshevism. They had by then begun to try and deal with the opposition in our country which was growing stronger. I had myself become friendly with one of the German teachers, these people were acting as managers to make sure the curriculum suited their own ideas. Obviously, we had to try and do the best we could in our dealings with them, although not bowing completely and certainly not trying to completely Nazify the pupils who in any case were bright enough to know the truth.

'Then, when the war began in Russia things became more difficult and the Germans began rounding up men for forced labour. But they offered an alternative, and this was to join the Legion Norwegen and assist in the anti-Bolshevik crusade, as they called it. I hated communism, so decided I would rather join this Legion than go to work in Germany. At my age I was eligible for deportation, so fell in with some other Norwegian lads who had also decided to join the Legion. I must admit that we had no idea at all of the horrors of war and certainly not of the kind of conditions we would meet in Russia. I suppose to some extent we swallowed the German propaganda which asserted that the Soviet Union was a rotten edifice that would soon collapse.

'Having said a tearful farewell to our families we were sent to north Germany. My father refused to speak to me, but my mother and sister saw me off at the station, though neither said very much, they were in tears. They felt that while I was possibly following my convictions I was in a real sense a traitor to my own country and would have to pay some price eventually.

'We were given uniforms and sent to an assembly camp to begin training with many other Norwegians. The training was quite hard and awkward as we were forced to learn the words of command and much else in German. We had a Norwegian emblem and an appropriate sleeve ribbon on our tunics and carried our own banners on parade.'

We shall see how Jutte Olafsen fared in his first taste of war on the Leningrad front later.

According to German source findings published some years after the war, Waffen-SS volunteers broke down into the following categories:

Germany and other West European countries — 410,00 Germans; 300,000 Racial Germans; 55,000 Dutch; 23,000 Flemings; 20,000 French; 20,000 Walloons; 6,000 Norwegians; 6,000 Danes; 800 Swiss; 80 Lichtenstein; 200 various, including Britons, Swedes, Spaniards.

East and South-eastern Europe — 31,000 Lettland; 20,000 Estonia; 20,000 Ukraine; 30,000 Cossacks; 8,000 Turkestan; 25,000 Caucasus; 14,000 Musselmans (from the Balkans).

The same source also quoted 83% of Germans joining the Waffen-SS as not having been Nazi Party members or ex-members of the General SS. Well over a third (37.3%) had been labourers and farm workers, 4.8% were ex-students or high school leavers, 14.4% office workers, only 1.8% were professional soldiers, the rest being made up of miscellaneous workers and employees. Their ages ranged from 17–19 years.

CHAPTER EIGHT

A German youth called Heinz Reinefarth — not to be confused with one of the same name later accused as 'a butcher' — joined the Waffen-SS following his conscription in 1941, and his story provides a very different kind of experience:

'I joined as an infantryman, but was then given some choice, which surprised me, so for some reason I decided to become a policeman. I volunteered for the Military Police with one other comrade, and we were sent at once to a police school run by the Army and SS to learn military law. This course lasted a month, after which we had to take another in field security duties which included very secret work on how to handle deserters and panic in the field, which consisted of immediate arrest of those found behind the front without valid reason. Such people were to be taken away and charged at once, and if proven guilty were likely to be shot without delay as an example to all others. However, in all my experience I never came across a single SS deserter, not one.

'At the end of the course we were sent to an MP unit in eastern Poland and then towards the front near Smolensk where we joined a mobile unit whose task it was to watch out for German deserters, Russian infiltrators and suspects. As the area was very large we were constantly on the move, and before long we had rounded up a number of suspects for interrogation. They happened to be fairly harmless individuals, but there was it seemed no question of releasing them at once since we were in a military zone, so they were sent to a makeshift prison in the rear.

'Then we received our first report of sabotage and possible guerilla activity in our sector. This concerned the interrupting of communications, the pulling down of telegraph wires, blowing up of roads etc and even the ambush of lone vehicles. So when we patrolled the area we decided to interrogate the nearest villagers who were trying to carry on their lives in what remained of their houses. We rounded them up and herded them into a makeshift office one by one for questioning. We had one man who had learned Russian as well as a Russian 'Hias' (volunteer helper), to act as interpreters.

'We got nothing out of these people, except for one, an old and very frightened man who said he had seen strangers passing behind the village carrying cans and implements one evening. He showed us the spot, and when we followed a track it did lead to one of our convoy routes not far away. So we took some of the villagers including the old man along the track in the opposite direction until we came to a small wood. We had a dozen men armed with

Schmeissers and a machine-gun and we had to surround the wood, although it was really a job for a much larger unit. When our officer blew his whistle we began to advance into the wood from all directions, and as soon as we did the civilians with us ran away.

'I walked forward through the undergrowth with my Schmeisser at the ready, and could hear all sorts of movements in the wood and then shooting and shouts. I knelt down at the ready and heard men running and saw a man in a dark jacket and cap coming towards me. He saw me and stopped and I realized he had a rifle, so I shouted at him to drop it. But he turned and ran, so I fired at him and he fell down. I rushed forward and found he was dead. There was still a lot of noise going on and I heard more men coming so I lay down and waited but saw no one. Then some of my young comrades came through the trees so I stood up and we searched the man I had shot. He carried a piece of bread and a party card, that was all. His rifle was loaded, so we took it away with us.

'Later that same day back at our HQ another squad brought in a suspect who had been found near the same wood so he was interrogated but said nothing even when beaten. He was therefore taken out and shot.

'Very soon after that we received information from a Russian peasant informer of more activity not far away. We went out in two patrols to a largely wooded area but surrounded by plains, so if they had look-outs they must have seen us coming from afar.

'As before, we tried to surround the wood, but it was much more extensive and we could see that we stood little chance of catching anybody without a lot more help which we did not have. We searched as best we could but found no one so we returned to our base, tired, thirsty and thoroughly frustrated. Our CO needed the assistance of larger forces otherwise we were powerless to prevent the growth of bandit activity. It was several months before a local militia was recruited from among the disaffected peasantry who had seen too much of Stalin's methods and did not like the 'bandits' who had infiltrated from other provinces. These Russian helpers were only given a 'Deutsche Wehrmacht' armband and some old rifles and were supervised by some of our NCOs, with a few more lent by the Army. We were then able to begin a large scale operation against the areas we believed contained bandits. The problem was as follows:

'Our lines of communication were over extended and had to be kept open to supply the great armies at the front. But the areas between these roads were so vast that it was quite impossible to occupy them or even patrol them very regularly, we hadn't the forces to do it. All we could do was to mount the occasional sweep with what men we had. In this the locals were always very helpful in this period as they only wanted to live their simple lives in peace, free of Moscow's domination with its insane decrees.

'We set off some two hundred strong in trucks, bound for the areas where bandits had been reported. Once again we reached the same wooded area, and this time we fanned out, leaving one force on the far side while the rest acted as beaters to comb through the trees. We certainly made enough noise doing it, but felt more confident this time.

'At last we heard a great commotion ahead of us and shots rang out, followed by the sound of men running, but these were our helpers who had encountered a bandit ambush. Some were killed or wounded, the rest were difficult to stop, though we managed to catch a few of them, though in some cases they had thrown away their rifles. This was bad and we were far from pleased. But we gave them some of our weapons and advanced again behind them, being very cautious as we did so.

'After about one hundred metres or so firing broke out and our people in front dropped to the ground in panic. We could hardly blame them, they were very ill trained and hadn't the stomach for a real fight. So we were obliged to advance on our own while our Russian helpers pointed out the many bunkers which were mere holes but very well camouflaged. We let fly with grenades and went in firing and several men and three women threw out their guns and surrendered. They were searched and marched off out of the wood, taken back to base and interrogated. All were roughly handled and then shot.

'This was a very small beginning in the anti-bandit war, and although we had succeeded there were thousands more lurking about the countryside and in some cases led by Russian officers who had parachuted in and received supplies by air later. It was impossible to comb the great tracts of land without larger forces and planes to help us. We did our best to organize intelligence networks of informers who were paid money and supplies to keep us up to date on the latest developments.

'A few months later we received the good news that Cossacks and other regular Russian forces who had come over to our side would assist us in another drive against the bandits who were growing bolder in their attacks. I saw these Cossacks arriving and they were rather impressive, very proud men with long traditions and very keen to show what they could do against the Reds.

'A few days later we had worked out a plan of campaign and our whole 'army' set off in a great column until we reached bandit country. We then split up into large groups to infiltrate the localities, well armed and with one week's rations. It was very tiring work as the only way to comb the countryside was on foot. In that particular part of the country it was quite hilly and we were in fear of running into an ambush. But our Cossacks scouted ahead on horseback and proved invaluable.

'In due course we heard a battle breaking out so hurried forward to join in. There was a very large hollow covered in sparse bushes and there we found that our Cossacks had cornered a party of bandits and were involved in a battle with them. Since we had the area surrounded and looked down into the hollow it was an easy task to simply lob grenades and fire our weapons into the bushes until at last all signs of resistance ceased. We then advanced down the hillside into the hollow, still cautious in case we were trapped. But all the bandits except one were dead. There were about twenty in all including the prisoner who had lost a lung through a grenade. He was taken away and his wound treated prior to interrogation, but died in silence.

'From our point of view this had been a very successful operation, but

Young SS gunners take shelter as a Soviet T34 tank is finally halted just yards from them. (Munin Verlag)

Well protected by winter parkas: SS panzer-grenadiers in Kharkov, March 1943.

SS prisoners unlikely to see their homeland again. (Ahnert Verlag)

SS infantry with Tiger tanks make ready to jump off in the ill-fated Kursk offensive, July 1943. (Ahnert Verlag)

Battle is joined: the Soviets were forewarned. Note Russian prisoner.

How the SS took care of its own: one version of elaborate grave sites in Russia.

A recruiting poster invites Belgian Walloons to enlist in the Waffen-SS.

Dutchmen leave for training in Germany. Few would survive the war.

North European volunteers are sworn in – German style.

Moslems in the SS division 'Handschar' were of little military value.

Christian von Schalborg rallied the early 'nordic' recruits but was killed in Russia.

A Flemish volunteer. Varied reasons induced such youths to join the Waffen-SS.

Leon Degrelle, a Belgian most fêted by the Nazis.
Degrelle receives the Oak Leaves to the Knight's Cross from Hitler.

Alleged members of the so-called 'British Legion of St George' or Freecorps on the eastern front 1945.
(Beadle)

Recruiting poster for the new 12th SS Division Hitlerjugend.

unfortunately there were other aspects which made things a great deal more difficult. It seemed that the activities of the police and SD units in our rear had driven the population into hiding and many of them had gone over to the communist bandits. This was the result of the insane, murderous policies of Himmler and co., which resulted in a lot more work for us and also incidentally stirred up a hornet's nest of opposition from the regional Gauleiters who desired to use these Russian civilians for labour. From that time on we were at daggers drawn with the SD and police in the rear areas and gave them no co-operation at all. Furthermore, the Gauleiters refused to co-operate with Himmler and he virtually lost all authority in the eastern provinces.

'But our problems were only just beginning, with ever increasing demands from the Army to clean up the bandit-infested areas and secure their lines of communication. It was an impossible task that we were not really equipped for. The involvement of more and more civilians meant that our supply of informers dried up, so we were at a loss for intelligence. There were times when we were forced to take the harshest measures with suspects who had been incautious and were apprehended. This was a measure of their increasing boldness and our own desperation.

'I remember three women who had been caught red-handed trying to hide weapons in a little wood for their menfolk. We marched them off and they were given a beating followed by the gentle treatment and then interrogated. They were not tortured but slapped and punched and questioned. They were of course guilty of transporting arms in a military zone, so we took them out and shot them. It was very tragic to see these girls barely out of their teens standing bravely before a firing squad. I felt terrible about that affair, but it was a brutal war and the bandits committed many atrocities against our own people.

'On one occasion we entered a village in the middle of bandit country and were about to haul out the inhabitants for interrogation when a single shot rang out. We leapt from our vehicles, weapons at the ready, and advanced cautiously from house to house until at last we came to one shack, and in this we found the body of a German soldier. He was tied to a chair with his tongue torn out, it was lying at his feet. He had just been shot in the back of the head, the blood was still warm. We ran out the back but saw no one, so we pulled all the remaining villagers out of their houses and lined them up. Our CO then went from one to the other questioning them, but none spoke. So he paraded them past the body of the German soldier, they were shocked but remained silent. They new perfectly well what would happen to them if they gave us information; the bandits would murder them all. We were therefore in an impossible position, so we promised a reward for information and left with the body of our soldier.

'During one of my rare leave periods I met a woman and was completely smitten by her. She new my "line of business" but asked no questions. As it happened she had lost her man in the East and found me an attractive substitute I imagine. We corresponded for some time but then her letters stopped and I never knew why, but since she lived in Hamburg I had to assume that she had been killed in the air raids.'

CHAPTER NINE

Faced with ever increasing losses in Russia, the German government dropped the call-up age to seventeen. Reinhard Bochel passed through the usual Hitler Youth and labour service and on conscription:

'was attracted by the SS posters in the town of Hanau. Every single town had its SS recruiting office, and in the cities they were larger.

'We would receive our papers telling us to report to the Wehrmacht or SS recruiting offices in town by a certain date; if you did not do this you would be arrested. In my case I was lured by their SS posters and reported to their offices where after taking my details they told me to report back next day for a medical examination.'

After taking his physical Bochel waited for the summons to attend a training camp and this came a week later. Taking the usual small bag of toiletries he travelled to Zwischenahn where at the railway station an SS NCO collected the group of conscripts and put them in a waiting truck. The camp was as usual set in the countryside: 'Bleak, but with warm huts, though this was early summer, just before the invasion of Russia'. Bochel went through the mill of drawing uniform and equipment, then joined the training unit with the rest of the newcomers, and receiving inoculations against various diseases. Then followed weapon training, lectures and country runs.

'Our big shock came when we had to advance under fire from live ammunition and exploding charges which was very frightening. But we soon got used to this and all the noise. We were taught how to march in parade step (marschschritt or goose-step), and inspected by higher officers who sometimes exhorted us with cries of "Long live the SS!" and "Long live the Fuehrer!"'

After a final bout of hard training Bochel was posted with a dozen others to the Wiking division in Russia:

'This we dreaded, for the country was such a vast wilderness, this we knew, yet we did look forward to the experience, though as mere beginners we had no idea of the horrors of war. It took us three days to reach the battalion, and when we finally arrived after a three-mile trek we found a kind of party in progress. A lot of soldiers were celebrating someone's birthday behind the front, and somehow

they had obtained enough beer and spirits to make it a lively affair. So we were invited to join in the fun and we did, even though we were very tired and hungry. There was a certain amount to eat, but it was a very informal affair in a large hut and the men were singing rude songs which we did not know. We had learned a number of songs in training which were part of the standard Army repertoire* but also some which were peculiar to the SS. But of course, soldiers being what they are, there were other songs with words not permitted to be sung in public:

> *She was fat and he was forty*
> *So when he put it into her*
> *She squealed like a fat pig in joy*
> *But he was far from up to the job*
> *So then he fell away in sleep*
>
> *She was fat and he was forty*
> *She knew not what to make of him*
> *First he boasted of his prowess*
> *Then he shrank to nothing at all*
> *Oh yea! Oh yea! Oh yea! Oh yea!*

German marching songs were usually tuneful and catchy, though the above lyric, like others of a more mature status, loses something in the translating.

'We soon learnt the words to such ditties which were sung with great gusto on certain occasions. But this kind of fun was a comparative rarity as a great deal of the time was spent in the line awaiting Russian attacks or mounting our own.'

Peter Zahnfeld entered Russia as an Oberleutnant, or rather an SS Obersturmfuehrer or First Lieutenant, being told that promotion would soon be forthcoming:

'We lost our first men to Russian fire and buried them on Soviet soil the same day. This was very sad, some of them had been with us from the start. We had a special kind of SS grave marker for the lads and this was attended to by a detail whose unfortunate task it was to deal with such matters. It fell to me as their CO to write short letters of condolence to the families concerned.

'The summer nights were uncomfortable as the heat grew worse. There were flies and other insects and we never knew exactly where we were. The maps were very inadequate, not that it really mattered; our chief aim was to destroy the Soviet Army, and judging by the vast numbers of prisoners we seemed to be doing that. There is no doubt that if properly handled these soldiers could have given us a hard time, but their generals and officers were poor and allowed great numbers of their men to be cut off, and when that happened they usually gave up.

---

* The singing of marching songs was all part of German military training and still is; the standard soldiers' song book containing about sixty songs.

'I remember one hot afternoon when we were moving across a huge plain via the only dirt road, when suddenly we saw what looked like a brown wave or tide coming over the horizon. It was raising huge dust clouds and when we looked through our binoculars we could see that it was a surging mass of humanity, all heading directly for us. We hurriedly deployed off our vehicles and set up our machine-guns etc and waited for what we assumed to be a mass attack.

'The brown herd came nearer and nearer, and then we heard the low, moaning grumbling noise of their voices. It was amazing, all these poor creatures seemed to be voicing in one way or another, mumbling or calling to each other as if all talking at once in some fashion. We then realized that they were without arms and only giving themselves up. We saw a few NCOs and officers among them, but they showed no sign of leadership at all. They simply surged past us in a great mass, almost ignoring us, having given up and been told by some other German unit to march west, and that's what they were doing. This great military procession took hours to pass by, they were that large in number.

'This was only one of the amazing sights in Russia. Another was the appearance of women. We saw some female prisoners, auxiliaries we thought, but later they appeared as snipers and were indistinguishable from the men in dress and outlook and showed every sign of hating us.

'It was during our early weeks in Russia that we first heard of atrocities. It is amazing how such tales circulate, especially considering the vastness of the landscape and that although the Germans had launched such a large force they were scattered across western Russia and reduced to quite small units in the advance. But with communications the stories soon became known.

'The first time I heard anything of this nature was one afternoon when a messenger on a motorcycle told us that another section of SS troops had been cut off by a strong Russian counter-attack and by the time the enemy had been wiped out or driven back the Germans had vanished. There was a farm nearby and some Russian civilians showed the German troops a pit where the prisoners had been executed by the NKVD secret police. I had no way of verifying this tale, but it came to be fairly common knowledge and I believe it was true.

'Inevitably, it incensed the men who acted accordingly when Russians fell into their hands, though I must say it would be a very rare occasion for Germans to take any Soviet secret police as prisoners, they were too adept at escaping long before we reached them.'

Zahnfeld recalls that the Fuehrer's order commanding all Soviet political commissars to be shot on capture was received during the first week of the campaign:

'I had no intention of carrying out such an order, no matter what my own feelings for such people were. But as it happened I saw one such individual who had been taken out of a group of prisoners by some SS field police. He was removed in a truck and I've no doubt done away with.

'The great advances continued throughout July and August, with our troops becoming increasingly exhausted. We had covered many hundreds of miles, mostly on the plains, and only occasionally stopping to fight a battle. These were at first against isolated units, but then we began to encounter more organized resistance, and this marked the end of my campaign.

'We had reached a small village under artillery fire which grew heavier and caused us some losses as we rushed towards the little dwellings, intending to envelope the area. Then we came under mortar and machine-gun fire. I remember something hitting me in the side, I cried out in pain and fell into the grass where I lay in agony. My sergeant ran to me and pulled open my jacket, trying to apply a bandage until the medics could remove me. I was faint, losing blood and passed out. The next thing I knew was a face looking down at me and I realized it was a doctor. I was in a dressing station, they applied ether and I passed out again.'

When Peter Zahnfeld came round again he found himself in bed surrounded by other wounded, located in a larger type of Russian building in a small town behind the front. An orderly helped him to sit up in bed and eat some delicious soup, he felt thankful to be alive. When the doctor came round he learned that he had a serious wound and would be evacuated back to Germany. This happened a week later when following a two-day journey the hospital train finally reached Berlin where he was soon being visited by his parents and fiancée who brought him small comforts of chocolates etc. He had suffered a smashed rib from a Russian bullet which would take time to heal; meantime as soon as he could walk he was allowed home on leave, and two months later pronounced fit for non-combat duty and assigned as an instructor to an SS training depot.

Accounts of the great German advances during the first phase of Operation Barbarossa tend to give the impression of negligible losses to the attackers. Perhaps in comparison to the enormous damage inflicted on the Soviet armies this is so. But one SS officer who survived the war to attempt a history of the Das Reich division refers to SS losses as 'bloody', citing various official returns for certain periods. For example:

During the weeks 22 June — 27 July 1941 the SS-Reich (as it was then known) suffered 2,411 casualties in killed, wounded and missing; by 17 August this figure had risen to 3,907. This division fought as part of the 24th Army Corps on the central sector whose other infantry components were the 268th Division and the élite *Grossdeutschland*, comparable figures for these two formations being 639 and 1,541 respectively. It is impossible to deduce with certainty the reason for this disparity which could be due to various reasons, even that of the SS reputation as the most aggressive attacking troops. Against such losses must be set the fantastic damage done to the Soviets which in this period was set out in an order of the day issued by the German Corps commander, Field Marshal von Bock on 4 July 1941..

This German army corps on the central sector including the SS-Reich had encountered four Soviet armies consisting of 32 Rifle divisions, 8 Tank divisions, 6 motorized brigades, and 3 cavalry divisions, of which the following were destroyed:

22 Rifle divisions; 7 Tank divisions; 6 Mechanized brigades;
3 Cavalry divisions

The Russians taken prisoner numbered 287,704 men, plus 2,585 tanks destroyed, 1,449 guns and 246 planes captured, plus great quantities of small-arms, munitions, vehicles and supplies including fuel. The planes captured did not of course include those destroyed in air combat or in Luftwaffe air attacks.

Such figures give an indication of the scale of these operations, and the German losses have to be seen in this context. Even so, the SS losses amounted to a comparatively small but frequent occurrence brought about by the kind of 'short, sharp battles' fought whenever the Soviet defenders managed to organize some real defence, though as seen, until the Autumn these were no more than small scale actions. It was the rapid panzer spearheads driving the prescribed 'wedges' deep into Russian territory which so upset and demoralized the Soviet forces, this coupled with the fact that their officer corps had been decimated in the mid-thirties purges by Stalin; this traumatic event helped or otherwise by the machinations of the SS intelligence chief Reinhard Heydrich whose faked documents are said to have helped convince the Soviet dictator in his paranoic distrust of his lieutenants.

Even so, and as with any army, the eventual, cumulative effect of a constant small drainage of casualties means an eventual complete turnover in personnel, which is virtually what happened to the SS and indeed Army units at the sharp end of the German attack after a few months of combat in Russia.

Karl Hummelkieir recalls that after a few months his unit had lost half its strength and only received a few replacements:

'We became tired out, but we pressed on until suddenly the Russian winter hit us, with heavy rain that reduced the terrible roads to rivers of mud and rendered us immobile.'

The mighty, highly mobile German Army and SS Divisions were stuck knee deep in muck which petrified the front. Having told the German people at home in frequent victory fanfares that the Red Army was smashed beyond repair the Goebbels propaganda machine was now obliged to switch its tune to one of suffering by the heroic troops at the front; the German illustrated papers began showing men, vehicles and horses struggling in amazing quagmires.

Paul Kretzler had taken part in a number of huge encircling movements with his Totenkopf unit in which complete Russian armies had been swallowed up, simply vanishing from the Soviet order of battle, scooped up by the Germans and trotted off westwards, a great number of them doomed to die of neglect, not all of it deliberate.

'A vast mass of dirty brown humanity marching across the plain or on the so-called roads'.

When he entered the next battle it seemed to be no more than one of the routine skirmishes:

'We entered a locality, ready for a rest, with no sign of the enemy, and climbed out of our vehicles to have a meal, when a great shouting began and a lot of Russian troops rushed out of concealment among the houses. We sprang to our weapons, but by then we were under fire and several men including myself were hit. A bullet went through the fleshy part of my side and I fell to the ground in pain. The next moments were hazy, a confusion of shouts and noise which grew louder and louder as some of our vehicles blew up and caught fire. I tried to crawl away but felt myself grabbed and kicked and then two men pulled me across the grass and I found myself in a house. The firing went on for a while and then I must have fainted. When I came to it was much quieter and when I opened my eyes I found myself in a dark house with some Russians including an officer. They were not unfriendly, perhaps anxious to get me to talk. One of them gave me a drink of vodka which choked me while they took off my jacket and began bandaging my wound. I was in a state of terror as I expected to be shot. The bandage was very poor and the blood seeped through it over the earth floor. I felt faint and asked for some water. They propped me up against the wall and the officer knelt down to ask me some questions in German. He said: "What is your unit of the SS? What is its strength? What are your objectives?"

'That sort of thing. I said nothing, so he shrugged his shoulders and left me alone. Then a lot more shooting began and the Russians ran outside and began firing themselves. The roof of the house was straw and it caught fire and pieces of burning debris began falling into the room. I tried to crawl to the open doorway, but my head seemed very painful and I collapsed on the ground with burning debris around me. Then I heard shouts as some men ran into the cottage, strong hands took hold of me and I found myself outside. I heard German voices that I recognized and was lifted up onto a vehicle which drove me out of the area. A few hours later I had been operated on in hospital and had a bullet removed from my side.'

A veteran of the armed SS from 1938, Karl-Heinz Anold of the Germania regiment also encountered the stiffening Russian resistance by September 1941, having to fight for possession of small villages before resuming the line of advance. Then he received his first wound during a Russian artillery bombardment:

'We were taking cover from the bursting shells when I sensed a blow on my helmet which I thought had been caused by a clod of earth. But then my scalp began to hurt and placing my hand there I felt blood and a comrade found a wound which though not serious needed attention. A small splinter had penetrated my helmet, but once it was bandaged up I carried on.

'But soon after that I was blown up by another shell. We had been advancing rapidly and as usual had little idea of where we actually were. It was not important so long as we were moving east and destroying the enemy. At times we made encircling movements before resuming our easterly advance.

'As often the Russians had followed our progress with artillery fire and this time they caught us as we were alighting from our vehicles. I felt a searing flash next to me, the breath seemed to be sucked out of me and I was sent flying through the air. I do not recall hitting the ground, I believe I was unconscious by then. But when I came round my head was singing and I could hear nothing. I had pains all over me and wondered if I had been killed. Then I felt someone turn me over and hands running over me as if looking for wounds. I was lifted up but could see nothing at first. Then I felt myself lifted into a vehicle and began to see light and gradually the things around me, but I was still deaf.

'I was taken to the rear with some dead and wounded and examined by a doctor who diagnosed concussion, and I was put in a bed for observation in the care of SS male orderlies. This was quite comfortable but I was still bothered by my lack of hearing. Several days went by and I ate well enough, the feeling came back into my aching limbs and I was allowed up. But I still could not hear anything. The doctor examined me and decided my eardrums must have been damaged, so I was sent back to the base hospital for more expert examination, and there they discovered that I had indeed suffered from perforation of the eardrums.'

Anold had also come to the end of his combat career, being returned to hospital in Germany for six months of comfort before being relegated to a safe job in a depot.

For Lothar Vogel of the Leibstandarte the summer had seemed long, hot, thirsting, one long pursuit without hot food, nights under the stars, and as always little idea of their location:

'The flat, featureless terrain seemed endless, we did not know which way was what, our maps were useless, the roads hopeless. Only when we reached some locality recognizable as a town could we orientate ourselves. This was the norm and went on for months until the resistance stiffened and the Soviets began to show some sign of better organization and we had harder battles. In these we lost men and never seemed to get the replacements we needed so were always under-strength.

'I remember one small battle in particular for it was then that our young Lieutenant was killed by a Russian sharpshooter. They were always very good at that sort of thing. If we were stuck in positional warfare then you knew it was always necessary to take extra care, for their snipers set themselves up at once. You only needed to show part of the body to be shot and our Lieutenant was exceedingly careless. He tried to observe the Russians through his binocularscope and received a bullet in the head at once. His deputy took command but was too upset to function for a while. So it was just as well we had a lull.

'When the rains came everything was ruined for us, the track roads turned into a morass of mud and immobilized us.'

Lothar Vogel survived the mud, but in November, after the big freeze had started he was struck down by a bullet:

'I was on watch in one of our dug-outs with a machine-gun. It was quiet after several days of snow and constant Russian artillery fire. I was trying to keep warm, stamping my feet and moving about as much as I could in the confined space of the dug-out when I felt a sudden blow on my temple and knew no more.'

The bullet had actually struck his skull a glancing blow, but it was enough to put him out of combat for the rest of the war.

Ex-camp guard, now Totenkopf infantryman, Gustav Doren:

'Our battles were just like any other unit's, we committed no atrocities at any time. I never saw a single act that could be called that. We used a few willing Russian men and women on daily chores and they took their pay in the form of food or rather meals. Some of them stayed with us for a year or so, but gradually disappeared for various reasons, and I do not mean they were killed by us. I believe one of the women was a willing sexual partner to one of our men, but this sort of thing was discouraged. These Russians were usually lice-ridden and we insisted they take measures or be dismissed. It was not my experience that Russian women were used sexually by our troops, though obviously there were exceptions when the officers were absent and the troops were not engaged in fighting.

'Small incidents became magnified. I knew that some German prisoners had been mutilated by the Russian secret police and I believe reprisals were taken at the time, but it never became the rule. The problem is that it takes but one incident to become common knowledge and that is the stuff myths are made of. There were cruelties on both sides and of course very many hostages were shot and hanged later when the partisans began their operations behind our lines. I believe there was some clause in the Geneva Convention excusing this practice*. I am not educated enough to quote it and in any case it was irrelevant in Russia, a country which refused to be part of such things, but then the brutal invasion of their country was bound to bring revenge.'

Having spent two months convalescing in Poland and Germany, Paul Kretzler returned to his Totenkopf unit to find a very different state of affairs. The summer had gone and it rained all the time.

'We were stuck in the mud and I had a terrible time trying to find the unit I was assigned to, for the old hands had gone — killed, wounded, or missing,

---

* This is correct. It was the clause which saved Field Marshal von Manstein when he was arraigned before a tribunal after the war.

and the replacements, although good lads, were not of the same calibre. We were unable to move or do anything owing to the terrible conditions. This went on for a while until quite suddenly it all turned to ice and snow and this was in a sense far worse for we had no winter clothing at all. There was much suffering as we tried to improve our position and keep our vehicles in motion. Everything froze and we were short of lubricants which made things worse.

'Then I received a second wound which put me out of the war.

'The Russians gave us one of their artillery barrages prior to an attack. When the shells exploded they tore up huge chunks of frozen soil which were almost as dangerous as splinters. One of these struck me on the head and I fell unconscious and it was some time before anyone could reach me and drag me to the safety of a vehicle. I was severely wounded in the head and evacuated the same day. I remember very little of this period as I had alternate bouts of waking and unconsciousness and was moved from one place to another until I realized I was back in Germany. I was invalided home to my mother in Dresden, a physical wreck.'

Paul Kretzler never served again and managed to escape the worst of the air raids later as well as the subsequent Russian occupation.

Borodino — a name from history: there, 129 years before, the Emperor Napoleon's *Grande Armée* had been brought to the brink of defeat. Now, the spearhead units of the SS-Reich division were thrusting straight at Moscow — only 62 miles distant. The Soviet dictator rushed up forces from his far eastern provinces, including the crack 32nd Siberian Rifle Division, three infantry regiments supported by two brigades of the deadly T34 tanks, these aided by the almost impregnable monstrous 52-ton KV2s.

On the left flank of the SS-Reich fought the Hauenschild Brigade of the 10th Panzer Division, the 7th Panzer regiment, a battalion of the 90th Motorized Artillery, and a motorcycle battalion of the 10th Division. Against these German units the Soviets launched massed tank attacks for the very first time; these supported by the charging Siberians, flak, 7.62 cm pak guns and some multiple-barrelled mortars.

A great battle ensued, and there were none of the famous 'eighty-eights' to hand, and the Germans' 37mm 'door knocker' pak cannon were useless against the Soviet armour, so the defending infantry of the Army and SS were obliged to tackle the Russian tanks with explosive charges. In the severe fighting the 3rd SS Infantry were almost destroyed, its remnants split between the other two regiments (Deutschland and Der Fuehrer). Every available piece of German artillery was brought to bear on the Soviet units, and the SS infantry charged forward in a counter attack 'with death defying courage'. The Russians had established a defence line, complete with flame thrower batteries, minefields, barbed wire, flak and pak guns, pillboxes, with their infantry using machine-guns, rifles and massed mortars. Above the hellish din of the battle roamed Soviet ground attack planes but these were at once intercepted by fighters of the Luftwaffe's VIIIth Air Corps.

Ferocious fighting took place, and before long the German SS and Army dead and wounded were being laid out in rows in the field dressing stations just behind the battle line — among them Lt-General Paul Hausser who had been struck in the right eye by a shell splinter.

But not all the Soviet units were of the calibre of the Siberians, some suffered up to 80% desertions, with officers the first to flee on horses, even changing into civilian clothes in the nearest villages to escape the Germans. Collective farms were 'liberated' of all their food, horses and carts being used to carry the supplies. The Soviet command resorted to using security detachments to prevent unauthorized withdrawals with orders to ruthlessly mow down recalcitrants. Greatly weakened though they were, the German units pushing on towards Moscow instilled panic into the capital, with anti-communist posters beginning to appear. The government and diplomatic corps prepared to leave the city, as did ministries, factories and institutions. Rumour mongers began their work, petty crime and looting took place, and Stalin declared a state of emergency with Moscow decreed a military zone, which meant that the army and militia had orders to shoot provocateurs and spies and all others calling for rebellion. Stalin knew that if Moscow fell the Red Army would be forced to give up all of the Western Soviet Union. In a mood of desperation he confessed in a remark to the American ambassador Harry Hopkins that he would welcome the appearance of US troops under their own unrestricted command in any part of the front.

Even in July, a 'Peoples' Army' of 100,000 men had been recruited by decree, given a mere 20 days training and rushed to the killing grounds. At the start of October a further 100,000 men were called up and these too rushed out to defend Moscow, while a further 18,000 men were formed into Worker's Battalions to help maintain order in the city; 40,000 boys and girls plus half a million women and old men were mobilized to dig and construct defence lines under military command, working in three shifts, day and night, in terrible conditions.

Yet even arrests, executions and constant patrolling by the security forces failed to prevent deserters and looters including children from wandering the streets. The worst point was reached on 27 November, by which time most of the attacking German divisions had been reduced to 5000–10,000 men, the panzer battalions in a worse state. On that day Colonel Hasso von Manteuffel's men had seized a crossing and established a bridgehead over the Moscow-Volga canal and the power station providing Moscow with its electricity was captured. Complete triumph seemed to be within the Germans' grasp, yet within two hours on the same afternoon the temperature dropped to 40 degrees below zero centigrade. The Germans had no winter clothing and suffered accordingly.

* * *

It was time for sober reflection on the Germans' part as their frozen units sank into exhausted immobility at the outer limits of the Moscow tramlines.

Back in June their huge army of 146 divisions (not counting those of their allies) had faced an estimated 139 Soviet divisions plus 29 independent brigades equalling 4,700,000 men, greatly outnumbering the attackers. But the estimates of Hitler and most of his experts were hazy and based on very inadequate intelligence. The panzer expert General Heinz Guderian had written his book called *Panzer!* in which he had estimated Soviet tank strength at ten thousand, for this he was accused by his contemporaries as alarmist. The Soviets in fact possessed *seventeen* thousand tanks.

By 1942 even Hitler was forced to admit to the Finnish Field Marshal Mannerheim that if anyone had told him that the Russians could field 35,000 vehicles he would have declared them mad; in fact they had already used that number in battle. The Soviet strength had come as a tremendous shock to the Fuehrer. But the crux of the whole Soviet defence set-up was its colossal manpower which manifested in the profligate use of infantry en masse at the front.

From a population of 190 million the Soviets could boast 16 million men of military age. It was this almost inexhaustible supply of manpower, plus Allied aid, that kept the 'Soviet colossus' from toppling.

On the other side, the German attackers were being bled white and found it increasingly difficult to maintain the strength of their units which, even when of usual numbers, were no longer of their old hitting power. A constant stream of hospital trains transported the wounded back to the Reich. In August alone (in 1941) the SS Police Division lost 2,000 men killed and wounded fighting in the Luga bridgehead.

But, just how seriously did Stalin really take the repeated warnings of an impending German attack? It is often said that he ignored them up to the last moment, usually blaming the British who he knew desired Soviet participation in the war against Hitler.

Yet, over a week before Operation Barbarossa began the Soviet NKVD secret police and militia began deporting 'suspect families' from its north-western provinces in the Baltic areas: 69,000 such families were arrested and deported to Siberia.

CHAPTER TEN

An order of the day issued by the commander of the German XLVI Panzer Corps described the action of one small SS group as 'an example of what defence means'.

This referred to an incident back in August when one small section of the 1st Company of the motorcycle battalion Langemarck held out to the last against a Russian attack. When the battle was over, one SS Corporal, one Lance Corporal and two privates lay dead around their machines, surrounded by the corpses of the Russians who had attacked them.

It was this kind of small action that gradually drained the Germans' strength in the months before the big freeze-up which brought thousands of frostbite cases and then the big Soviet counter-offensive. Yet, the hardening of the ground did help restore some of the Germans' mobility:

Karl Hummelkeier:

'The temperature plummeted and everything froze. This enabled us to move again but our weapons and vehicles froze up too so this became a new factor. The Russian resistance stiffened and they did not seem to be greatly affected by the climate, probably because their army was not a mobile one. It was almost impossible to dig into the frozen ground and we suffered accordingly. The shell bursts sent clods of frozen earth flying which were almost as dangerous as shell splinters. I remembered my will and thought it had been a good idea.

'When we were able to move forward the Russians struck just as the snow came and chaos resulted. Far from being beaten to nothing the Bear had sprung up again and gave us a very bad time. However, it was the weather which continued to be a worst enemy. We froze and were immobilized again. What little cover we had could not keep out the terrible cold, yet the winter had only just begun. We had our first frostbite cases and it seemed as if the proud élite were in dire trouble. The Russians made gains but Hitler ordered everyone to stand fast and the line held. It was a nightmare as our highly mobile forces were made redundant. Our weapons continually froze up and we were all but turned to ice statues by the cold. I cannot understand even now how we survived that nightmare winter, for it was many weeks before any winter clothing reached us. All we had was our usual SS camouflage jackets over our grey uniforms. I have never experienced cold like that, it was impossible to deal with. To sleep meant to risk death from freezing, yet to try and keep awake indefinitely was impossible. Men fell asleep over their weapons from sheer exhaustion. And the Russians shelled us continuously and gave us no peace.

'We were reduced to mere shadows of our former selves, I was amazed how the young men I had known for so long became old in the face, haggard, grey looking, unshaven most of the time, gaunt skeletons. Yet we never gave in. It was a question of survival. The enemy knew we were suffering, they used loudspeakers to call on us to surrender. Inevitably, they had taken prisoners and one of these agreed to broadcast propaganda for the Russians. We did not fancy our chances as prisoners, there had been ugly rumours of what they did to SS men. There had certainly been atrocities on both sides and it had become a savage war. The Russians had no respect for the Geneva Convention, in a way we could understand their hatred and they probably saw SS troops as the epitome of Nazism.

'A number of our men were lost in the Russian attacks, some of them captured and wounded, and those would never see their homeland again, along with large numbers of others who were taken prisoner. On the rare occasions when we now took prisoners they proved much more bitter and unco-operative, though occasionally we found a Russian who was almost fawning in his desire to please us, begging to be allowed to stay with us and do various menial tasks. These were usually the non-Russians of the provinces such as the Ukraine where there was so much hatred of Stalin and his regime.'

The fast moving SS units had won many victories in the great advances of June to October 1941, it was the Der Fuehrer regiment of Hausser's division Reich that had taken Borodino, to advance along the Moscow highway with their Army comrades, only to be struck by Mongolian regiments in sub-zero temperatures. Hausser's men had got within forty miles of Moscow but having lost 7,000 men in the combats were no longer in a fit state to continue.

The enormous difficulties described by the witnesses were added to by the lack of visibility in those murky days, a dim light penetrating the darkness from about eleven in the morning; by three o'clock it was dark again.

Yet the SS-Reich division clung on, suffering a further 4,000 casualties before it was finally withdrawn in March 1942.

The Norwegian volunteer force had finally reached the front in February. Jutte Olafsen describes what he found:

'After two months training and a big inspection we entrained for the East. We were in fairly good spirits, though I'm sure that some at least were having second thoughts, but there were field police on the train to make sure we didn't desert. It took us two days to reach Russia where we detrained and boarded trucks which took us forward over the frozen ground, this being the winter of early 1942 after the worst had passed. I doubt if we could have survived that real winter in the first campaign season when the Germans were caught without proper clothing and suffered greatly.

'We reached our sector on the front and were marched on foot to our positions. It was our very first experience of war and I will give my impressions.

'We were near a wood, but all before us was frozen plain with not a tree to be seen. There were deep dug-outs with interconnecting lines of trenches, little foxholes (schutzengraben), and machine-guns set up every few yards. The enemy we were told by our German hosts were about a mile ahead and occasionally made attacks across the plain with tanks and infantry. But since they had no cover our artillery always took care of them so there was nothing to worry about! This sanguine forecast was not borne out by events.

'The harshness of the conditions disappointed us. We had not expected to find the conditions of World War I but tried to make the best of it. Our German officers had tried to inspire us as some kind of fellow Nordic heroes, but we no longer felt like the would-be heroes some of us had been I suspect.

'We settled down to our first night in Russia, quite well provided with warm clothing, although this was of little use if you remained still for too long. We heard various strange noises through the night — strange to us, plus occasional shelling, but not near us.

'After a rudimentary breakfast next morning we were told we would be selected for indoctrination patrols and I was one of those picked out to make up a group of twenty or so who would reconnoitre the territory before us. I was terribly afraid as the ground was so open as we crawled out in single file and began a zigzag route towards enemy country which lay somewhere on the horizon. It was still cold and we wore winter clothing and carried rifles, submachine-guns and grenades. Every so often we paused to look and listen. It was amazingly quiet, apart from the slithering of our bodies over the hard ground there was not a sound.

'Then we came upon a dead Russian who stank horribly and gave us newcomers a nasty turn. I will not forget his face which was decomposing and looking up at the sky, his hands like two claws. I forced myself to look away as we edged past it; it was only the first of many bodies I would see.

At last we reached a slight dip in the ground, and there we paused while our German patrol leader, a Lieutenant, went forward with a Sergeant. When he came back he told us to split into two groups and go off under command of a Sergeant in different directions to approach the Russian positions. He told us not to worry if we came under fire and in no circumstances to stand up or try to run away as we'd be shot down because there was no cover.

'I felt terribly frightened as we set off again, and about this time we heard the first small-arms fire not too far away, but had no idea who was doing the shooting. Our other party went off to the right and we to the left and we lost sight of them. The sun came up and it grew warmer and I thought that at any moment we would be seen and shot at. Yet every time I dared look up towards the enemy I could see nothing at all but bare ground and a few very tiny hillocks. It was not as I had imagined it would be; I had thought of hordes of yelling Russians charging at us, with our guns shooting them down. In fact that morning went so slowly and uneventfully that I began to wonder if the enemy was there at all.

'After about thirty minutes of this slithering along our patrol leader stopped to peer at the supposed Russian positions through his binoculars before passing word that we would now return. It took us a whole hour to regain our old positions by which time I was in a great state of nerves as I imagined our own men shooting at us. We were very relieved to have got through this first 'action', such as it was, and pleased to get the hot drinks which soon reached us.

'Our lives then took on a deadly routine, for day after day we were either on watch or sleeping in the dug-outs, with very little sign of the enemy at all. An occasional shell whistled over our heads to explode some way behind us, but apart from that we seemed to be in a quiet sector.'

The Norwegians had indeed been inserted into such a location to enable them to be broken in gently, though they were soon to get their full share of the action:

'All this was to change very dramatically, as a Russian attack came at us a few weeks later.

'By then we had been taken to the rear a few times for a rest, there we lived in huts built for the purpose and these were quite comfortable. We would spend three or four days there doing nothing much but eating and sleeping. But after we returned to our front positions one night we were suddenly hit by an artillery barrage, and this was the first time we had been under fire of any consequence and it was terrifying. The sound of the shells as they came over was like one long, howling whistle. Then came a fluttering sound and terrific detonations that shook the earth round us and sent over great clods of frozen earth, stones, and bits of timber when some of the dug-outs were hit. We heard yells and screams and commands. Then I heard a whistle which meant the Russians were coming. I was as usual very frightened, I'm sure we all were. But we leapt out of our holes and into the firing trench as the German NCO rushed along to get us organized.

'When we dared poke our heads over the rim of the trench we saw long brown lines of Russian infantry advancing towards us behind several tanks. The artillery fire had shifted elsewhere and I was now terrified by the tanks as they looked impressive and invincible. Our training had included this kind of thing and our NCOs told us to keep calm as the Russians would be stopped.

'We sighted our weapons and tried not to shake too much with fear and sure enough there were loud bangs not far away and at once two of the Russian tanks were hit. One of them had its turret blown clean off and blew up with a bang, the other just stopped coming. Our NCOs then told us to let loose at the Russian infantry who were yelling like mad, half running and half dodging about as they came on. A lot of them wore greatcoats and helmets, but others had fur caps on.

'Our anti-tank guns were blazing away from concealed positions and two more of the enemy tanks went up in flames. The noise was tremendous, one great racket as we opened fire with all our weapons and we saw lots of Russians falling and staggering about, but many more came on. There were three long lines of them but the first had melted away to nothing as our bullets hit them. I had no idea if I hit any of them. I had a Mauser rifle and was firing as fast as I could. They were still several hundred yards off and I was not an especially good shot and could not say if I hit the mark or not. But the second line of Russians came on until they too began to wilt as they were mown down, most of the execution being done by our machine-guns. It was terrible to see so many humans dying like that and I felt upset.

'Our NCOs were shouting at the Russians, partly to encourage us I believe, but still the remnants came on, and these were now firing with rifles and machine carbines and you could hear the whistle and whine of the bullets. I wanted to run away or at least hide in a dug-out, but I forced myself to stay where I was. One or two men cried out and I saw them fall to the ground. One of them I had known as a good man, he was hit in the eye and died.

'The remaining Russian tanks were knocked out, but not before one of them had almost reached our lines where its guns did a lot of damage. It was then attacked by resolute NCOs and went up in flames. The remaining Russians now lay on the ground and fired at us, but they were terribly exposed and before long our machine-guns had searched them out and they were all put out of action. The noise died down and we were able to take a better look at the battlefield.

'It all happened in about five or ten minutes, and during that time the Russians had lost twelve tanks, all T34s, and I don't know how many hundred men. There were clouds of smoke rolling across the scene, the ground was littered with brown lumps, not one of them moved, though there must have been some still alive. Our machine-gunners remorselessly mowed the terrain, so I guessed they must have been intent on finishing off the wounded. It was all terribly brutal and I felt sick. I sat down in the trench and drank some water and the German NCOs went through the trench system making sure we were all in good shape, and our dead comrade was hurried away to the rear. I believe he was the only man killed. The wounded were also removed and I think survived.

'That night the Russians gave us no peace, mortaring us for hours as if in revenge, so that we were obliged to remain in our deepest dug-outs as the cursed bombs dropped all over our trenches. We got no sleep at all that night, and when dawn came yet another Russian attack developed and we knew we were in for it as an air raid preceded it. Low flying Stormoviks came over, bombing and machine-gunning. They were met afterwards by some of our fighters but it was too late. At the same time a heavy tank attack took place on our left, followed by masses of infantry who created a lot of noise with their yelling. This time our guns gave them a pasting as soon as they appeared and a lot never got started. But there were so many of them behind that they just kept on coming all along our sector — thousands and thousands of them. This was a terrifying ordeal as we could not see how they could be stopped, yet the concentrated fire of all our weapons soon thinned their ranks and then the artillery cut them down still further. Then Stukas came over and finished them off. The dive bombers screamed down on them, dropping anti-personnel, fragmentation bombs, and that was the end of the attack.

'Yet this was only an introduction to the Russian front, within a week we had been shifted to another sector that was rather different as the terrain was covered in gentle slopes and there were woods and ruined villages. The enemy was very active here and able to concentrate in the gullies and other places of concealment to make some surprise assaults on us, so we needed to be on the alert at all times. I saw several attacks, one of which succeeded in penetrating our lines to the left of us, but an immediate counter-attack restored the situation. Yet even more Russian assaults came in which gave us no peace.

'After a week of this with us constantly on the alert we grew exhausted and longed for a respite. In fact by then we wished we had never volunteered for such a lunatic war, even labouring in the Reich would have been preferable. But there was no turning back though, we could not be taken out of the line because of the constant pressure and begun to suffer casualties from mortar and artillery fire. To me it seemed probable that we would never see our dear homeland again.

'Then came a lull and at last we could be taken out for a rest in a village behind the line where we could have a good clean up and eat reasonable meals. This was a week of luxury and during this time I grew very friendly with a fellow called Lars who was actually Swedish I believe. We became very close friends for the rest of my service in the Legion.

'Just before our return to the front we were inspected by an SS general who thanked us for our service and great contribution to the struggle against Bolshevism, and we had to cheer him afterwards with several loud "hurrahs". Then we had a drink of schnapps and were taken off by truck to the front again and what I felt increasingly was certain death.'

Reinhard Bochel also had to be indoctrinated into the war in the East:

'All of the new men were taken out in a big patrol towards the Russian positions. It was the half light of dusk and we had to crawl over many shellholes filled with rubbish, discarded equipment and even one or two dead Russians who were well past the decomposition stage. These were awful sights for us, but we saw many hundreds later. In due course our progress was slowed so that we were hardly moving at all. There were obstacles, lumps of trees, the remains of a tank and a road. These were useful for concealment and those behind the senior NCO took cover while he went forward to listen and observe before we moved on. We were over twenty strong and armed with machine pistols and grenades, our object to assess the exact enemy positions but also to break in the new men like myself. It was very quiet, but then we heard Russians singing and a few guns fired, the shells passing over our heads. We were out in this 'no man's land' for over an hour and I saw no sign of the enemy, which was perhaps just as well, though they were there and not very far away.

'About a month later we were put into the attack on a local level as the Russians had been edging forward their positions little by little and we wanted to drive them back. After a short but heavy bombardment we rushed out from *our dug-outs across the open terrain. It was dawn and not too light, but our NCOs had shown us where to expect the Russkis who were very good at camouflage. I was terrified as I ran at full speed behind the other men. Then the machine-guns started up and the bullets were singing over our heads and then slapping into the ground near us. I fell down in fright or over some obstacle, I'm not sure which. Our NCO urged us on in bounds as we raced along the remains of a track we had seen earlier and from there we set up our machine-gun to start spraying the enemy while other sections rushed them. I was one of the assault squad, carrying a grenade in one hand and my rifle in the other.*

'*The noise was very considerable as the Russkis started using mortars, but the bombs fell behind us. Then we were near enough to fling ourselves down and hurl grenades. I heard some screaming as one of our men was hit, then we had to rush on behind the NCO who was apparently fearless. He shot off all his ammunition and then threw grenades with us close behind him. Until that moment I had not seen a single Russian. But then I saw them, their heads were bobbing up and down out of their little dug-outs. They had helmets and caps on and were in a great state of excitement, shouting to each other and at us. Our machine-gun cut some of them down and our grenades burst among them, the NCO vanished into one of the enemy dug-outs with us close behind.*

'*It was all confusion in the half light and I saw some Russians running away from their positions and fired at them and then jumped down into a hole on top of a dead one. He was half staring at me with bloody eyes and looked awful. I leapt out again to find a better place and saw several more Russians nearby who had their hands up in surrender, but they were mown down by fire from someone who rushed up with his machine carbine. Our people were now in full possession of the Russian line, but suddenly it all went quiet, and as I knelt in a hole I could hardly see a soul. Then the NCO appeared, grinning, and told me to watch out as the Russkis would likely counter-attack. So I set up my rifle facing the right way and saw most of our lads doing the same thing. Some of them were removing the Russian corpses, and then another squad arrived to reinforce us so we felt more secure. I thought that surely some of our men must have been killed and wounded, and looking around I saw some being removed by the medics.*

'*After a while the NCO passed round a water bottle filled with schnapps and we took a swig. Then the Russians began mortaring us and the earth shook with sharp detonations. This was bad as they had the range and splinters were flying all around us. But we kept our heads down and I don't think anyone was hit. Some of the veterans had even used dead Russkis to protect their holes, propping them up to provide cover. It was all a horrible experience and I shrank down into my hole, heart beating madly and wondering when the Russian infantry would rush us.*

'*Well, after about fifteen minutes the mortaring stopped quite suddenly and I heard a great volume of yelling and shouting and our NCO bawled — "Catch the bastards, here they come!"*

'*I forced my head up and to my horror saw the Russians were only twenty yards away. So we all began firing like mad. I'm not sure how many there were as we had no time to count them before they were upon us in a flash and we were fighting like demons for our lives. I could not fire my damn rifle fast enough so threw my last two grenades and tried to get out my bayonet but it was too late — the nearest Russians were on us and had those well-known machine-guns with the round drums and were shooting in all directions. I hit the nearest one with a bullet and he crashed down over me which was fortunate in a way as it prevented one of his comrades getting at me and I shot him too. They fell over my dug-out to make a protective roof and I lay still for a moment while all the yelling and shooting went on. Then I struggled up, still terrified, and saw some of our men out of their holes and fighting the Russians who were all round us.*

'There must have been twenty bodies lying around the dug-outs. Then I went to help a comrade who was fighting two Russkis who for some reason were not using their weapons and were probably trying to capture a prisoner. I hit one Russian over the head without thinking about it, and as the other one turned on me my comrade stuck a bayonet into his chest and he gasped and fell down. We then rushed at the others and managed to knock them down too, but then I felt a blow on my knee and fell down myself. The noise went on all round us, and then the damned Russian mortar bombs started falling again, even though the Russian infantrymen were still around us.

'I had no idea of what had hit me but I started to crawl away just as the Russians began running back to their own positions. I fell into a dug-out next to one of our lads who was trying to shelter from the mortar fire. The bangs went on for a long time, and then we heard great yelling, and sure enough the Russians came at us again. But this time they were all killed by our machine-guns, not one survived.

'This was my first battle and a bloody one. My comrade in the hole with me was also a newcomer. He looked at my knee and found it had been struck by a bullet, and when it grew quiet he received permission from an NCO to help me back to our main line for aid. This was only managed with a lot of difficulty as I was in pain and we had to crawl on our bellies as the Russians were using machine-guns to sweep the whole area in order to prevent the newly captured position from being reinforced.'

An hour later Reinhard Bochel was being expertly attended to in the rear and was soon evacuated to Germany where he spent six comfortable months.

'When I was completely fit again I returned to the front to my old unit and found many changes. There were no more than three of the old faces, all those I had gone to the unit with had been killed or were otherwise out of action. It was not long before I received another wound which put me out of the fighting for good.

'We had gone forward in trucks to help the Army and went into the attack, but were hit by Russian tanks, not all of which were hit by our pak guns. They shelled us and one of the explosions buried me in dirt and muck, so that I

almost suffocated. In fact the weight on my chest was so great that I fully expected to die. I fell unconscious, but then felt strong hands tugging at me, but the Russians were using machine-guns and my comrades had to take cover for some time until they could come to try and rescue me again. By the time I saw daylight again I was in a bad way and was taken to hospital. The effects of being buried alive were peculiar.'

Bochel relates that the deprivation of oxygen had affected him, especially his lungs, so once again he spent several months in Germany:

'By the time I was released and re-assessed I was no longer the young man I had been and was downgraded, posted to a depot and sat out the rest of the war in odd jobs, office work, instruction, but I found I was unable to speak for long periods, so I remained working for the Adjutant until escaping to the West following the Russian advance of 1944-45.'

CHAPTER ELEVEN

Paul Giske joined the SS 'for much the same reason as most. They seemed to be something special', and having passed all his tests and been approved as of true Aryan stock he went through the usual infantry training, but then decided to volunteer for the panzers:

'Although the SS armoured formations did not really come into being until 1942, in the year before some units were receiving training in old tanks, mostly IIIs and IVs. These were the first SS tank companies and I was attracted to them as they seemed so much more invincible and safe to me. This was an illusion of course, but this is what I thought at the time.

'We were quartered in Wunstrau training area and went into it with enthusiasm under army instructors at first. I was very keen to become a gunner and soon learned how to handle the 75mm cannon in those tanks. We had a few old wrecks to shoot at, sometimes on the move and at times in the stop position. It was very bumpy riding in a tank, very confining and very smelly. In fact I soon began to regret my decision, but the life was quite easy as there seemed to be no urgency in our training which was soon taken over by newly qualified SS instructors who I suspect did not have much experience themselves at the time in armoured warfare.

'We had six tanks in this unit, but it was usual for at least two to be out of action through mechanical trouble. We wore overalls for our training but of course on parade or for formal occasions the army type black coverall uniforms with SS insignia. There were some with us who had worn this uniform for some time as they had been in armoured cars and had fought in Poland and France. But as a tank formation we were a new cadre, and in 1942 the authorization came for us to be greatly expanded into an armoured division, or rather to join one of the existing SS infantry divisions as armoured support. In our case we were expanded to regimental size and were sent to the Das Reich division still fighting in the East.

'We now entered large scale training with new Panther tanks and had a lot of problems at first with these, though they were obviously very good. Once the firm making them had sorted out the mechanical problems they became very good medium tanks on all fronts and were generally more than a match for the enemy.'

The Germans had been shaken by the early appearance of the T34 tank in Russia, and only the inept Soviet handling of armour had prevented them from gaining greater successes with this weapon. The Mk V Panther weighed around 45 tons and was armed with a 75mm long barrelled cannon and proved an excellent all-round panzer once its teething problems had been eliminated.

'Then the SS divisions were withdrawn from the Eastern Front (March 1942) and we met our new unit for the first time and entered into fresh training comprising infantry and tankmen combined in columns to form battle groups which included anti-tank guns and armoured cars etc. After a while all was ready and we entrained for the Eastern Front, some of our tanks being the latest Mk IV type with side armour (skirts).

'We were thrown into the battle at once and I tasted action for the first time. In my position as a gunner there was little to see, I sighted the weapon and pulled the trigger, the commander in the turret gave the orders, the loader attended to the ammunition. I remember the first enemy tanks we saw. They were T34s and moving fast across the horizon and were a good target; but we were ordered to let them get nearer.

'I sighted on one of the Russians as it came nearer and turned towards us, and I thought our CO would never give the order to fire. We were half concealed behind some rising ground and old stonework. At last all our tanks opened fire, the solid shot bounced off the front plate of my T34 to go ricocheting away. I tried again and this time blew off his track so the enemy tank slewed round, and my next shot set it on fire. The crew did not appear so we switched to another target.

'All of the Russian tanks were advancing at full speed with hundreds of infantrymen coming up behind them. My next shot caught not my intended tank target but some of the infantrymen who were blown up. The Russian tanks were now firing continuously and shells were whizzing past us. I fired again and again, and this time saw a tank go flying through the air as a shell struck home and the T34 blew to pieces. We remained stationary in our positions and fired and fired until all the Soviet tanks were destroyed, though some of them managed to get within yards of us. We lost one Panther and one Mk IV, but the crews escaped. Our loader then took on the Russian infantry with our machine-gun and they were beaten back.

'The heat in the tank became almost unbearable, so when the action was over we leapt out for some fresh air. By that time all we could see was the smoking wrecks of the T34s and the field littered with corpses of the Russian infantry. We then changed our positions as the Russians began shelling us, pulling back to a ruined village near a forest where we took a break. This was our privilege, our poor comrades in the infantry stayed where they were.

'Our first real action on the move came soon after that. We were ordered to restore the position a few miles away where the Russians had broken through the army lines. We drove across country and at once came under fire from artillery so that the infantry with us were obliged to take cover under our hulls or in shell-holes. We pushed on and attacked the Russian concentrations of tanks and infantry who were stationary as we had been *earlier, but not so well sited. The Russians never did learn how to use armour properly.*

'We raced towards them with guns blazing and at once I managed to hit a T34 in the flank and it blew up in flames. But the enemy had some pak guns and two of our tanks were hit. Then we were among them, the Russian tanks failed to manoeuvre and prevent us from overrunning their infantry who were then dealt with by our own infantry. We churned through the broken ground and shot up their tanks from the rear, and when they were all destroyed we turned on their infantry and finished them off in small packets. Many prisoners were taken as the Russians gave up in large numbers.

'We remained in that sector for some time and it was very uncomfortable owing to Russian artillery fire so that we had to continually change position. My CO was wounded by a splinter and replaced by another who was very experienced and a Knight's Cross holder. The war of movement had now ceased and we were used in defensive positions most of the time, which was not what we had been trained for. Being stuck in a tank for long periods under fire is bad, the air becomes foul and you cannot perform natural functions very easily and it is hard to get hot food as the ration parties cannot reach you in a barrage. We had to do the best we could in the tank until things improved. We tried to change our position as often as we could but this involved difficulties. For one thing the ground was becoming so churned up that it was easy for a tank to fall into a shell-hole and get bogged down, especially when the rains came and everything was reduced to mud. In any case, our infantry were all around us in their holes so we could not easily move in any direction without great care.'

The veteran Karl Hummelkeier, having survived the terrible crisis winter of 1941-42 enjoyed a rest out of the line, now eligible like all the rest of those veteran combat troops for the *Ostmedaille*, the East Front Medal, enjoying the 'heaven' of a bath, clean clothes and decent meals in peace and comfort. Then they learned of the big changes with the SS divisions converting into panzer and panzer-grenadier divisions (it was in this period that Hitler decreed that all German infantrymen would henceforth be designated 'grenadiers'). It was a time to accept replacements and commence fresh training:

'The SS never stopped trying to recruit men and the best available, until the dire times when the eastern volunteers were accepted. That whole period was one of amazement for us, after all the concepts of racial purity, the true Aryan race and how precious the SS were, the need to be kept pure, and all the rest of it. To see the huge variety of soldier material bearing the SS insignia was rather staggering. Those of the west and north who joined the SS were fairly good, but their hearts often wilted in the wastes of Russia. Some in any case were mere adventurers. When we began the new season of campaigning in Russia we felt re-invigorated, and knew that if we had to face another winter there we would be well prepared.'

Hummelkeier achieved the rank of Sergeant, much to his surprise, and went into the great German summer offensive of 1942 with a bunch of new recruits:

'I did my upmost to teach them all I knew, but it would be a time of testing when they entered battle. Our new weapons in tanks and rockets proved our superiority, but the Russians had also learnt and we had tough battles and lost men including those new to the unit. Yet huge gains were made in the East and the enemy again lost tremendously. Then came the siege of Stalingrad which fortunately did not involve us. This was the greatest disaster to German arms and signalled the end for us. It marked the turning point, for despite Manstein's great victories in the Crimea it could not go on, even our huge army was being bled and by the next winter we were back where we started.

'I remember one particular incident before that winter came. I had been resting with my men in a village just behind the front when some Russian planes came over looking for targets. Our flak hit one of them and it came down about a mile from us. We raced to the spot and found the pilot hobbling away from the wreck and discovered it was a woman. As soon as she saw us she spat in our direction, making some remark about SS troops. One of my men grew angry and was about to slap her but I stopped him. At this point she laughed and opened her blouse, exposing her bare breasts to me, and I believe she was suggesting that I was trying to be nice to her so that I could have her. We took her away for removal to a prisoner-of-war camp.

'I also remember a wonderful leave at home in that period marred by air raids, then back to the front and some very large battles. The Russians seemed to be in possession of an inexhaustible supply of men, no matter how many we put out of action there were always more and more. And their tanks were appearing in ever increasing numbers and joined in mass attacks, suffering heavily but achieving breakthroughs by sheer weight of numbers. The Russians were very well supplied with mortars too* and knew how to use them well. As for their artillery, this was always their dominant arm and gave us a great deal of punishment.

'As a result of these battles all of our unit were killed or wounded in a short period. Companies were reduced to a quarter of their strength and the men remaining grew exhausted. The Russian attacks were almost incessant and though not all on a great scale even the smaller ones were often accompanied by great artillery barrages, so we always took casualties. But we had our successes when working with our armour and inflicted terrible losses on them.

'Yet the tide had irretrievably turned, we were gradually forced to give up our carefully constructed positions. There was no longer any question of advancing further, but of desperately trying to hold on to what we had, and this was beyond our strength. When we received replacements they were incompletely trained and we had no time to complete their education, so these

---

* The Russians had a new angle on an old saying, that every German soldier might (metaphorically) have a Field Marshal's baton in his knapsack, for the Russian soldier it was a mortar.

seventeen or even sixteen-year-olds had to learn on the job, but too often they did not live long enough to do so.

'The Russian landscape was pitiless and very rarely attractive, mostly vast areas of plain and forest, and we learned to avoid the woods as they were controlled by partisans. An ever-increasing number of units had to be diverted to combat their forays on our lines of communications and there were many battles and I believe it was during those that most atrocities occurred. Fortunately, we had no part in such operations which were usually conducted by second line troops and police as well as Russian volunteers who showed no mercy whatever towards their fellow countrymen when they caught them.

'It is impossible to adequately describe the war in Russia, it was a cruel one, and yet it would be wrong to say it was all savagery, there was humanitarianism on both sides. It was not the case that Russian POWs were ill-treated by combat troops on our side, any ill-treatment in the form of neglect did not occur in the forward areas but was part of the higher policy back in Germany and this was disgusting. As for our own SS prisoners of the Russians, I can only repeat from a few who had been captured and escaped that they had been reasonably treated and interrogated like any other prisoners, fed and kept under guard. But in those cases they escaped during a German counter-attack; if they had been taken to the rear and off to Siberia then their chance of survival would have been zero. The Russians did all they could to avenge the rape of their country and we could hardly blame them for that.'

A more unusual career in the Waffen-SS was experienced by Richard Helm who, following his entry into the Wiking division in 1942 suffered a stomach wound on the Eastern Front and was convalesced in Germany. Then he was posted as an infantry training instructor at a depot near Leipzig:

'This was not an easy life as it entailed leading recruits in mock combat and after a time I was relieved as unfit owing to my old wound. I was then sent to the NCO and officer pool to await a new job and after a week or two despatched to a recruiting centre in a little suburb of Berlin. This was an apparent back-water, but in a built-up area with plenty of potential recruits. It was our job to attract them and up to the staff to fulfil a certain quota if possible. In this we were of course competing against the Wehrmacht, so we were always trying to make our window displays as attractive as possible with posters and medals.

'I believe we succeeded, although with my experience of war I was in two minds as to sending boys into combat, for they had no idea what lay before them. No amount of training can prepare young men for the horrors of the battlefield.

'We had a Captain of almost retirement age in charge of our little unit, he had never been in combat and had originally been in the General SS but had somehow got himself transferred to the Waffen-SS. I believe he was an old Army man but had not been in combat at all. He insisted on interviewing every prospective applicant himself and was full of enthusiasm. He told them of

the glorious deeds of the Waffen-SS heroes and even had copies of newspaper stories on the walls of his office, as well as large photos of SS troops and tanks so that when the applicants were seen he would walk them round the office with a fatherly air, one arm round their shoulders, explaining what a grand life it all was and what good fellows and comrades were to be found in the Waffen-SS.

'My own duties were not quite like that, I simply filled in forms with the applicant's details, a mere checking job, but I had no objection to this, it was better than being shot at. I was no hero of combat and had no desire to be. But every so often an inspector from the Waffen-SS HQ made the rounds and we had to convince him that we were doing a grand job in recruiting, and he usually went away satisfied. I must admit that our Captain had a very persuasive manner, and very few boys left unconvinced, usually signing up before they went back home to their parents.'

Another 1942 entrant was Siegfried Karlsen, born in Breslau and thoroughly imbued he admits with Nazi propaganda as to his view of the world, which was inevitable. When his time for call-up came the war had yet to turn against Germany, and having heard that 'they treated you very well in the Waffen-SS' he signed up with them:

'But, by the time I had completed training everything had changed. The battle of Stalingrad was entering its final, disastrous phase and we had lost in Africa. It was a bitter time after all our sacrifices and we grew afraid that we might lose the war after all. I finished my training and was sent to Italy to join a new SS division then being formed up of various volunteers that received the name Reichsfuehrer (16th), which was not too appropriate. But although we stayed there for some time we had no fighting to do.'

Karlsen was about to become a member of another division in embryo, the 12th *SS Hitlerjugend*, and would receive a very full share of combat in Normandy.

Matthias Hensen also joined the Waffen-SS as a conscript in 1942, being sent after training to the Das Reich division where he fought many a hard battle before being withdrawn as an NCO with the formation to France for a rest and refit. It was there that he experienced an adventure of a rather different kind later in 1943.

But, in the Spring of 1942, before the last German offensive to make any real gains and take the attackers to the shores of the Black Sea and to Stalingrad, the Norwegian volunteer Jutte Olafsen had experienced an uplift in morale:

'The warm weather brought an uplift of spirits, and then came the long awaited mail from home which made us all homesick. I must say that although there were a few among us who believed in our cause, there were those including some Germans who were rootless men or like myself to an extent faced with a situation we could not escape from. We hoped that somehow our Legion would

be returned to Norway, but there seemed no chance of that. In fact, we learned that as soon as the weather improved the first of the year's big German attacks would begin, this a kind of preliminary to the big summer offensive which gained the Germans much that year and was their final big fling in Russia before the retreat began in 1943.

'We took part in the first attack. By then there were large multiple-barrelled mortars and these had the power of artillery battalions and were very fearsome in action. We watched in amazement, never having seen them before. Several units were positioned behind us and the missiles curved up over our heads trailing smoke and making a terrible screeching noise, and when they landed on the enemy lines the detonations were very great. After fifteen minutes of this we advanced and the crescendo of noise grew even greater as our artillery and Stukas joined in. You would imagine that nothing could survive such a barrage, yet when we finally neared the enemy positions there were still some of them in action, the flame from their weapons visible through the fog from all the explosions. We rushed on, our NCOs urging us to keep moving, though we dropped down occasionally to take cover.

'One of our Sergeants was killed in this attack and several more men wounded, I among them. I was hit in the leg by something and went spinning over, losing my weapon and doubling up in agony. The other men ran on and I thought I was abandoned, but the medics were very good and soon attended to the wound. I had a smashed shin bone and was carried back to a temporary dressing station, my wound attended to, then removed to the rear by truck. While we were there the building was hit during an air raid and several of the wounded killed. Then I was taken to a hospital of sorts further in the rear and began to imagine I would get home. It was a great relief to escape the fighting. The doctors examined my leg, had it properly splinted, and evacuated me to Germany.'

Jutte Olafsen was permanently out of combat and spent six months in convalescence before being assessed for instructional duties at a camp in north Germany where it was hoped a continuous flow of replacements from Scandinavia would come:

'But this did not happen. The supply dried up owing to the hardening resistance to German occupation and of course the small population. In the end the Germans had to accept the inevitable so the camp was turned over almost exclusively to the training of Germans and a few other mixed nationalities for the various SS formations.'

Hans-Jurgen Welle entered the SS in 1943 at the age of seventeen, by which time the German nation had been shaken by the disaster at Stalingrad, where Hitler's obsessive interference had cost the Wehrmacht a complete army. Welle went through the usual infantry mill before opting to become a gunner on a 50mm 'pak' cannon and was sent to the Leibstandarte:

'We were told this was a very great honour, but I can tell you we had no desire to go to the Eastern Front at all. When we arrived in the desolate wilderness our morale was not good, but we were made very welcome and introduced to the lads of the unit who like ourselves were gunners, they had already scored many victories against Russian tanks. They showed us the white victory rings round the barrels of their guns and we were very impressed. At that time there was a lull in the battle, but a very large German offensive was being prepared in the Kursk area and we helped stack the large amounts of ammunition into trucks ready for the attack. Then we were briefed by an officer on the great importance of the coming battle which we were assured would do great damage to the Soviet Army. In view of the fact that this army was supposed to have been annihilated in 1941 we were rather dubious.'

Matthias Hensen, having fought with the Das Reich division in Russia, now enjoyed a life of calm after the formation was again withdrawn for a rest, this time to France:

'It was during my stay in France that I developed a relationship with a French woman. This was at Tours late in 1943. I had been promoted to Sergeant and was often off duty in the town and at that time we were not engaged in any difficulties with the local population and were free to spend time in the bars and cafes, though we usually went about in groups.

'It was while we were enjoying a small meal in a cafe that I noticed a woman watching me with some interest and I saw her about the town on other occasions and was much attracted to her. One evening I was in the same cafe with some comrades when the same woman entered and took her place at a table not far away from us. As a result, when my comrades left I decided to speak to her, much to their surprise and amusement. I asked her if I could join her and she did not object, so I bought her some coffee, such as it was, and we got into conversation.

'She was not unfriendly, but I believe under some restraint, not unnaturally since few French women wished to be seen fraternizing with the occupiers. She told me that she was a war widow, her husband having been killed in the fighting in 1940, so I expressed my regrets. I showed some pictures of my family including my young sister back in Nuremberg, and she told me that she was looking for work and had considered going to Paris, so I said that if she was willing I might be able to find her a post with the occupying forces. I should explain that I knew some French from my school-days and enjoyed trying to make some conversation in the language, even though I was far from competent. She told me that to work for the Allemande would be tantamount to suicide with her people, some of her relatives were extremely anti-German, but as for herself she no longer hated anyone. The Germans had not really done her harm, it was the war, and though she thought Hitler was a bad man she seemed to take a fatalistic view of the whole situation.

'I told her that if she so decided I could ask at our HQ if they could use a French woman on general duties of some kind, there was always the need for some kind of liaison personnel, even though security was strict. Yet as soon as I made this offer I wondered if I was being naive and foolish, but I was so attracted to her that I let my tongue run away with me. She got up to go and I wanted to go with her, but she told me it was too dangerous, but I could join her for a little supper later on. I was overjoyed, and decided to follow her at a discreet distance so that I would know were to go. This I did, and saw her enter a block of flats. Then I walked the streets for a time until it was curfew and I could go to her address. I had a two-day pass, but it was a rule in our unit that liaisons with the locals be avoided, or at least strictly controlled for obvious reasons. But I swept aside all thoughts of security and went to her address which she had scribbled on a piece of paper and I had no difficulty finding her.

'The place was in darkness, but I found her door on the second floor and knocked. She opened it at once and took me inside, it was a comfortable place consisting of a living room, bedroom, a small kitchen and a tiny bathroom and toilet. It was quite attractive and especially so to a soldier in civilian surroundings; being quartered in barracks, it was always the same in the army. You were with your comrades all the time in sparse surroundings, so a change was very welcome. Apart from which I had rather fallen for this French woman and felt all caution slipping aside. In short, I wanted her.

'She asked me to sit down and served some tea with a few cakes. We chatted as best we could on the war and how she lived on a small pension and I gained the impression that it was very difficult for her as food was becoming scarce. So I offered to try and supply her with a few small items, though we ourselves were not exactly overfed. She said she was grateful but could not allow this, but I insisted that if I could help her I would. She then asked me if I was not on duty, so I told her I had a short leave but could not get home to Nuremberg in such a short time. Then we fell silent until I asked her if there was a small, safe hotel I could stay at nearby so that with her permission I might call on her the next day. She replied that this would be very dangerous for me, as it was she had a nervous feeling about me being there, although she did not think I had been seen as it was dark and her neighbours kept to themselves.

'So I stood up to leave, but then she told me that if I did not mind sleeping on the sofa I could stay in her flat. She had some spare blankets — otherwise — well, I assumed she meant I could go back to the barracks. So I accepted her offer of a bed on the sofa, assuring her that I would be no trouble. So we listened to the radio in front of the electric fire for a while, and then she told me she would retire and went off to the bathroom. So I removed my tunic and waited for her to bring me some blankets, but to my amazement when she came out of the bathroom she had a negligee on and said to me: "If you would prefer it, there is room for both of us in my bed. It's up to you." Then she walked off into the bedroom, so in a daze I followed her, and we spent a wonderful night together.

'Next morning she went out, leaving me to ponder on the strangeness of my situation. I had begun to wonder about the risks I was taking, my comrades would miss me and guess I had gone with the French woman. When she returned from shopping I told her of my fears in all frankness, was she mixed up with the Resistance? She laughed and told me not to be so foolish, telling me she was in more danger than I was, for there would certainly be some who would mark her down as a collaborator. And what about our Gestapo she said, would they not be watching us? I told her I did not know, I had never met a Gestapo agent. In any case, what harm were we doing? Just the same, I became worried for her safety in case any of her people decided to take revenge, and wondered if she could move to another town, but this she refused to do. She had always lived in Tours, and would stay there, whatever happened.

'We went to bed once more before I left for my barracks that evening where I encountered a certain amount of ribald comment from my comrades who wanted to know all the details. But when they saw that I refused to speak of it they assumed I was serious about the woman and one of them told me I was being a fool and should take care. Well, I took heed of his remarks, but next evening went straight to her and once more ended up in bed, such was our need.

'A few days later however, I received a shock. My commander sent for me, and this is what he said:

"You are having an affair with a woman in town?" I admitted that this was so.

"Then I would advise you strongly to end it at once", he said. "You must understand our situation here, we are an occupying force and discipline has to be maintained. For security reasons I cannot allow my men to attach themselves to French women, it is obvious why, you could become a liability to us."

'I told him that this could not be the case, for I was loyal to my unit and comrades. He then asked me point blank if I was sleeping with her and with a red face I admitted that this was so. Whereupon he told me that if I did not cease the association he would have to take measures. He then dismissed me and said he would see me again shortly.

'I was very embarrassed and upset by all this and became aware that everyone in the barracks seemed to know of my affair, so things became very difficult for me, especially as I was an NCO. I did not know what to do for the best, I went to see Marianne the next evening and told her the situation while we were in bed. She was very sad and told me I must do what I thought best. There was no question of her wanting to cast a spell over me to get me into trouble, I would have to make my own choice. I left her later in a state of upset.

'But just after that, before I had a chance to make up my mind what to do, we were sent away on training to the south and the matter was taken out of my hands. But I wrote to her and explained the situation, telling her I would return to her as soon as I was able. Then the invasion came and we became embroiled in fighting the Americans and when we retreated I had but one thought which was to return to my love, but this proved impossible. However, after the war was over I was able to return to Tours on a short holiday to find her, but when I found her flat there was another family in occupation who knew nothing of Marianne. They told me the flat had been empty for some time when they arrived and they had no knowledge of the previous tenant.

'So I went to the same cafe and enquired, but they knew nothing of her whereabouts and I never saw her again.'

Georg Lanfelde opted for the SS artillery and following the usual recruit infantry training was sent to a gunnery school to learn the rudiments:

'We were shown various howitzers of all calibres before entering a course of lectures followed by drill at the gun which was an old 75mm howitzer. We learnt the purpose of guns in battle in their various roles, and how to tell the difference between enemy gun work. This was concerned with barrages, harassing and counter battery fire. We learnt something of the principal enemy artillery pieces, but in the main the instruction was concerned with support for our own troops.

'We were then shown how to operate as a team behind various weapons except the pak gun, for we were only concerned with field artillery. Then came firing exercises in open countryside, working first as single units and then as a battery. We were then assessed as good enough to be sent to the front.

'In that period of the war we had largely lost the initiative, but still had a great deal of force in artillery. We were sent as a gun squad to the Leibstandarte division in Russia and joined a battery of veterans as a relief team. This was to enable leave to be granted to a few men at a time, they had been under a great deal of pressure and were very tired, so to escape from the front was a godsend to them. Our first action soon came, for the Russians were putting in a lot of attacks. Our role was to break up their massed tanks and infantry before they got near our own troops. In this we rarely saw the enemy at all, as we were simply given observations of azimuth and elevation and fired on command. At that time we had adequate stocks of ammunition so put down quite a barrage of fire which helped the infantry stop the Russian attacks.

'Our accommodation consisted of well constructed dug-outs that were covered over and camouflaged, the shells and charges stacked well away from these dug-outs and well covered in bits of bushes etc. We spent some hours on duty in that first battle and were quite exhausted at the end of it. We had to clean out the gun barrels before taking tea and biscuits and later an evening meal.* But any question of snatching some sleep was off as the Russians were using artillery and we had to commence counter-battery fire. This was not so easy as we no longer had complete command of the air and our spotter planes could not operate as they had done in the past. But we had other methods of locating the origin of enemy shelling and the necessary co-ordinates were passed to us, but how successful we were was hard to tell, the Russians had many more guns than we had and excelled in barrage fire, so it was impossible to know how many of their weapons were knocked out.

---

* The official daily ration scale for a German Army soldier in the field in 1941 comprised: one loaf of bread — 650 grams, Butter or fat substitute — 45 grams, Wurst sausage — 120 grams, Fresh meat — 120 grams, Jam — 200 grams, Real coffee —59 grams, Coffee substitute — 109 grams, 6 cigarettes. This scale could not always be adhered to and considerable variations occurred including extras when available (especially from home) such as chocolate and liquor.

'Then we were forced to retreat in a hurry by a large Russian breakthrough. All our weapons were limbered up to half-tracks and towed away to a new site. But the Russians came on so we were forced to fire a barrage over open sights and I saw the enemy for the first time, only a brown mass with an occasional tank between them on the far horizon, but in artillery terms they were close enough. We had a good 'shoot' and the attack was stopped. So we breathed again, but not for long as over the coming weeks we were forced back and had to find new battery sites every few days. Then some Russian fighters attacked and damaged our own gun beyond repair, so once again we were used as a relief crew. Then we received new equipment and went into action once more, this time trying to stop a Russian tank attack. They were now using tanks in mass and we just poured HE shell into them and before them to deter them as they were difficult to destroy with our kind of weapon. But I believe we did some good and actually obtained some direct hits; a plunging shell can destroy a tank if it strikes in the right place, even though some shells were of low velocity. This particular batch of Russian tanks was finished off by Tigers and Panthers firing from hull down positions, plus a battery of eighty-eights.'

Hans Welle, it will be remembered, had arrived in time to participate in the last great German offensive in the East. The SS forces had already distinguished themselves in 1943, commencing in February when the Russians recaptured the city of Kharkov. Paul Hausser had now taken command of the newly constituted SS Panzerkorps and this formation was rushed forward and after a heavy battle lasting five days succeeded in retaking the city, although it was lost again soon afterwards. But the German Army Generals had good cause to be grateful to the SS units which like the paratroops were used again and again in the 'fire brigade' role.

But by July 1943, the Soviets, well informed by various intelligence sources of the imminent German offensive which was delayed for a while, laid extensive minefields and put hundreds of anti-tank guns in place. The SS Panzerkorps was part of the pincer designed to trap the Soviet armies around Kursk in the southern sector. The Germans finally began their assault with a short artillery barrage at 3 pm on 4 July, a hot afternoon, after which 700 tanks of the SS were launched at the enemy; this mass of armour well supported by the usual mobile infantry in half-tracks and pak guns trailing along behind across the sun scorched hills and cornfields. Apart from the minefields and massed anti-tank cannon the Soviets had gathered 850 of their own tanks, these being held back at the start.

Hans Welle records his impressions of that day:

'The weather was very warm, I was nervous but encouraged by the masses of armour and guns and men all over the fields. It was a truly inspiring sight and I suppose we felt confident. The barrage from our artillery and rockets was tremendous, then the Stukas and other ground attack planes went in to attack

the Russkis. The noise was far greater than anything I had heard in training. Then we boarded our vehicles and moved off in grand style, led by Tigers and Panthers which soon ran into Russian fire on a considerable scale. We had to deploy at once and make our pak guns ready in case the Russkis put in a counter-attack with tanks. But none came, yet the battle was very fierce. The Russkis had masses of pak guns in well concealed positions and we could see were destroying all our tanks, in fact the sky was soon full of black smoke columns. We were pushed forward to try and help knock out some of the Russian guns, but it was very hard to see them.

'But we began firing, using HE shells against probable targets, though it was hard to really assess the results, which was very unsatisfactory. We were trained as anti-tank gunners, not as field artillery, so we felt we were being wasted. Then, at last, after a day or two the Russian tanks began to appear in growing numbers and our chance came.

'I remember our first victory. All our crew were newcomers like myself, but we were directed by an experienced NCO who pointed out the targets. There were a dozen or more tanks within range at about one mile, but we let them come much nearer before opening fire. We saw our target flying sideways as our solid shot struck it slightly in the flank. Our second shot set it on fire. We switched to a new target at once but missed. But the other guns nearby us struck this Russki and he went up in smoke. The crack and bang of our guns was continuous and this fire helped our recovery vehicles to rescue some of our own disabled tanks.

'This battle lasted about an hour before the Russian artillery fire began to arrive in great volume and we were forced to retire. But we had done our job and the Russian tanks had been stopped. Yet our own great offensive was a failure, we left many of our tanks wrecked on the battlefield and most of the crews were killed.'

Operation Zitadelle had seen the greatest tank battle of the war, both sides losing some 300 panzers, but by 13 July the Germans had made little headway and Hitler was reluctantly forced to call off the offensive. Welle continues:

'We were gradually forced back into our original positions and static warfare again with our unit doing very little until the Russians mounted a counter offensive. Their artillery fire was terrible and some of our guns and vehicles were lost. So we watched as our field artillery struck the hordes of Russian infantry, but there were thousands and thousands of them and they came on and on until the Leibstandarte infantrymen opened up with their machine-guns while we went into action against the Russian tanks. But the enemy broke through elsewhere and we were forced to withdraw to prevent being outflanked. We were then attacked by Russian planes and given a going-over with cannon and machine-guns but several of the enemy were shot down by our flak, one of them near us so we went to see the wreck and capture the crew if still alive, but the mess was unrecognizable, just burnt metal and scorched human flesh.

"The Russkis attacked again and again and in the terrible rocket fire our own gun was destroyed, so we were given hand weapons and told to dig in. This was terrifying as the Russians numbered thousands and they came on despite our fire. In the end we were forced to run for our lives with bullets flying about us and shells churning up the ground nearby. Some of our lads were lost, and when we re-assembled we were a very weak unit. I remember the look on our CO's face when he counted us, he was shaken and angry that no replacements had arrived. And when they did they looked like schoolboys, but they were terribly keen. Yet not one of these poor lads survived in the coming weeks when the Russkis attacked us again and again, driving us back by violent artillery barrages and constant infantry and tank attacks. We received new guns and again took up position and in one battle our weapon was hit by machine-gun fire from a T34 that got too close so we were put out of action again. Fortunately, the Russian tanks were destroyed by very brave infantrymen. We then took over another gun whose crew had been killed, it was tragic to see those lads who had stuck to the gun to the last, but a Russian machine-gun had caught them.'

The German armies in Russia had now begun their long retreat, and the military policeman Heinz Reinefarth indicates the effect of the reverses on his war:

'After the disaster at Stalingrad we knew the war was lost and the event gave encouragement to all the bandit forces. We fully realized that they were fighting for what they believed in, but we had the protection of our soldiers in mind. I saw too many innocents as well as bandits shot or hanged from then on. We were forced to employ whole divisions of troops to scour the rear areas to keep them passive, but we never succeeded. When at last we began the long retreat we were forced to evacuate all civilians, many of them came willingly with us, plus all livestock and to burn everything to prevent the advancing Russian forces from finding anything of value.'

Once again it is necessary to remind oneself of the great scale of these operations where the front ran for some 900 kilometres. The German Army Group South in the pre-summer battles comprised 60 divisions of 720,000 men, while facing them were 264 Russian divisions numbering 1,700,000 soldiers. The German retreat began in the late summer of 1943, first to the river Dnieper, then on and on, ever backwards towards the Reich itself, and in this retreat the Germans copied the Russian's own 'scorched earth' policy, but carried it out far more thoroughly. Not a house, barn, factory or building of any kind was left standing; the railway tracks everywhere were torn up, and above all every living piece of livestock was moved westwards in a vast trek: 153,000 horses, 200,000 cattle, 270,000 sheep, plus pigs, chickens, every edible creature was taken away with the retreating armies or destroyed, and as Heinz Reinefarth says, many of the civilian population went along too.

Karl Hummelkeier took part in this exodus:

'We had orders like all the German forces to leave absolutely nothing behind for the Soviets. We were following their own example for they too had finally adopted the scorched earth policy in their retreat, burning and destroying everything so as to leave us nothing. Yet they left very many animals in the western areas of the Soviet Union, and when we retreated, every one of them was shepherded to the west. Every hovel, barn, factory, in fact everything of any use to the enemy at all was blown up or burnt. This was pitiful as it deprived the population of their meagre possessions.

' It has to be said that we were quite ruthless in suppressing resistance activity, with hostages being taken wholesale owing to Russian attacks behind the lines which sometimes took the form of individual murders of sentries etc in the most brutal fashion, or even kidnapping with the mutilated bodies being left for us to find later to terrorize us. In general I saw little of this and it was the cause of harsh reprisals. It was a terrible war, but when the civilian population became involved in such activities in a fighting zone then reprisals are inevitable. I saw two hangings and that was enough for me.

'We were out of the line for a short respite and passing along a small road in a rear area when we saw a group of field police and army troops with several Russian prisoners who were obviously civilians. As we passed the first two were strung up on a makeshift gallows. This was a mile or so from a village, but I have no idea if the victims were partisans or hostages. There were orders from on high to deal severely with all forms of resistance behind the lines, but we were never involved in such operations. There were those specially detailed to carry out such operations and the wholesale extermination of the Jews. This last question is a vexed one, for although no German could be unaware of the Nazis' attitude to the Jews, when it came to killing them off very few knew anything of this. The fact that the Einsatzgruppen were operating in the rear areas was also largely unknown to the combat troops at the front. It has to be borne in mind that these SD men only comprised a few dozen out of millions of men in Russia.'

Such a comment can give a misleading impression. Hitler had already warned his army generals before the campaign in Poland that there would be unpleasantness behind the front which was none of their business, and in April 1941 the then Chief-of-Staff General Brauchitsch agreed at a conference to the use of special police groups providing they stayed clear of the operational areas. The German armies for the invasion of the Soviet Union were organized into four groups: North, Centre, South (W.N. & E) and South (S), and behind each army group was set up the equivalent Einsatzgruppe of the SD, being A. B, C, and D, and in Action Group A the strength in October 1941 was 989, which is far more than a 'few dozen' and included Waffen-SS troops, motorcyclists, administration, security, Criminal Police, Gestapo, Auxiliary Police, Order Police, female employees, interpreters, teletype and radio operators, plus no doubt sundry other employees such as cooks etc. So it is fair to say that each 'Action Group' numbered close to one thousand, making four thousand in all, and one authority has stated that there were times when these highly mobile groups followed so close on the heels of the combat units that they actually became involved in the fighting.*

All of these staffs were of course part of the Himmler police set-up and had no direct connection with the fighting units, yet in view of the huge numbers of ordinary German service personnel involved in supply, administration etc behind the front it is not easy to imagine that the activities of the Einsatzgruppen did not become known. But apart from these groups who had been given special tasks, various security units of battalion size or over were raised behind the front from the willing Russians mentioned and these sometimes included expatriate Germans, and very often it was these non-Germans or part-German police who carried out the worst atrocities and were from time to time disbanded as too difficult to handle. The complications are too long to be gone into here, but it is a fact that some of these irregulars wore SS uniforms or insignia at various times.

Hummelkeier:

'Naturally, the fighting men hoped that rear area security was being attended to by the anti-bandit units, but the wholesale murder of innocents was a different matter. I can only say that justice was meted out to some of these people when they were caught by the Allies later.'

It seemed a miracle to Hummelkeier that he had survived into 1944 when all the old faces had long since vanished, most killed, but a few surviving with wounds in Germany.

'Eventually we were fighting for our lives on German soil. The once proud SS divisions still fought hard, but it could never be the same again. The Russian fire power had grown tremendously, and their use of men profligate, so that we were compelled to give ground over and over again and grew weaker. Towards the end of 1944 I was finally knocked out of the battle:

'I had been promoted a few times, inevitably because of losses, and was now the battalion commander, weakened as it was. We had dug ourselves into yet another 'stop' position in Prussia and were expecting the next Russian attack. And when it came it was preceded by a terrible rocket attack which kept our armour in the rear, so that when their masses of infantry fell on us we were unsupported and overrun in some sectors. I was fighting hard with a group of lads when a bullet struck my right elbow and put me out of action, so I crawled away in a useless condition to get aid, and as I did so my men were overwhelmed. I barely escaped that fight with my life and was taken to the rear with my right arm out of action. A few days later I was back in a Berlin hospital.'

---

* Andrew Mollo in 1971

So ended the combat career of an SS veteran who had fought in Poland, Holland, France and Russia, surviving to escape to the West before the Soviets reached the Reich capital.

The SS panzer gunner attached to Das Reich, Paul Giske, records that his unit was hit by a deluge of Russian artillery and rocket fire and forced to withdraw, things made even harder by heavily increased Russian air support:

'After a few weeks we were withdrawn from the front for a rest and refit and to our great delight sent into southern France which was heavenly after the terrors of the Russian front. All the men enjoyed themselves and had some leave of some sort, even if only at local level. We had no problems with the population at that time and the men were able to walk the streets and stay in commandeered hotels with no bother.'

Pak gunner Hans Welle also found himself back on German soil by early 1944 with the Russians in hot pursuit. Although originally attached to the Leibstandarte, Welle had remained on the Eastern Front when the division was sent south into northern Italy to take part in the occupation following that country's collapse as a partner of Hitler in September 1943, though the formation would soon be rushed back into Russia to rejoin the rest of the SS Panzerkorps. However, by early 1944 this original SS combat unit would be withdrawn once more from the East for a rest and refit and to help combat the Allied invasion in Normandy. Even then, Hans Welle remained in the East and to his own fate:

'I remember seeing the columns of refugees fleeing from the advancing Russians. They looked very pathetic with their tired, worried faces and bundles and carts, only a few were in trucks or cars, many in those in Nazi Party uniform. We hurled insults and jibes at them, we had to remain in place and this we did until the Russians were upon us and all hell broke loose. We had some of our latest Tiger tanks dug in nearby and they were very effective, repelling all the Russian tank assaults, with our help of course. It was heartening to see all those burning wrecks on the field before us, with here and there some surviving crewmen trying to escape. Very few did.

'The Russian artillery fire was the worst part and put paid to our defence; some of the Tigers were buried in the explosions, others simply ran out of ammunition. So once more we were obliged to retreat and this time we lost our guns as our towing vehicle was damaged. We ran as fast as we could with the Russians on our heels and barely escaped with our lives. We entered a village and an empty house to get warm and try to find something to eat, but the cupboards were bare. We waited while our NCOs tried to assemble some kind of unit again with some new guns, but until then we would have to defend the village as infantry. This was hopeless as the Russians simply deluged us with artillery fire and it became impossible to survive. I saw troops running away in panic under that shellfire which went on and on until every house was a

blazing wreck. They used HE and phosphorous, anything to raze the place and again we barely escaped with our lives. Our NCO was killed so we had no alternative but to run as hard as we could to the next village.

'We were exhausted, starving and leaderless. But then we found some prepared positions and some officers who took good care of us, sending us away to recover with food and sleep. By the time we were ready to fight again the battle was over and we were in full retreat again, caught up in a refugee column on Tiger tanks but unable to move in a nightmare situation. It was like that when the end came for many. Russian planes attacked the column which was broken up, civilians and troops fleeing across the fields in all directions, many of them being killed or wounded. But the tanks and many of the soldiers escaped.

'I had been lying in the road with my hands over my ears while a lot of civilians ran past carrying their baggage. The planes were merciless, machine-gunning everything that moved. A bullet hit me in the back and I passed out, lying unconcious for some time until on coming to I felt myself lifted up and carried some way to be placed in a truck. I heard German voices and the truck raced off and then I heard a lot of gunfire, but then passed out again. I remember a lot of banging about, then a period of calm, and when I finally woke up I was lying in a hospital bed in Berlin.'

Like other SS wounded, Hans Welle was evacuated to the West before the Russians arrived.

The SS artilleryman Georg Lanfelde was also caught up in the great retreat into East Germany:

'It was heartbreaking to see our refugees and the pretty villages deserted before the advancing Russian hordes who included Mongolian troops who were very savage. They had of course been urged to "kill the fascist beast in his lair", and when they caught up with our people this is what occurred. The dwellings were turned into whorehouses and often burned. Fortunately, we managed to stay ahead of them, we did not relish being sent to Siberia for the rest of our lives.

'In East Germany we almost ran out of ammunition as the convoys could not get through owing to the refugee problem and roads and railways blocked by air attack. At one moment we were on the point of destroying our guns but suddenly a truckful of shells arrived and this helped us to stave off the Russian assault. But the end result was not in doubt and we tried to retreat but were almost cut off and forced at last to abandon our guns after putting them out of action. It is always a very sad moment for a gunner to lose his weapon. We had some small arms and fell back mile after mile until reaching a new defence line where we were ordered to fight on as infantry. Our CO asked if he could go off to find some more guns but this was refused. So we did our best and helped drive off several Russian attacks.'

Just before yet another Russian assault a convoy of new guns arrived and with these Georg Lanfelde and his fellow gunners managed to hold off the enemy, though it was only a matter of time before the retreat began again. For every German gun there were ten Russian. Eventually, the German forces were back in the suburbs of East Berlin and the final battles of the 'East Front' began. By that time the recruiting office clerk Richard Helm had found increasing difficulties:

'When the bad air raids came to Berlin so did a lot of refugees start flooding into the safer areas and this put a strain on accommodation. Curiously enough, it also affected recruiting, because the lads began coming to us before they were of age. I cannot adequately explain this, but we did not accept anyone before they were due for call-up, the age having quite disgracefully been lowered to sixteen. Every youth had to complete labour service, though the term served grew shorter and shorter as the war progressed. By late 1944 we were finding it very hard to get men owing to the manpower shortage. This was met in part by taking in older men from the SA who had been on homefront duties. And then conscription direct into the Waffen-SS began, so they were no longer volunteers. This came about as an order from Himmler which affected a number of age groups. There was a great comb-out, but even so, those who had been former Navy men or in the Luftwaffe were directed into the Army, not the SS. We tried to maintain our standards of recruitment, but it was extremely difficult in the circumstances, and in the last months of the war we were obliged to close down. I was put into the Volkssturm in command of old men in the defence of Berlin.'

When the Russians came Richard Helm escaped with others to the West.

Gustav Doren had just enjoyed a home leave in Mecklenburg and returned to his Totenkopf unit when they were hit by a sudden artillery barrage:

'I was caught out of cover and hit by a splinter in one eye. It hurt terribly and I was evacuated at once. There was no chance of saving my eye so I was pensioned out of the SS.'

Karl-Heinz Roberts had had it easy from the start, simply exchanging his civilian suit for a black SS outfit when he was conscripted in 1939. His duties as an interpreter had been light, and when things turned unsavoury he simply opted out, leaving the lush posting in Paris to return to the more dubious offices in Berlin. Back in Himmler's RHSA building he found there was no work for him, and to his great consternation was told he would be sent to the Waffen-SS infantry. He had time only to go home for a brief visit before returning to pick up his orders and go on to the barracks at Lichterfelde:

'So for another week or so I continued the course which was very hard. And then I was again sent for by the CO who told me that he had received new orders for me. I was to report to the Waffen-SS headquarters in Berlin at once

where I would receive a new job. I said goodbye to my new comrades and left the next day, and when I found the Waffen-SS department in Berlin they told me that I was specially suited to a job they had open. I was to liaise between the various commanders in different places, though I could not see how my knowledge of other languages fitted me for such a job. However, I was in some ignorance, for plans were clearly afoot to form various volunteer legions, including French and Belgian ones. So I was bundled off to Paris and Brussels again where I had no contact with the SD but with the Waffen-SS staffs who were liaising with the French and Belgians in setting up the foreign legions. There was plenty to do in the way of translating documents as well as meeting the various people involved.

'There were quite a few volunteers and these swelled to come thousands who were apparently anxious to join in the so-called 'anti-Bolshevik crusade' in the East. These poor chaps were fitted out with German uniforms and weapons and after some training bundled off to the Eastern Front where most I believe were killed or wounded. Very few returned to their native lands, and those that did later were arrested as traitors and in many cases executed.'

The run-down of the foreign volunteer campaign in the West would lead Roberts to another kind of task, one nearer to the actual combat zone.

Similarly, the ex-Leibstandarte infantry officer Peter Krollman had, following his wounding in the east, been slotted into a plum job in the Waffen-SS intelligence staff:

'My duties were wholly concerned with the evaluation of foreign and especially enemy ground forces. This was accomplished by reports from our front units and other sources such as foreign publications which came to us through neutral sources, which meant that we had been able to build up a good library on the combatants opposing us. The results of these researches were used as a basis for lectures to student NCOs and officers in the training schools. For example, it became my special responsibility to assess any new developments in enemy armour and this was very interesting as it did occasionally involve my going to inspect captured examples which had been brought back from the various fronts. We had copies of the giant Russian KV7 and of course the T34 series and its later derivations, the English Crusader, Sherman and Matilda and one or two others including the General Grant. These were assessed from the point of view of driving, accommodation, and of course firing capability, and suitable tables issued. All such data was collected by me with the help of an NCO and another man and our tables and comments drawn up for issue to the combat units and schools.'

Krollman also evaluated other weapons such as anti-tank guns. When his department was driven out of Berlin by the air raids the staff were set up again in a camp outside the city until the war's end.

The artilleryman Georg Lanfelde found himself back in the suburbs of East Berlin battling the oncoming Russians:

'The battle was continuous and very fierce and we soon ran out of ammunition and were forced to fight as infantry. The Russians squandered their men in these street battles, but they seemed to have an inexhaustible supply. We were trapped several times and had great difficulty in fighting our way out again through the houses. Our problem was a dwindling number of men and lack of ammunition, and eventually we simply had nothing left to fight with. In one battle I became separated from my remaining comrades for a short time but then found two of them again. We crossed a canal in a small boat and escaped. Then we found more men who provided us with weapons and some food and we fought on for some days until the battle was over.

'This was a testing time for us, we were determined not to surrender to the Russians so we hid in an abandoned apartment block, threw away our uniforms and put on some civilian clothes. After a few days the Russians began scouring all the houses for stragglers, shooting every so often, and our position became desperate. However, they did not enter every house and we managed to escape detection. Our problem was how to find some food and water, but there was nothing to be found, so we began to starve. Eventually a small boy found us and with his help we managed to evade the Russian patrols and ended up in his house with his mother who was very kind to us. She had a few morsels of food but was terrified the Russians would find her and rape her. We did our best for her, and after a week were able to take her to a small family who looked after her and the boy while we hid elsewhere.

'By some miracle we survived as kind neighbours brought us scraps despite their own privations. But it was several weeks before we could show ourselves and try to join the work of reconstruction. But a number of Germans hiding in the city were found by the Russians and in some cases shot on the spot.'

CHAPTER TWELVE

By 1943 Hitler had become a prisoner of his own conquests, for he no longer had the strength in military power to hold them; the Wehrmacht and SS forces had become overstretched and despite their power unable to stem the enemy on all fronts. The disasters at Stalingrad and in North Africa had cost Hitler close on 600,000 soldiers; German morale had plummeted and even the Fuehrer had been forced to change his attitude. His favourite architect Albert Speer was given almost unlimited powers to put the German economy on a total war footing, for even after three years of war many factories were still producing consumer goods, women were not conscripted and Hitler refused to reduce the meat ration. Speer would achieve miracles of war production, so that by early 1944 the Wehrmacht and SS forces were better equipped than ever before; the panzer units fielded over 11,000 tanks.

Despite this, German military manpower continued to shrink, attempts by Hitler to build up a strategic reserve failed as the new divisions raised were swallowed up on the Eastern Front. The great gamble at Kursk in the summer of 1943 had cost the Germans dear and proved their last offensive on that front.

In June 1944 the German armies comprised a grand total of 286 divisions, including Waffen-SS formations, many of the Wehrmacht units far below their former establishment, so that one top German Field-Marshal complained that those divisions in the West were worth only half their nominal strength in fighting power. The German dispositions were:

Norway — 12 divisions; Denmark — 6 divisions; Eastern Front — 163 divisions; Balkans — 21 divisions; Italy — 26 divisions; North-west Europe — 59 divisions; Germany — 9 divisions.

These figures did not include those of Germany's allies (Finland, Romania, Hungary) which numbered a further 30 divisions.

Yet despite the gloomy outlook for the Germans, Hitler insisted that all would come right, the Soviets 'would wear themselves out', the Allies were bogged down in Italy and their army massed across the Channel for the much heralded invasion was largely composed of inexperienced troops who faced battle-hardened German units. In fact of course the Fuehrer's 'Atlantic Wall' with its defences 'one thousand times stronger than at Dieppe in 1942', included second-rate units and foreign intakes such as Mongols with no intention of dying for Germany. The German defence in the West rested squarely on a hard core of army and Waffen-SS troops, the latter including the remaining cream of the original volunteers of the old guard, the 1st SS Leibstandarte, the 2nd SS Das Reich, with more of proven renown about to join them from the Russian front, plus of course the brave lads of the new 12th SS Hitlerjugend division.

It has been said that early in 1944 the Waffen-SS still, despite its great expansion, less than 5% the numerical strength of the Wehrmacht, yet contained 25% of the panzer and 33% of the panzer-grenadier divisions. The German Army was still largely composed of infantry, and according to Keppler had never really taken to the SS concepts of battle tactics.

The campaign in Normandy which followed the Allied invasion of 6 June 1944 was to test the Waffen-SS commanders as never before, for despite their years of experience in Russia this new battle was a very different one in several important respects. It was the kind of battle they had not trained for, experienced or even expected, though it cannot really be said that they were found wanting. In a sense the short campaign can be seen as the highpoint of these men's careers at least from the point of view of testing them; it certainly forced out of them the utmost in military experience and ingenuity, much as it taxed the capabilities of the young SS soldiers, many of whom had never been in battle before.

Having won his spurs so to speak in the Balkans, Kurt Meyer had gone on to gain very considerable combat experience in Russia, where the Leibstandarte had at first fought in the Army Corps commanded by Major-General Kempf, a man who, following the triumphant encirclement of 100,000 Russians at Uman had nothing but praise for the part played by the Leibstandarte. The division had gone on to win new laurels at Kharkov, after which fight Hitler had crowed:

'The SS Panzerkorps is worth twenty Italian divisions!'

But the Fuehrer's favourites had then been thrown out of Kharkov and finally thwarted in the great battle of Kursk. Then the Leibstandarte during its 'rest' in Italy had briefly taken part in anti-partisan operations during which it is alleged to have wiped out the population of a whole village. After being rushed back to the Eastern Front to take part in more 'rescue' operations it was again withdrawn to rest and refit in France. All of this experience involved Kurt Meyer.

By mid-1943 the idea of a 'Hitler Youth' division had taken hold, supposedly the brain-child of Arthur Axmann, the Reichsjugendfuehrer who had succeeded Baldur von Schirach after the latter had gone into the forces. Following Hitler's approval the new division's headquarters unit was set up at Beverloo in Belgium, and some ten thousand recruits placed under NCOs and officers of experience to begin training. On 24 June 1943 the new formation was officially named the 12th SS Hitlerjugend Division, and by the following April had completed its training and was stationed south of Paris as part of Hitler's counter-invasion strategic reserve. In its ranks stood Kurt Meyer as commander of 12th SS Panzer

Regiment; as a field commander Meyer would be in the very thickest of the Normandy fighting almost from the beginning.

Obergruppenfuehrer Sepp Dietrich was put in command of the 1st SS Panzerkorps and set up his headquarters in Rouen. His units included the 1st SS Leibstandarte, the new 12th SS Hitler Youth, and the army's crack Panzer Lehr Division, so on the face of it Dietrich had been provided with some top troops to defend the eastern sector of the invasion area. Although some German soldiers in the area had sat out four years of war with no action and grown comparatively soft, the Panzer Lehr troops were considered something special.

Formed early in 1944 from experience men of the panzer training schools the division was intended to serve as a demonstration unit. But in the last week of March it was rushed to Poland with 9th and 10th SS divisions to help stem the Soviet offensive. Then came the Spring thaw and the Russians became bogged down, so Panzer Lehr was turned about and arrived back in France. It was the most powerful armoured division in the Wehrmacht and trained in anti-invasion tactics, its strength included 190 tanks, 40 SP assault guns and 612 half-tracks to carry its infantry component — double the usual establishment. But none of these highly trained troops under Dietrich were prepared for what hit them early in June, certainly not the untried teenage soldiers of the Hitlerjugend.

Meanwhile, Obergruppenfuehrer and General of the Waffen-SS Paul Hausser's old 2nd SS Division Das Reich, likewise withdrawn from the east, had moved across southern France to rest and refit in the Bordeaux area. It has to be remembered that these 'original' SS divisions, though good, were no longer as effective as they had once been. Most of the highly selected, original volunteers of the earlier days had long gone, their places increasingly filled by more hastily trained and less motivated soldiers who despite all the Nazi promises concerning 'wonder weapons' must have been increasingly sceptical of total victory. Even so, since all the SS units were panzer or motorized and well equipped they still possessed plenty of punch and their leaders were as cocky as ever. But the old SS arrogance was about to take a very severe shaking once the unrealized power of the Allied air forces and artillery was let loose on them.

When the Allies landed in France Paul Hausser was in command of 2nd SS Panzerkorps in the western sector, and like the other German commanders his priority was to rush up his somewhat scattered units to beef up the infantry divisions fighting to contain the Allied lodgements. Movement of the German formations stationed inland proved to be chaotic, though the SS units were more fortunate than some. For example, the parachute corps had enough transport for one regiment only, while some other unit commanders were forced to commandeer ancient French buses to move their men northwards. Many German soldiers rode on bicycles or simply started marching on foot. But all had to contend with complete Allied control of the air which had been wrested from the Luftwaffe, and this made all daylight movement dangerous. The Allies were well informed of their enemy's movements by the network of agents, radio intercepts including Ultra and of course constant aerial reconnaissance.

In some areas the French Maquis rose up to intervene and make these German movements even more hazardous and later we will examine some of the events of 6 June in more detail. Frederik Hutten went from the labour corps into a Waffen-SS training camp and then into the Hitler Youth division early in 1944. He had enjoyed only one short leave to his home when the division was sent to the invasion front in Normandy:

'We had a very hard time getting anywhere near the fighting zone' he reports, indicating the preventative measures taken by the RAF 2nd Tactical Air Force.

Siegfried Karlsen, already trained into the 16th SS Reichsfuehrer, found himself transferred to the Hitlerjugend where he says he was forced to go through the same training all over again with new recruits:

'Our new commanders told us we were now something very special and had been given the great honour title of Hitlerjungend Division of the SS, which meant that we would have a great responsibility on our young shoulders as representatives of the SS spirit, with big things expected of us. We were still in training with our armour when the invasion came, so we were at once alerted and drove off through Holland, then Belgium and into France, and that is where we received our first terrible baptism of fire. We came under air attack and this was an awful experience. The Allied jabos (jagdbomben — fighter-bombers) found us and never left us alone, we were continually forced to leap from our vehicles and hide in the ditches while they bombed and machine-gunned us and fired rockets which made a terrific noise as they came down, exploding in great sheets of flame. We lost many vehicles and boys before we got anywhere near the front.'

When the German Supreme Command (OKW) confirmed that a large-scale landing had indeed taken place on the Normandy beaches, General Jodl issued an order stating 'the bridgehead there must be cleaned up not later than tonight (6 June)'. This order was confirmed by Field Marshal Rommel's HQ in the West which instructed Seventh Army that the enemy had to be annihilated by evening — 'it is the desire of OKW'.

Since most of the German armoured forces were at least a day or more away in travelling time from the beachhead this order was obviously impossible to carry out. Nevertheless, Field Marshal von Rundstedt, as Commander-in-Chief West, ordered the Panzer Lehr division plus 12th SS to move on the vital communication centre of Caen and its adjacent airfield of Carpiquet in the eastern sector of Normandy. But both these units were part of the strategic armoured reserve controlled exclusively by Hitler and the movement was angrily cancelled by OKW on the grounds that the enemy's intentions were not clear. This referred to the threat, deliberately fostered by deception measures on the Allies' part, of a further, even main landing in the Pas de Calais area. In any case, the Fuehrer was still asleep in his bed and did not learn of the invasion until afternoon. But a battlegroup under command of Kurt Meyer was on the move by mid-morning, his column finally reaching Lisieux by 3 pm and racing on to Evrecy, some nine miles to the south of Caen. Meyer's orders were to join forces with the Army's 21st Panzer division and throw the enemy back who had penetrated almost to the airfield north-west of the river Odon.

But as Meyer and his men saw the black smoke rising from burning Caen, so did they for the first time encounter something new in their experience — a sky totally dominated by the enemy's air force. The British General Dempsey, commanding Second Army, had called on the RAF to interdict all roads to the south-east of Caen city to prevent the arrival of German reinforcements. This was all part of the Allied plan to isolate the battlefield from the air in order to allow them to build up their strength on the beaches and enlarge the bridgehead before starting to grind down the enemy forces opposing them.

Inevitably, the Allied fighter-bomber pilots attacked anything that was moving towards the battle area and especially transport, so that when Meyer and his convoy neared Caen they were held up by debris blocking the road. A French bus was blazing, the occupants trapped inside, while the bodies of Germans and civilians lay scattered about the roadway. It was after midnight when Meyer finally burst into the German HQ at Caen, his confidence not too shaken by his experiences on the road, to confront Major-General Edgar Feuchtinger, commander of the 21st Panzer division which had itself been delayed en route, though its leading elements were now in action. Also present in the HQ was Lt-General Wilhelm Richter whose 716th Infantry was in the process of being destroyed in the beachhead. Meyer was, reportedly, 'brimming with confidence', the British were 'little fish' who he with his Hitler Youth division would soon drive back into the sea.

Meyer had with him, he told them, his *Kampfgruppe* (battlegroup) consisting of one tank battalion equipped with 90 Mk IV tanks of the latest kind, plus three divisions of infantry and some artillery. When combined with the 21st Panzer they could therefore total 160 tanks and five battalions of infantry. Meyer's advance force would moreover soon be backed up by the rest of the formation, two more tank battalions and two of infantry who were on their way. On the surface his confidence was not unjustified, even though this force could not be expected to deliver a knockout punch. As for the Panzer Lehr, they could expect no help from that quarter for this division was still strung out over 130 miles of road, its tanks forced to travel on their own tracks through lack of trains and the destruction of the railway system by Allied bombers and sabotage.

While an odd collection of German armour and infantry tried to contain the Allied advance, the main counterstroke against the British was scheduled to take place at noon on 7 June. But the SS troops were delayed by the shortage of fuel and were still not in position by dawn on that morning. Meanwhile, the assembling troops and armour of the 21st Panzer were forced onto the defensive by a British attack on Lebisey wood. Meyer had himself set up his advance command post in Ardenne Abbey, yet the bulk of his 12th SS were still strung out along four miles of the Falaise-Caen road and under constant harassment from the RAF. It was then that Meyer's plan for a concentrated offensive began to come apart, for to his consternation he observed his own leading units threatened by an attack by the 3rd Canadian Division which had almost reached the airfield at Carpiquet.

The rough, tough Canadian infantrymen of the 9th Brigade were doubtless in their minds avenging the fiasco and carnage of the Dieppe raid (16 August 1942), and were supported by Sherman tanks of their own 27th Armoured Regiment. About to clash with these brave warriors, every one a volunteer for overseas duty, were the largely teenage kids of Meyer's Hitler Youth, average age eighteen. The lads of the 12th SS tank units had come into black U-boat leathers during the winter which had been supplied to the Italians but never used. These they had of course now discarded for the lighter tanker's coveralls including some of the latest spotty camouflage suits. Unusually for the Germans, these kids preferred to paint girl's names on their tanks, just like their opponents. Both sides had come through one ordeal; the Germans the constant interference from the sky, the Canadians the dreaded beach landings which had gone so well with only light casualties. Unlike the unfortunate Canucks in 1942, these men had come ashore largely unscathed, only wet, and had pushed inland, meeting only disorganized opposition which they quickly brushed aside.

As always, the Germans reacted swiftly to a changing situation.

Meyer ordered his battlegroup to deploy rapidly into the cover of a wooded hollow and arranged a perfect ambush, impressing on all ranks the need for perfect fire discipline while despatching a message by motorcyclist to HQ to tell them his intentions. The Canadians marched on unsuspecting, the big Sherman tanks halting every so often, their cannon probing the air like insects scenting danger. But the Canadians saw none, and blundered straight into the welcoming muzzles of Meyer's concealed armour and infantry who now blazed away into the ranks of the shocked Canadians, routing the infantry and blowing up their tanks with hits in their vulnerable flanks. Many of the Canadians were mown down by the rapid, tearing fire of the German MG42 machine-guns, the rest fled to escape further slaughter.

But now Meyer and his men were served up their second terrible lesson in twenty-four hours, and this was to be the pattern for their campaign in Normandy. No sooner had the surviving Canadians withdrawn from the ambush area than they called down supporting fire, and within a few minutes the huge fifteen and sixteen-inch projectiles from the British battleships anchored offshore began to hurtle down on the SS troops and their panzers, sending up great geysers of earth and debris — bang on target. The British artillery and tanks joined in and the battlegroup of the 12th SS were pulverized with fire. Meyer himself was forced to leap for cover, choosing one of the huge shellholes left by one of the naval projectiles.

'Because of this concentrated shellfire, such as I had never seen before on any European battlefield, both officers and men became demoralized and had to dig in', one SS officer said later.

These events absorbed the forces of 21st Panzer and 12th SS, so that instead of a concerted drive to smash through the British-Canadian armies to the beaches the Germans had been completely frustrated and forced onto the defensive. The hours lost were crucial, for during all this time the Allies were pouring in men and material from the great fleet anchored at sea in a race to build up sufficient forces to hold any German counterstroke. Above all, the greatest factor in this effort was the massing ashore of a great force of artillery, hundreds of guns and crews being pushed ashore into the increasingly congested beachhead; time and time again these gunners, in concert with the air force, would defeat every German attempt to regain the initiative.

The planned counter-stroke of 7 June having failed, Meyer attempted to reassemble his forces the following day, but this comprised just 17 tanks and one battalion of infantry. The chance that Meyer thought existed to drive to the sea had vanished, for the British and Canadian armies had firmly linked and would never again be threatened by any crisis. The OKW order to annihilate the enemy lodgement by the first evening had been a futile one because of its own dispositions forced on them by the uncertainties of the situation. After years of preparation and expectation the much vaunted German military staff had been caught on the wrong foot, with quite insufficient forces on hand to smash the Allied landings.

As for the role of the Waffen-SS divisions in these crucial opening days of the campaign, their great dash, élan and expertise had come to nothing, frustrated by dispersal, the terrain and Allied air power. The speed and 'blitzkrieg' manoeuvrability of the German panzers counted for nothing in the bocage country and was the exact opposite to that experienced in Russia. The speedy SS units were forced into a new kind of warfare, into a static role which in view of the terrain was ideally suited to the defence, yet it was also well suited to the kind of set-piece battle that Montgomery had in mind for them at this stage of the campaign, to draw them into the trap and killing ground he had set for them in which the massed Allied air and artillery power could grind them to pieces. Even then the trap could have been escaped from but for Hitler's intervention, so it became a strait-jacket for the Germans.

So far, the SS forces had only been committed against the British and Canadians on the eastern sector, but one SS formation was about to enter the battle on the American front, with another to follow.

The sorry saga of the Das Reich division has been documented in this period most thoroughly by Max Hastings*. Considered by some the best of the SS divisions it would, like others, have its reputation tarnished. Unfortunately, the one eye-witness quoted here was not in the best position to ascertain exactly what happened later, but his experience typifies that of many German units trying to reach the battle zone:

Paul Giske:

'The division was ordered north, a long journey towards the battle zone which took many days and involved various difficulties and ended in the terrible conditions in Normandy. Our progress along the French roads was reasonable until we reached a certain point when the first delays occurred. In a long column of vehicles stretched out over many miles it is not always easy to know what is happening. We had not really been bothered by any air raids up to that time, but there were a certain number of incidents with Maquis units who did all they could to delay us or even prevent us from reaching the battle zone. The advance units were fired on several times from hedgerows and houses, with the result that our men began shooting back in self defence, that was inevitable.

'All our tanks were on the road, mixed in with armoured cars, personnel carriers, trucks etc, the whole Das Reich division was stretched out for mile after mile and I was somewhere in the middle of this slow moving cavalcade. For much of the time I was sitting outside on the turret top with my CO enjoying the fresh air and keeping an eye out for enemy aircraft. But nothing much was seen, though the delays grew worse as we crept northwards.

'Then we heard a lot of shooting in the distance, and after a long delay we reached the little town of Oradour. A column of smoke rose into the sky, and as we passed through the streets we saw troops of our division and some police near a burning church and heard that some terrorists had attacked the column and hidden in the church. There had been a fight and the church burned. We moved on and had no reason to believe otherwise. At the time we were all in a state of tension as we reached the battle zone, this was to be our first fight against the Western Allies.

'When after much difficulty we reached the war zone we were shown our deployment area against the Americans and this is where our baptism into a very different kind of warfare began.'

What had actually occurred in Oradour will perhaps never be known, but one thing is certain, the involvement of civilians in the battle against the Germans was bound to bring reprisals. This particular unit had been

---

* In *Das Reich* (Michael Joseph 1981)

harassed and goaded almost beyond measure, and as one other writer has commented, if troops are trained to and regarded as élite in battle then if sufficiently provoked they will hit back. Specifically, the accuracy of Paul Giske's mention of 'all' the unit's tanks being on the road is open to question. Quoting a more contemporary account, the tanks of Das Reich were forced to wait four vital days for a train to be assembled. Moving a division by rail is no small undertaking, even apart from air raids and French sabotage. In the case of Reich it involved around 18,600 men with 3,482 vehicles, and the loading of the armoured segment had just begun when the rail marshalling yard at Montauban suffered a heavy air raid which delayed loading for another week. The mass of its non-tracked vehicles and personnel proceeded by road, with the divisional reconnaissance unit in the van, and it was these men who were most the victims of Maquis ambush, for the Germans had to pass through country largely controlled by these French Resistance fighters. These attacks were said by one source to have become so heavy that whole battalions were forced to dismount to try and deal with them. But more subtle methods were also employed by the French to delay the German forces moving north.

At midnight the SS Colonel commanding the 3rd Battalion of the 4th SS Panzer Regiment was found to have vanished. The unit had halted for the night north of Limoges, and nothing was done until dawn when troops were despatched back along the route to search for the missing officer. Not until midday was the Colonel's car discovered abandoned in a village 40 miles back, with no signs of struggle and the vehicle still in running order. The SS soldiers spent nearly 24 hours vainly searching for the officer but he had vanished for good.

The state of mind of the troops as they encountered these frustrations can easily be imagined, especially as every bridge bar one ahead of them had been knocked out by Allied bombers. On the one bridge still not collapsed the SS vehicles had to be very slowly edged across one by one.

Then, one report states that the recce troops of Das Reich discovered the bodies of 62 German soldiers who appeared to have been mutilated and executed by French 'bandits'. As a reprisal, 99 French hostages were taken and hanged as suspected members of the Resistance.

Then an SS officer was killed by a sniper. Troops who had endured all the terrors and hardships of the Eastern front were now in no mood to use kid gloves when confronted with armed civilians in a war zone. Some 400 inhabitants of Oradour-sur-Glane were rounded up and herded into the town church, garages and barns nearby and the SS troops began firing in to them and throwing grenades, fires broke out and 393 people including children died.

It took the Das Reich Division 10 to 14 days to reach the battle, 450 miles from Toulouse. But this was only part of its travail, for when its units began forming up to attack and drive a wedge between the American and British armies their armour was held up for lack of fuel.

These delays fatally hampered Paul Hausser's attempt to carry out Rommel's orders, but all the German formations were in a similar predicament. The so-called 3rd Parachute Army and the new 17th SS Panzer-Grenadier Division Goetz von Berlichingen were likewise stuck, only able to send a few units forward in piecemeal fashion.

One German Army regiment loaded all its transport including horses onto a train, destination St Lo; it had travelled half-way by 7 June when it was discovered by American bombers in Fougeres station. The ensuing air attack produced chaos worthy of a fiction film: one bomb severed the train in half, so that the rear portion containing the regiment's horses rolled back down the line for four miles. By the time the galled German troops caught up with it the French had spirited away all the horses so the soldiers were obliged to continue their journey on foot.

Siegfried Karlsen describes his experiences when he reached the battle zone with the 12th SS:

'One afternoon we had pulled under some trees and very carefully camouflaged our vehicles before we had something to eat. We had only just arrived in France and knew no better. Someone shouted "Jabos", as some of our vehicles had been spotted by the Allied planes which were up there the whole time. We should never have stopped on that road, we had much to learn. We dived under the trees and into ditches. A host of fighters queued up to strafe us, flying over again and again, using machine-guns and cannon until most of our vehicles were flaming wrecks. The noise was continuous, our flak put out of action and we were helpless to stop the enemy. Of course, there was no sign of the Luftwaffe.

'We had to pick up the pieces and continue on foot. Thankfully, we had suffered few casualties, but this was to change. We had no armoured cars or tanks and moved off as soon as we could. Owing to the nature of the country we were forced to use the roads in order to approach the battle zone which was very dangerous. In fact, we were ordered not to move at all in daylight if possible, which seemed fantastic, and this meant we could not arrive where we were most needed until it was too late.

'At last we reached our assigned positions. I was in the infantry, and as we had lost all our vehicles we were no longer SS panzer-grenadiers but reduced to mere foot soldiers. We were facing the British and Canadians and the battle began for us with a terrible artillery barrage which far surpassed anything we had expected. We fell to the ground, hoping to dig holes or find ditches, but the shells and splinters seemed to search us out everywhere. It was a shambles, a terrifying experience for boys of our age who had never been in a battle.'

Frederik Hutten was also shocked by the terrific artillery fire, and explained that their whole training had concentrated on tank-infantry co-operation, for these lads were élite panzer-grenadiers who had expected to race into action in armoured carriers from which they would spring to deal with the opposition, hopefully in short, sharp and victorious battles.

It did not work out that way: the repeated emphasis on speed and more speed during training simply did not apply in the close country of Normandy where the landscape was of English type, with small, rolling fields bounded by hedgerows, sometimes in double thickness and just as unsuitable for the German panzers as it was for Allied tanks. An enemy could remain unseen just yards away.

'We were very keen,' Hutten continues, 'many of us under eighteen years old. I remember seeing Kurt Meyer, who became our CO, he always called us his "pimpfe" after the days in the Hitler Youth. We were very shocked by the terrible artillery and air bombardment which reduced us to impotence. Our expectations had been of a hard lightning thrust to the coast, that is what we had been expecting. But we had lost so many vehicles including tanks on the way, that by the time we reached the front we were reduced to a group of foot soldiers under constant attack from land and air, and at one point from the sea also. I and my friends of the squad had survived, but many had not. We had a very tough NCO of Russian front experience and he led us forward into a zone of heavy fire and told us to keep moving fast. But he was killed at once and we were left alone. So we hid under a hedgerow until another NCO came and told us to watch our front and flanks.'

It was the failure of the German Army's infantry and tanks to push the invaders back into the sea and the tardiness of the Leibstandarte's advance to combat which resulted in the premature commitment of the penny packets from 12th SS. Thrown into the fire zone in small groups the inexperienced, unsupported youths were to become a sacrifice in a hopeless situation, even though their extraordinary stand did buy the Germans time, though this was of little avail in the long run.

It has been alleged that neither Rommel nor his ageing chief Gerd von Rundstedt had any faith in the ability of Sepp Dietrich to handle a major operation, despite his apparent successes on the Russian front. The truth is of course that neither Dietrich, the 'Desert Fox' nor the old veteran von Rundstedt had the means or experience to deal with the kind of situation presented to them by the Allies in Normandy.

The failure of the Hitler Youth division resulted in a fresh plan to split the Allied invasion front in two from the south. This grand offensive was to be more carefully planned under the command of General der Panzertruppe Freiherr Geyr von Schweppenburg, a man descended from the Master of the House to the King of Wurttemburg. This general had come from the Russian front in a hurry to form a headquarters in a new and curious command set-up, one that was already bedevilled by very un-Teutonic complications, boundaries and rivalries topped by Hitlerian interference.

Panzer Group West was set up a few miles south of Caen, but was at once discovered by British intelligence and given the 'treatment', plastered by RAF bombs in a precision attack which killed

Schweppenburg's Chief-of-Staff and seventeen others, destroying most of the HQ transport and rendering it inoperable. But it took the Seventh Army twelve hours to learn of this disaster, and as a result Sepp Dietrich was placed in overall command of the sector; in other words, the direction of battle had fallen to the Waffen-SS, for Rommel, the once tactical genius of the desert war, had been reduced to a mere figurehead in Normandy, and a temporary one at that. The old days when the master had run rings round the British in North Africa had long gone. The man who had been at Hitler's side in command of his Fuehrerhauptquartier in 1939 had gone on to fame as commander of the 7th, so-called 'Ghost' division in the battle of France the next year, earning Hitler's amazed acclamation, so that it had seemed a natural choice when a vacancy came up to take a small German corps to contain the British in Libya. Whatever the sour opinions expressed among his seniors of the Army in Berlin, Rommel had won the hearts of the Afrikakorps and the people at home and had been hoisted by a grateful Fuehrer to Field Marshal. But from this pinnacle he had sunk into decline, eclipsed by a new star on the Allied horizon, a man who by the Normandy affair was still in the ascendant. The initiative and bloodletting was now directed by Montgomery.

As for Sepp Dietrich, he had come too far, the so-called 'butcher-bully boy' of the 1920s now commanded a whole army, but by mid-June it was clear he was at a loss and quite as incapable of influencing events at the front as were his colleagues. On 16 June he reported to his chief that the last reserves of his 1st SS Panzerkorps had been thrown in to try and stem the British. Then:

'I am being bled white and getting nowhere . . . we need another eight to ten divisions in the next few days or we are finished.'

This was a dire warning to Hitler, coming as it did from one of his favourites, though one who had already lost faith in his Fuehrer while on the Eastern Front.

Frederik Hutten:

'Then the Canadians attacked and it was my very first experience of enemy infantry. We stuck our weapons through the bottoms of the hedgerows and fired as fast as we could, but the enemy machine-guns were rattling the hedge with fire so we were forced to take cover. But the Canadians had been decimated and the next thing that hit us was more artillery fire which tore open the hedges and reduced us to wrecks. It was the worse experience of all, and we had to run back to where we had started from as soon as the fire had lifted. Then I saw Meyer frantically trying to organize a new defence line, and this he succeeded in doing.

'We dug little holes in the ground near a sunken lane and it started all over again. Terrible artillery fire and constant attacks from the air, with fighters using cannon, machine-guns and rockets, so we had no chance of keeping proper

observation. Then came the Sherman tanks along the lane, shooting at everything. Two of them were knocked out at once, but we could not stop them all so we ran back to a new position. Then some Tiger tanks arrived and restored the situation. But the cursed artillery began again, everything was churned up and the Tigers destroyed, so we were once more left alone. I remember saying goodbye in my mind to my family as the Canadians attacked again, and I found myself completely alone as all my comrades had been killed or wounded.

'I saw these big men in khaki coming along the lane behind Sherman tanks, shooting their weapons into the hedgerows, jumping over the shellholes and cursing all the time. I tried to fire my Schmeisser but it jammed, so I put my hands up just as they started firing again and a bullet went through my arm. I fell to the ground in pain and they rushed at me, kicking me, and telling me to get up. So I struggled up, received more kicks and was sent to the rear.'

Frederik Hutten's war had lasted two days.

The experience of Siegfried Karlsen with the 12th SS was hardly different:

'When the Tommies attacked our NCOs somehow pulled us together, those that had survived the artillery barrage, and we opened fire as best we could. These were the first enemy soldiers I had seen and they were very brave to come rushing at us over the fields and under the hedgerows. The countryside was very attractive but being torn up and ruined by the battle. There were many dead cows lying around with bloated bodies with their feet sticking up in the air; you could smell death everywhere because of the unburied carcasses.

'The khaki figures were rushing and yelling at us, even though I doubt if they could even see us. The noise was very great, and there were planes in the sky all the time, and the continuous bang and rumble of artillery. Then we heard tank engines and their guns firing, the constant stutter of machine-guns and the rattle of carbines. Above all this din came the yells of the Canadian soldiers as they attacked us. But we were well trained and disciplined and hidden under the hedges and in the ditches with as much camouflage as we could gather in the few moments before they hit us.

'I remember the shock and surprise on the enemy faces when we opened fire with all our weapons, they were that close to us as we had deliberately held our fire so as not to disclose our positions until the last moment. The Canadians were wiped out. It was terrible to see all those fine young men falling and cut down and their cries were awful. But then we ourselves came under heavy fire from machine-guns and all kinds of weapons and were forced to withdraw a little. The enemy licked his wounds and then sent in a tank attack, but the country was such that they were too slow, held up by the hedgerows and ditches, and as we had a few pak guns most of them were knocked out. The enemy faltered, but now we had to get under cover again as the fighter bombers hit us once more and we thought they would never stop.

'In all our long training we had never been prepared for this kind of warfare. We had never been under such air attack or in fact any kind in our training

areas so it was all the more terrifying. The Allies had complete control of the skies and all our movements seemed to be observed and we were attacked continuously.

'The yelling of the wounded men on both sides was terrible to hear. I lay in a ditch, soaked, exhausted, terrified, and hungry, my friends either dead or wounded, with only a few strange comrades nearby, wondering how much longer it could go on for. Then an NCO came to us and handed us some English chocolate, telling us we were heroes! I did not feel like one. I was filthy, starving and very frightened.

'Then the next attack came in and this time they knew exactly where we were, so we were moved out to the field behind us. It really mattered very little whether we lost a few fields, what did matter our NCO told us was that the enemy should be so bled that he was unable to advance further. We had to hold on till reinforcements came. We found a safer place to hide and some more Tiger tanks arrived so we felt more cheerful. All the old Mk IV tanks we had brought seemed to have been destroyed. Those Tigers were invincible and they took up defensive positions near us, the crews having to place broken trees and leaves all over them before the enemy planes saw them.

'Then the artillery started up again, the shells finding their way all over the fields, and soon it was our turn. We huddled with our heads down, rolled up like a ball in a ditch, quite unable to fight at all as the explosions ripped open everything around us. It was a terrifying experience and even worse than the earlier barrage. But it ended and we were given a few moments of peace before the enemy machine-guns began raking the fields and hedges. Then we heard tanks and looking up saw Shermans with infantry behind them, trying to advance. Those Tigers that were still in one piece waited until the enemy came nearer before opening fire. All the Shermans were destroyed or forced to retire and the infantry ran back or tried to hide themselves. Our fire drove them out of the shallow holes and they lost a lot of men. It was a terrible battle and we ran out of ammunition.

'We then withdrew for a short rest and received a small meal which came up in a wagon that by some miracle had survived. Then the enemy's artillery began again and everyone dived for cover. The jabos joined in and the whole serenade drove us crazy. Some of the boys were whimpering in terror as the flames and splinters flew about us without pause. I cannot imagine how anyone survived that barrage which was even worse than those before. When the pause came I think most of our officers, NCOs and men had been killed, wounded or driven insane. I myself lay in a ditch with my head in my arms, unable to move, completely demoralized and in a state of shock. At last I heard voices and saw enemy soldiers moving towards me. I was petrified as they came nearer, firing their weapons into the hedges and ditches. I sat up, expecting the worse, but as soon as I was seen they shouted, "Put your fucking hands up kid!" And I did so.

'I was roughly handled, given a slap or two on the face, searched, given a kick in the rear and told to march away with two others from our unit, lads I did not know. There were smoking craters, destruction and rubbish all over the

place and bodies which were hardly recognizable, some just pieces of flesh with shreds of uniforms or jackets which I could see were SS. We had one man guarding us as we ran back down a little lane, he had 'Canada' on his shoulder and I could see that he seemed as frightened as we were, as there were still shells and bullets flying about.

'At last, after we had passed lots of soldiers and trucks and other vehicles and a lot of wounded men we reached a little tent and were shown inside where an officer interrogated us in bad German. There was little we could say. My two comrades were in no state to speak so they kicked us out — literally — and after a little while we were given some tea and a biscuit and sat on the grass in silence. It was the end of our short war.'

Paul Giske had finally arrived with his unit of Das Reich to combat the Americans:

'We had already heard enemy planes in the sky and heard the constant rumble of gunfire. Officers met us in some consternation and told us to get all of our vehicles out of sight and camouflaged at once — "Or the Ami jabos will get you!" they shouted. Everyone was rushing about and in a short time we had our first air raid. It was as if they had been expecting us. A fleet of medium bombers came and dropped their loads all over the area, but caused few casualties. But from then on we were never left alone. There were American planes coming over all day long, so we seemed to spend more time hiding from their bombs and rockets and machine-gun fire than fighting a ground battle.

' Much of the time we were leaping into our tanks to get under cover. We had never experienced anything like it before and were certainly unprepared for it. Whenever we tried to move along the roads to meet the advancing Americans we found the way blocked by the wrecked vehicles of our own or other units. It became chaotic and difficult to restore order as we came under constant air attack. I saw many corpses and dead horses of army units who had long been killed, but no one had time to bury them or even move them. It was a rather desperate situation, but such was our morale that we still felt we could stop the American advance given a respite from air attack.

'We then came under enemy artillery fire and could see their spotter planes in the sky and then saw the American tanks and infantry advancing towards us. A great battle developed and we inflicted heavy losses on the Americans whose attack was halted. Then my CO took our tank into a hull-down position in a gully off the road, in fact all our remaining tanks and vehicles were off the road by now and trying to find concealment. Every time we saw enemy vehicles we fired. The country was of course extremely different from our Russian experience, very, very enclosed and ideal for defence. At least, it would have been but for the accursed jabos who had us in their sights all the time. If it had not been for this great enemy air superiority the Americans would never have got past us. As it was, we lost vehicle after vehicle to air attack so that our units were gradually ground to pieces and we were unable to confront the Ami ground forces who were very timidly trying to advance.

'At last we were alone and still in action and running short of ammunition and unable to get re-supplied owing to the air attacks going on all round us. So we shot off our last round, leapt from the tank and raced away for cover with the American infantry advancing on all sides. We had no chance of escape as the enemy were firing into the hedges and ditches and at last the inevitable happened and we were captured. A Sergeant saw us and motioned us to put our hands up, then several Amis came along and searched us, removing all watches and badges as souvenirs, laughing with excitement as they pocketed this and that. Then they gave us a few slaps and kicks and sent us off under guard. I remember one very big Ami soldier who said in German:
"You so-and-so krauts of the SS, you're not so tough after all, are you?"

CHAPTER THIRTEEN

At dawn on 13 June a column of tanks and infantry of the British 22nd Armoured Brigade moved on the village of Villers-Bocage, meeting no opposition and being greeted by French inhabitants; two Germans fled in a Kubelwagen. The leading tanks then probed on towards Point 213, a hill half-a-mile along the road to the north-east, leaving their accompanying infantry to dismount from their half-tracks to stretch their legs.

The Tommies had barely begun to unwind and light up cigarettes when a single gun cracked out not far away and to their consternation they saw a dreaded Tiger tank lumbering towards them over the fields from the north. The high velocity shot from the Tiger's eighty-eight struck the leading half-track which burst into flames. Panic reigned as the lone Tiger crunched down the tree-lined lane, its long barrelled cannon swinging around towards its next target. As the British soldiers ran for cover the German tank began its unopposed work of destruction, cruising leisurely along the roadway, its gunner pumping shell after shell into the row of British vehicles, brewing them up in turn, eventually dealing with the light armour of the regiment's reconnaissance troop — destroying the lot. A single 27-ton Cromwell attempted to challenge the raider with its 75mm gun, its shells bounced off the Tiger at a few yards range before it too went up in flames.

Twenty-five British vehicles were left blazing wrecks, the work of SS Hauptsturmfuehrer (Captain) Michel Wittmann, the most successful tank commander of the war, his score in that month rose to 138 enemy tanks and 132 guns destroyed. Wittmann had started his war with an assault gun in the Polish campaign as a member of the Leibstandarte, taken part in the invasion of Holland, then the campaign in France. In April 1941 he was in action in Greece before going to Russia in Operation Barbarossa where he scored most of his kills. In January 1944 he was awarded the Knight's Cross, the Oak Leaves being added by the end of the month, and on 22 June he became the 71st recipient of the Swords for his actions in Normandy as commander of the 1st (Heavy) Company, 501 SS Panzer Abteilung of the Leibstandarte.

Wittman's gunner, Sergeant Balthasar Woll, also held the Knight's Cross, and their comrades knocked out those British tanks which had reached Point 213. But the Germans were slow in assaulting Villers-Bocage, when they did they were repulsed by the reinforced British units, losing six precious Tigers and several Mk 4s.

Wittmann was killed south of Caen on 8 August, possibly in an Allied air attack; he was thirty.

On the same day that Sepp Dietrich sent his urgent call for support (16 June) the Panzer Lehr division collapsed, frittered away by the British-Canadian blitz.

Also on that day, the commander of 12th SS Hitlerjugend, the very experienced Fritz Witt, was killed in his own headquarters by naval gunfire. His place was taken by Kurt Meyer. In this period occurred an incident or incidents which would be later be termed an atrocity and this will be covered later.

Paul Hausser's planned counter-stroke from the south depended on the arrival of yet more SS divisions, the 9th and 10th, and on 23 June Hausser reported to Rommel's deputy General Dollman that both formations had arrived in France. These two divisions had moved west after their triumphant rebuff of the Soviet offensive in the Tarnopol area. They had left Poland on 12 June, but after four days travelling they had still only reached Lorraine in Alsace where they were brought to a standstill because the railway ahead of them was out of action through Allied bombing. The two SS divisions were therefore obliged to make a hazardous 400-mile journey by road, which was doubly unfortunate for the German commander in the west, for a fierce Channel storm, the worst in forty years, had so interrupted the Allied build-up in Normandy that a lull had ensued, which was exactly when Hausser's offensive should have gone in. The SS general had hoped to strike hard at the junction of the British and American sectors with a solid, extremely powerful punch using the combined weight of 1st, 2nd, 9th and 10th SS, but because of the delays imposed his plan never came off.

The 1st Leibstandarte had managed to move from Belgium, hopelessly late because of Hitler's belief in a second Allied landing in the Calais area, and the unit passed through Paris on 23 June. Because of Montgomery's tactics the SS units, like those of the German Army, were drawn into the battle piecemeal fashion, pulled into the cauldron in the eastern sector by constant pressure which though resulting in heavy casualties for the British and Canadians also saw some grinding down of the German divisions and of course resulted in far less problems for the Americans. Montgomery's front acted as the pivot, gripping most of the German armour in continuous battle while the Americans tried to break out south and west. Some British and Canadian units were bled white in this battle while the Americans failed to make any significant impression on their front, suffering set-backs and delays and when finally able to get started hampered by the errors of their own air force. Yet, in spite of their apparent inability to break the comparatively thin German crust in these weeks they would soon begin to snipe at Montgomery and his armies which were so heavily engaged against the bulk of the German armour.

Only the 9th SS Hohenstaufen reached the front, together with elements of LAH, so Hausser proposed a holding action until he had the strength to hit hard. He continued to build up his army, so that by 25 June not one panzer division had been in action against the Americans. The sole responsibility for Seventh Army had now fallen to Hausser, for both Rommel and Rundstedt had left to confer with Hitler and plead for a general withdrawal. Then the Americans at last captured the port of Cherbourg, which prompted Hitler to order a 'Court Martial' enquiry into why this had been allowed to happen. Then, on the morning of 28th General Dollman collapsed from a heart attack or stroke in his bathroom, with his dying order to Hausser that the attack must go in without further delay.

By next day (29th) Hausser's so-called 2nd SS Panzerkorps had at last received the 10th SS Frundsberg division which he now proposed launching as a diversion, reinforced by one regiment from the Leibstandarte. But by 10 am, long after the attack had been due to begin, Hausser reported a delay till the afternoon:

'Our concentrations are under continual air and artillery bombardment.'

At one-thirty he reported that the constant enemy fighter bomber attacks were causing heavy losses, while his panzers were immobilized through lack of fuel. The pride of the German armoured forces had been reduced to impotence, but those units surviving finally made a weak start at two-thirty in the afternoon. But this was much too late, for by then the British had occupied Hill 112 which afforded a magnificent view of the German assembly areas and enabled the British to swamp them with heavy shellfire.

Although itself overlooked by high ground elsewhere, Hill 112 was a vital point for advancing across the river Odon to the Orne, in fact, 'the back door to Caen', as well as permitting access to the more open tank country beyond and therefore a key to the battle of Normandy. These facts were certainly known to Hausser.

The planned diversionary attack by the 10th SS was therefore a failure from the start, compounded by the capture of an officer from the 9th SS who was found to be carrying both a map and notebook outlining the German plans. When Hausser's assault finally recommenced it did so at only half its original strength, the rest of the troops having been decimated and disorganized by British bombardment. Well forewarned, the guns and infantry of the 15th Scottish Division routed the SS infantry before destroying the few isolated panzers which had managed to penetrate a few miles. By now the very powerful British 17-pounder anti-tank gun had reached the units, and along with the 6-pounder was well able to deal with even the heaviest of enemy tanks.

The Germans' misery and frustration was sustained by the British artillerymen who blazed away through the night, shelling all the villages, copses and fields suspected of hiding enemy forces, thus preventing any dawn renewal of the attack. But the SS also made heavy use of artillery and especially mortars and managed to dislodge the British off Hill 112. The British infantry, probably those of the Hampshire Regiment though not named as such by Alexander Baron in his brilliant book *From the City from the Plough** had advanced through the high corn, and despite heavy casualties captured the hill. But later their armour support was withdrawn, which is when desperate attempts by the SS troops succeeded in retaking it. Hill 112 twice changed hands in bloody battles, some Germans dubbed it 'the Hill of Calvary'.

Hausser was now officially appointed commander of Seventh Army, but by the evening of 30 June, despite some local successes and support from 1st SS Panzerkorps under Dietrich he was forced to call off the attack, reporting to Rommel's HQ that the offensive by the two SS armoured corps had been suspended 'in the face of intensive enemy artillery fire and supporting fire of unprecedented ferocity from naval units . . . the tenacious enemy resistance will prevent our counter offensive from having any appreciable effect'.

The 'naval units' referred to were of course including the monitor HMS *Roberts*; at one point in the battle two of these armoured leviathans were pouring one 15-inch shell into the Caen crucible every half-minute.

In response to Hausser's plea for a withdrawal to husband his dwindling resources, General Speidel telephoned from Rommel's HQ to advise that permission would be granted as soon as it was authorized by OKW, in other words the Fuehrer. But Hitler had already refused to yield an inch to Rommel's arguments, the Caen area had to be held at all costs; he thus sounded the death knell of the German armies in the west, including the élite SS Panzerkorps. It was also in a sense the final chapter in the careers of these SS commanders.

Sepp Dietrich was hardly in his element, and by his own later admission no more than an average general. In his situation this was not good enough, though without a huge increase in his strength on the ground and adequate air support there was nothing he could do to prevent the Allies bursting out of their bridgehead. On 26 June he had again clamoured for help:

'If reinforcements are not sent up, a breakthrough cannot be prevented.'

This was during the battle for Cheux. Two battalions of SS Leibstandarte were promised him, but became stuck — out of fuel — four miles away; they might just as well have been forty, given his desperate situation. An appeal to Rommel's HQ for help from Hausser's corps was refused, for the 2nd SS Panzerkorps was in no position to assist. But somehow Dietrich managed to scrape together a force of 80 tanks to try and restore the situation, but their attack was driven off by the anti-tank screen on the flank of the 15th Scottish.

---

*Jonathan Cape 1948

Dietrich, well known as one of Hitler's oldest cohorts, was appealed to by his army colleagues and some of his own officers, surely he could get Hitler to change his mind and allow a withdrawal? To this suggestion he replied:

'If you want to get shot that's the way to do it!'

It had been the survivors of Meyer's 12th SS division that had largely held the troops of Montgomery's 21st Army Group at bay throughout June, yet by holding fast they were actually helping their enemy fulfil his strategy of using Caen as the pivot and focal point of the battle. The city acted as a magnet for the German commanders, and there was and has been since no indication that they realized what the enemy commander was up to. Even if they had done, there was not a thing they could do about it. Monty launched one 'operation' after another, throwing in hundreds of tanks and thousands of troops, massed artillery and 'air', including eventually four-engined bombers somewhat reluctantly loaned by Bomber Harris who forever frowned on any attempt to divert his force from what he saw as their true role — the strategic bombing of Germany. In these successive assaults Montgomery did however hope not only to continue pinning down the bulk of enemy strength, he also longed to be in possession of Caen and its vital road net so that his armour could break free of the accursed bocage country and go 'swanning' over open terrain.

Famous British regiments with proud traditions going back for centuries were reduced to company strength and less; one unit virtually ceased to exist, with a complete breakdown in morale and discipline. Inevitably, amalgamations took place and the War Office staffs began to cast about for new sources of manpower, finally coming to an agreement with the Air Ministry who handed over a number of ground airmen to be remustered much to their dismay and disgust as infantrymen. Despite all Monty's experiences in the First World War and his use of mass artillery and armour and 'air' it was the infantrymen who suffered most and their losses brought an ever increasing manpower crisis, though certainly not on the German scale. There is no doubt that a real comb-out in Britain would have produced sufficient men, but there would not have been enough time to train them.

The lads of the Hitler Youth division were thrown away by the thousands in Normandy, yet there is no question that their stand was a very brave and tenacious one. They remained in their foxholes until they were killed, wounded or captured, and certainly stood up better to the storm of steel and fire than the older soldiers of the German Army. It is hard to be precise, but the only logical explanation for their courage and steadfastness is pride in their unit, the same old military *esprit de corps* that sustains the élite troops of any army in the most difficult situations. It is no more fashionable now half a century on to give such credit than it was during the war, any mention of 'the SS' in the press is accompanied by the standard lines on Himmler's criminal order. The very worst of human traits are equated with the SS, and no newspaper journalist seems willing to risk his editor's ire by stating the facts on this subject.

'The astonishing young grenadiers of this unit were indescribably brave', commented one German tank crewman quoted by Alexander McKee in his fine book *Caen — Anvil of Victory**, while General Dwight Eisenhower stated in a report — ' . . . in attack or defence they fought to a man with fanatical courage'. Not that such a report made in wartime could ever see the light of day.

'The troops of 12th SS . . . fought with a tenacity and a ferocity seldom equalled and never excelled during the whole campaign', wrote the late Australian war correspondent Chester Wilmot in his excellent post-war book *The Struggle for Europe***.

On 26 June the 1st Panzerkorps had 114 Panthers and 200 Mk IV tanks still in action. By 9 July the Hitler Youth division had lost 60 per cent of its original manpower and only had 50 tanks left in action. The remnants were withdrawn to Falaise where they would provide the bastion against a great British-Canadian assault that would enable too many German troops to escape the pocket.

On 1 July Hausser made one last attempt to smash the bridgehead established by the British over the river Odon, launching elements of all four SS divisions against the 15th Scottish and 49th Divisions. Despite the power of the attack which was sustained, the British held firm against all the SS assaults, for the days when these élite troops carried all before them had gone. The British infantry opposing the SS were not intimidated into panic and rout, they stood their ground while the 6- and 17-pounder anti-tank guns knocked out the Tigers, Panthers and Mk IVs.

But on this decisive day the weather closed in, which might have been good news for Hausser, for it meant that the Allied Tactical Air Arm, as well as the heavies of Bomber Command were grounded, so their intervention was prevented. Yet the British, as ever, relied on a tremendous weight of artillery concentrations, the guns were indeed the 'Queen of the Battlefield' in Normandy, so that the SS troops in their vehicles or on foot were decimated. It was this latest disaster to German arms which allegedly prompted Hitler's toady Field Marshal Keitel of OKW to cry out to von Rundstedt by telephone 'What shall we do? What shall we do?' To which the veteran Field Marshal replied: 'Make peace, you fools!' When Hitler heard this from Keitel his reaction was to write von Rundstedt a mild letter relieving him of his command, supplanting him with one of his favourites, Field Marshal Gunther von Kluge. The new appointee had led the drive to the Channel in 1940, then the push towards Moscow in 1941, but had been absent from duty for nine months following a car crash. Hitler had shown his gratitude for von Kluge's

---

* Souvenir Press 1964
** Collins 1952

This guitar-strumming NCO of the Hitler Youth division wears U-boat leathers.

A Mk 4 panzer of 12th SS; note armour-plate 'skirt'.

The highly-successful Tiger tank commander Michel Wittmann with his gunner in Normandy before their death in August (1944).

A Hitler Youth SS tank company about to be inspected by Field Marshals von Rundstedt and Rommel and high SS officers including Dietrich and 'Panzer' Meyer. (Ahnert Verlag)

Troops of 17th SS parade in full rig-out before meeting their American opponents.
(Vowinkel Verlag)

One of the luckier ones: a young SS prisoner who survived the British air and artillery blitz in Normandy.

One of the 'old fighters' and essential cog that made the armed SS possible: Josef Sepp Dietrich.

Paul 'Papa' Hausser did most to elevate the armed SS to real military value. (Munin Verlag)

Felix Steiner, pioneer of tactics in the 'new model army' and champion of the foreign volunteer 'European ideal'. (Munin Verlag)

Georg Keppler: CO of Der Führer regiment and believer in the new army. (Munin Verlag)

Joachim Peiper: held partly responsible for the Malmedy massacre; murdered 1976.

Werner Ostendorff: Chief-of-Staff to the Reich Division in Russia, later commanded 17th SS in France. (Munin Verlag)

Kurt 'Panzer' Meyer, archetypal SS field officer who became the youngest general.

Hitler's last great gamble: the Ardennes offensive, December 1944.

SS troops pass a disabled American armoured car. Loot was plentiful.

The vehicles of Dietrich's 6th SS Panzer Army were bogged down in road jams. (Ahnert Verlag)

meritorious service by giving him a gift of 250,000 Reichmarks (about £20,000 at the time), allegedly from his own purse.

But by 1944 von Kluge had been inveigled by one of the dissident generals into the anti-Hitler plot, and although mentally committed, felt his oath of allegiance to the Fuehrer prevented him from taking any active part until Hitler was actually dead.

Like his predecessors, the new Commander West arrived in Normandy brimming with confidence and determined to succeed where others had clearly failed. Yet in that summer of 1944 von Kluge's great experience of European battlefields counted for next to nothing, he was no more able to retrieve the desperate situation than his fellow generals, for while isolating and devouring the German divisions the Allies now won the battle of the build-up, so that after seven weeks on French soil 1,500,000 men with all their equipment and supplies were in place, transported across an uneasy English Channel where one of the worst storms in living memory had raged and through a modicum of German interference. On 29 July Allied strength stood at 1,566,356 men, with 332,645 vehicles, including tanks, and stores amounting to 1,602,976 tons.

By then Germany, and above all its leaders, had been traumatized by the attempt on Hitler's life on 20 July. It was also the month which saw the removal of Monty's opponent Field Marshal Rommel: the car containing his party had been caught in daylight by Spitfires of RAF 602 Squadron, knocked out and Rommel seriously wounded.

Then a much delayed American offensive finally got under way, preceded by heavy bombing which did more damage to the attackers than the Germans. Seven of the nine German panzer divisions plus four heavy tank battalions and all three brigades of the dreaded multi-barrelled nebelwerfer mortars were concentrated on the British-Canadian front. Fourteen German divisions with some 600 tanks and assault guns still faced these Allied units as against a collection of nine German divisions with about 110 tanks in the American sector. Hausser once again called for a withdrawal, his front under tremendous pressure, with one flank dangerously exposed, but Hitler again refused. Between 6 June and 23 July the German 7th Army and Panzer Group West suffered 116,863 men killed, wounded and missing, but received only 10,000 replacements, but this figure did not include a further 10,000 men drafted to the 2nd Para Corps under Meindl from the Luftwaffe of whom 6,800 had fallen out in a short time due to lack of experience.

Then on 30 July the British drove a deep wedge into Hausser's front which split 7th Army from 5th Panzer Army (formerly Panzer Group West) on its eastern flank. The increasing momentum of the American advance was only slightly stemmed by a counter stroke delivered by 116th Panzer, 17th SS, and elements of the Leibstandarte and Das Reich, some of the latter being intercepted by the British.

The 17th was a new panzer-grenadier division placed under the command of Werner Ostendorff who had spent much of his career on the

Russian front with Das Reich which he commanded for a short time. He had been a general staff officer with the original V-Division in the Western Campaign of 1940, and during the invasion of Russia had served on Hausser's staff, graduating to the post of Chief-of-Staff SS Panzerkorps in Russia in 1943. On 26 November of that year he was appointed commander of a new division then forming in the Tours area of France, its designation of 17th SS Panzer-grenadier division *Goetz von Berlichingen** having been bestowed by Hitler on 3 October. At this time, Ostendorff held the rank of Oberfuehrer (one step above Standartenfuehrer or Colonel), but was promoted to SS Brigadefuehrer or Lt-General on taking up his new challenge.

When Ostendorff joined his headquarters staff at Thouars south of Le Mans in January 1944 the component parts of the division were still forming and training in other locations, but by end-March the formation was about ready and placed under command of the Army's 80th Corps. At this time it was still possible for a newly formed SS division to be 'christened' by ceremonial in some style, so on 10 April the Reichsfuehrer himself travelled from Berlin to the town hall in Thouars to attend a function which included Sepp Dietrich and the Army's General Gehr von Schweppenburg.

The commandeered town hall had been suitably decked out for the occasion; the new unit's SS Musikkorps arranged on stage, its backdrop a huge eagle and swastika backlit to form a sunburst in the Nazi manner, while a speaker's podium in front was draped with a black banner marked by large SS runes in white. Speeches and dedications in solemn manner doubtless included the usual oaths to struggle for the Fuehrer and Fatherland, and during the next hours inspections of the troops were carried out and the customary SS unit sleeve ribbons distributed; the division's emblem was a mailed fist.

The 17th SS had an establishment in personnel of 13,571 but although classified as an 'armoured infantry' division most of the foot grenadiers would be transported in Maultier trucks of which it had 1,921; added to this were 973 cars of one kind or another, 24 heavy armoured cars, 42 assault guns, 35 lightly armoured s.p. vehicles, a few APCs, anti-tank guns, supply trucks, motorcycles etc. Obviously it had no tanks, but it did have 18 of the indispensable 'eighty-eights'.

When the invasion came the 17th SS moved off, direction north-west, but like all other German units suffered delays from Allied air attack and French snipers before eventually entering battle against the Americans during the night of 11/12 June. It was not actually the first time it had fired its guns in action, the flak details having the first alarms against Allied air incursions, a British Halifax bomber being shot down by the 1st Battery on 2 June. It is said that not all of the men of the division were German, a few racial Germans including Romanians being included, but

---

* A German hero of an earlier century.

the success against the British terror-bomber was of some significance as the division had been adopted by the much battered German city of Stuttgart, the men having collected three-quarters of a million Reichsmarks towards the town's bomb relief fund.

Other 'highlights' of this unit's combat in the following days was the dismissal of their commander Werner Ostendorff through a wound on 16 June and hearing themselves named over the British-run 'Soldatensender Calais' radio station. The division was like the rest of the German units subjected to almost non-stop air assault and during operations one of its battalions was cut off by the Americans and taken prisoner. In this period among other supporting units on its front was the remains of the Panzer Lehr and paratroops under the command of Baron von Der Heydte who had survived the Crete invasion in May 1941.

That the whole ethos of these SS commanders had been formed by their Russian front experience is confirmed by comments made later by Kurt Meyer, who, when he became the youngest German general at the age of thirty-four already had the Knight's Cross with Oak Leaves slung about his neck, the Swords being added in August 1944 for his work in Normandy. The Knight's Cross was a comparatively common award and hardly comparable to the Victoria Cross: it had been instituted by Hitler on 1 September 1939 (the day Poland was invaded) to bridge the large gap between the Iron Cross 1st Class and the Grand Cross. Whereas only one of the latter was ever awarded (to Goering who lost it when his Berlin home was hit during an air raid), no less than 6,973 Knight's Crosses were given, and although one of the first recipients was an Army private in the Western campaign of 1940, most went to officers. But only 150 Knight's Crosses with Oak Leaves and Swords were awarded, and there is little doubt that Kurt Meyer won his decorations.

'Having come from Russia,' he said later, 'I and my fellow officers had grown into a certain way of thinking which had been bred by the type of fighting there which was dictated by the Russian mass attack. Of course in the earlier period we trained for and carried out a war of movement. We did not favour the so-called "set-piece" battle on World War I lines for the simple reason that it required no guile or science, simply a slogging match with the side having the most men and material the certain winner. Apart from which, all military thinking in the Waffen-SS, despite what was said about us, was concerned with gaining swift victories at a minimum of casualties. This means that all our troops were trained to move very fast, rather like the paratroops, but with more equipment.

'However, as soon as the East Front reached stalemate and became a war of attrition all our training went for nothing. We were reduced to positional warfare which was the very antithesis of all we had learned and believed in. As we knew we could not win because both the Russians and the Western Allies had a plethora of overwhelming superiority in material which reduced our superior infantry training and the use of armour to nothing. The results are well known.

'Long before we reached the front in Normandy we were spotted by air reconnaissance and the jabos began their assaults on us. Their attacks never ceased the whole time we were in battle. This was something beyond our experience as the Russians, although gaining the ascendancy in the East, had never developed the degree of ground-air co-operation which we saw deployed in the West. The result was a terrible baptism of fire for my boys and the loss of much material before we ever entered combat. We really never recovered from this.

'However, in the short respites we were able to move up into position, but as soon as we went into the attack we were struck by a hurricane of artillery fire and fresh air attacks, the like of which I had never experienced. The Allies had applied their own kind of "blitzkrieg", and it was the death knell of our division which with others was attempting to drive back the British and Canadian forces to the beaches. We had some local successes, but these could never be consolidated owing to the terrific artillery and air power laid on us. The fighting was some of the most intense I had experienced and came about because of the close nature of the terrain which was of course the exact opposite to the Eastern Front where we were used to never-ending plains, and even after we were reduced to static warfare in that region we did at least have complete, commanding views of the ground before us, and were able to bring fire to bear almost anywhere.

'However, the country in Normandy was ideal for defence, the only problem was that we had insufficient time in which to set up proper positions and were not trained for it anyway. We were thrown straight into the attack as we arrived in piecemeal fashion, we had lost this battle before we had started, and despite all the tremendously heroic efforts of those boys who were in many cases only seventeen-years-old, we were gradually ground down to nothing. It was a constant, hellfire battle dominated by artillery and air from the Allied side. I can honestly say that in straight, man-to-man infantry combat our lads always proved the better, even though as mentioned from the point of view of defence we did hold certain advantages. We took terrible losses which could not be replaced and never were.'

'I myself was involved in the actual fighting as the British and Canadian pressure grew with one offensive after another, each accompanied by huge air attack which reduced everything to chaos. The four-motor bombers did not achieve their objectives, rather did they create obstacles for the massed enemy tanks. But they did create a great deal of effect and confusion. But the chief reason, for our defeat, apart from the terrible British artillery fire, was the never-ending harassment along our roads of supply by the jabos which were always there, so that movement by day became impossible.'

It could be suggested that the British had ample time in which to develop similar swift-moving battlefield tactics as advocated by the SS, they certainly had the time in which to prepare themselves for a more modern kind of warfare, from 1940 until 1944 in fact, many thousands of troops waiting first for an invasion that never came and then one of their own. Old tactics and old thinking bedevilled all British army operations against the Germans so that in the end it was always the artillery and air force who came to be the bedrock of attack and defence. Montgomery's reputation as a 'master of the set piece battle' as described by Meyer in which the man with greatest amount of material wins was cemented in Normandy, and very expensive it proved to be. Yet, in that kind of country there seemed to be little alternative, apart from cutting the Germans off completely from their supplies and starving them into surrender. This is quite feasible, the enemy were not far short of that prospect and would certainly have collapsed through sheer lack of the wherewithal, thus saving very many lives. But the political and military thinking of the day were not geared along these lines, as exampled by the smashing of Le Havre by RAF bombers on the insistence of the army commander which cost only French lives, not the enemy's.

On the evening of 7 August the troops and armour of 51st Highland and the 2nd Canadian divisions were assembled south of Caen in six columns comprising tanks, self-propelled artillery and anti-tank guns, followed by infantry in carriers and other vehicles. Each column was tight-packed on a four-tank front, this phalanx headed by flail tanks whose whirling chains were designed to explode German mines.

The proposed corridor to be smashed through the German defences was also to be made with the aid of 'experimental measures', massed attacks on the flanks and ahead of the columns by heavy bombers aided by pathfinders, plus green target indicator shells and tracers each side of the route fired by 40mm Bofors guns. The light of the moon, due to rise before midnight, would be supplemented by the glare of searchlights.

Half an hour before the air bombing began a rolling artillery barrage was put down and at last the armoured spearheads began to move, keeping at first to each side of the Caen-Falaise road. But several factors now combined to frustrate this great set-piece attack. On the face of it, the great armoured cavalcade should have achieved an overwhelming breakthrough, and it should be understood that the intention was not merely to keep the Germans occupied while the Americans executed their own pincer movement to the south and east, but to finally break through the stubborn crust of the German defences which in some places despite all the awful punishment meted out to them by countless thousands of shells and bombs were still three or four lines deep. Once through these defences there would seem to be no limit to the victories beckoning beyond.

The bombing and shelling took its toll in effect and actual losses, but as usual, the (in this case) Poles and Canadians of the infantry units bellied their lack of understanding of what was required of them due as always to lack of the right training in Britain, even though as indicated many of them had been confined on the island with no action for up to four years, restlessly pining for battle. These infantrymen leapt from their carriers and trucks to begin mopping up every small island of resistance they encountered, instead of rushing forward towards their goals beyond. This involvement in small battles on each side of the march route dissipated the strength of the attack and brought momentum to a crawl or even a complete stop.

Night attacks were often avoided in the war for the very good reason that in darkness confusion is all too easily arrived at, which is precisely what occurred in this latest of Montgomery's assaults. The commander was under increasing pressure from above to break the supposed 'stalemate' around Caen. Increasingly isolated from his superiors by a series of gaffes in which his rather bombastic press briefings gave one impression after another of imminent and total triumph. To many it appeared that every one of his grand assaults had foundered, with hundreds more dead and the fields and lanes clogged with knocked out British tanks. Whether his bosses ever really understood his handling of the battle as overall ground commander is even now open to question. In the event, and unknown to his public at home, Monty came close to being dismissed for what was regarded as failure on the battlefield and some imprudent exchanges with Eisenhower, who was himself being fed a string of complaints and gossip by the British Air Commander, Tedder at SHAEF HQ. Only the intervention of his mentor Field Marshal Sir Alan Brooke saved him, for even the Prime Minister's patience seemed to be wearing thin.

Monty's desire to 'put everyone in the picture' had long come to include the press, in fact one critic has alleged that the General never did anything without giving a press handout, which for a British commander was extraordinary. It was well known that the American commanders were wholly conditioned to the power of the press and therefore public opinion back home which according to one Ike homily, 'won wars'. But Monty had the great knack of delineating a battle both before and during it, apart from giving copious and precise accounts of how he won them later. So even that famous Monty-hater General Patton had been impressed when first encountering one of the Britisher's briefings in England prior to D-day. However, later on the Americans and indeed some of the British would appear baffled by his strategy for the Normandy campaign, even though Montgomery's surviving notes on a General Officers' briefing he delivered on 7 April 1944 give an outline of his broad intentions.

Now, yet another Monty special rolled forward, and chaos was the result, brought about by the enormous amount of smoke and dust caused by the artillery fire and bombing. In the latter segment of the assault over 600 American bombers hit the 51st Highland Division, causing heavy casualties and disruption. The orderly lines of armour began to waver as the moonlight and glare of the searchlights was obscured, they lost direction; and behind the tanks and SP guns the infantry, coming under fire from those small surviving pockets of the enemy, diverted themselves to mop up. Then, to add to the confusion, some of the dreaded '88s' began to bark from the dust, Shermans were dismantled, brewed up and burned.

Yet, despite these inferno-like scenes of confusion and death, a breakthrough had occurred which even the 'fanatical' resistance of the SS troops could not prevent. Monty's Operation Totalize was not the decisive breakout he had hoped for, but it was sufficient to bring Field Marshal von Kluge close to despair. The victor of campaigns in France and Russia was reduced to impotent frustration as the coloured chinagraph squiggles on his situation map confirmed the enemy steam-roller moving inexorably south-eastwards.

Often the Allied troops were far too slow to exploit their success and when the first stream of demoralized German soldiers began streaming back from the blitz zone they were met by a determined young SS general. Kurt Meyer stood in the roadway, ordering the waverers back into new defence positions, and so effective was his leadership that he managed to set up a new blocking force, aided by a scratch collection of tanks and pak guns. Yet even 'Panzer' Meyer was unable to hold up the great force of men and armour pressing down on him, and despite some local successes against the Poles, the German defences were completely disrupted, and continually under attack by the RAF's 2nd Tactical Air Force and USAAF.

Now the American Third Army under Patton wheeled east and the whole German Seventh Army was threatened with encirclement, the key objective Falaise; if the Americans could link up swiftly enough with the Poles and Canadians then a whole German army would be trapped. Yet General Bradley's objective was a wider encircling movement — and Paris. Patton's pursuit corps began its race, the German counter-attack at Mortain at first contained and then pinched out, smothered by Thunderbolt and Typhoon jabos which had been held back for a time by fog in England.

'The activities of the fighter-bombers are almost unbearable', complained one German report, and — 'The Leibstandarte reports air attacks of such intensity they have never before experienced. Its attack has been stopped'.

The few Luftwaffe fighters which tried to intervene were intercepted and destroyed on take-off. One German commander reported:

'The 116th Panzer has not advanced one step today (6 August); neither have other units.'

With the German counter-attack blunted and halted the American advance continued, and von Kluge, on Hitler's instructions, ordered Hausser to divert two of his SS divisions from the British front to help stem the American thrust, to which the SS general replied:

'This, at the moment when strong enemy tank units are thrusting into our flank could deal a death blow not only to the Seventh Army but to the entire Wehrmacht in the West.'

But von Kluge merely repeated that it was a *Fuehrerbefehl,* a Hitler directive, and as a result of the subsequent battle around Caen the Field Marshal confessed to Hausser on the evening of 8 August:

'A breakthrough has occurred south of Caen such as we have never seen.'

Yet, within 24 hours von Kluge had recovered his nerve and become more optimistic, the reason for this turnabout being a 'decisive conference' he had attended with Hitler at OKW. This was the effect that Hitler had on most, and von Kluge was now inspired to a new counterstroke against the Allies in Normandy. But this was delving into fantasy, for the reality of events soon overcame him as it did all other Germans in Normandy as their front collapsed. By 16 August the Canadians had entered Falaise and von Kluge dared Hitler's wrath by allowing Hausser to begin withdrawing non-combatants with their transport from the trap. The Allies now squeezed the German Seventh Army inexorably into a shrinking pocket which by 17 August measured some twenty miles by ten. Within this trap were herded 100,000 German troops, the remains of fifteen divisions, plus stragglers from twelve more. Once more von Kluge was thrown into despair, and was now suspected by Hitler of treason, the Fuehrer's suspicions hardened when the Field Marshal went missing from his HQ for some hours. But for Gunther von Kluge, the man who had accepted the Fuehrer's golden bounty, the end had come: he shot himself in his car.

As for Kurt Meyer's once proud 12th SS division, some 500 grenadiers aided by about fifteen tanks held off the Canadians while the rest of the German forces attempted to escape. Then at long last sanction was finally given by Hitler for a general breakout. In this holocaust of battle one young SS officer cadet recalled later that in his hour of need he 'felt God was near', and the words of the psalms came to him. From an original strength of 21,300 men only about 300 troops with ten tanks remained of Meyer's 12th SS to flee eastwards out of the cauldron and carnage around Falaise. Of this their commander said:

'The débâcle at Falaise put an end to all the slaughter in Normandy, but very few of my division were able to escape the cauldron. It was a tragedy that so many young lives were lost.'

The last few square miles of the area around Falaise became a place of terror and nightmare for those thousands of German soldiers trying to flee eastwards; great numbers of men and horses were slaughtered in the Allied air and artillery blitz. Paul Hausser managed to ride out of the fiery cauldron on a tank, but was again wounded; the paratroop general Meindl also managed to escape with a squad of his men, while curiously enough Kurt Meyer is said to have been led to safety by a French civilian. There were certainly those among the French who were not very sympathetic to the Allies and hostile in some cases to the British. In the first place the notion that *le Tommy* had run away at Dunkirk without giving due notice to their ally was not only believed by many Frenchmen but apparently true. The feelings engendered were then hugely exacerbated when the Royal Navy attacked the French Fleet at Oran in North Africa to prevent it falling into German hands. These events were a wonderful windfall to German propagandists. Then there was the undoubted fact that the Normans preferred to live their lives in peace, undisturbed by friend or foe. Peace they had to a large extent enjoyed under the occupiers, the Allied invasion brought death and destruction — especially to their livestock.

The Mortain-Falaise pocket brought the greatest disaster to the Wehrmacht since Stalingrad and the surrender of Tunis in May 1943. It was also a disaster for the Waffen-SS which saw several of its finest divisions crushed and their reputation as invincibles further lowered. Most of the German generals and corps commanders however escaped, leaving around 10,000 of their men dead on the battlefield and a further 50,000 as prisoners. The material losses included some 500 tanks and assault guns. And the retreating army had yet to cross the river Seine where all the bridges bar one had been destroyed by Allied air attack. Sepp Dietrich was in command of this operation and commented later that in terms of further equipment lost it proved almost as great a disaster as Falaise. The desperate Germans, caught on the wrong side of the river, were forced to improvise in order to try and effect their crossing to the eastern bank; some lashed trees together to make rafts, many had to discard their gear and swim for it.

Of 2,300 tanks and assault guns committed to the Normandy battle by the Germans, only 100 to 200 were saved, the average strength of the panzer divisions after the battle was a mere 15 to 20 tanks each. Yet, in the three-month period May to July 1944 the Wehrmacht received 2,313 new tanks from the factories, but owing to the Allied air blockade was unable to get them to the troops on the western front.

For the Fuehrer the crunch point had come on 15 August which he later cited as 'the worst day of my life', previous 'worst days' one assumes not withstanding, ie, the recent attempt on his life and the two surrenders mentioned above that deprived him of around half a million soldiers.

Montgomery closed the books on the Normandy battle on 19 August, totting up the enemy's debit column as follows:

20 army, corps and divisional commanders killed or captured and two wounded (Rommel and Hausser); 2 C-in-Cs dismissed (von Rundstedt and von Kluge); 40 divisions wiped out or severely mauled; 3,000 guns destroyed or captured, over 1,000 tanks destroyed. The German's actual losses in men he could not accurately estimate, but reckoned on up to 300,000, though admitting the Germans had allowed 200,000.

It was of course the end of the road for Rommel, Montgomery's old adversary. Militarily he was spent, having had his day as a battlefield general and facing a charge of complicity in the anti-Hitler bomb plot he chose suicide, the option permitted him by his accusers; von Kluge had preceded him by the same exit.

But the Allies had paid a considerable price for their great victory: by 11 August the British and Canadians had lost 68,000 men in killed, wounded and missing, the Americans 102,000. It is as well for the younger generation to bear such huge sacrifices in mind and of course they make subsequent squabbles such as the Falklands campaign appear the tiny affairs they were by comparison.

General Montgomery was promoted Field Marshal with effect from 1 September, but by prior agreement lost overall command of the Allied ground forces to General Eisenhower. From then on Monty became even more irked as he believed American home politics were affecting operations in Europe.

It was the end of a four-year German occupation of France and Belgium as the battered remnants of the German Army and Waffen-SS divisions streamed back into Holland and Germany, closely followed by the Allied armies. Once again Sepp Dietrich narrowly escaped capture by the British when handing over his command post to General Eberbach who went into the bag.

CHAPTER FOURTEEN

By early September 1944 the Allied armies stood poised on the Reich borders and there were many who imagined the war to be practically over. The Wehrmacht appeared to have been almost beaten into submission, while at home the civilian population had suffered greatly from air raids. Belief in Hitler's promised 'wonder weapons' was fading fast, the V1 had come and gone without appreciable effect, and although V2 rockets were being launched against England and the Belgian port of Antwerp these too did not seem to be causing the Allies great concern.

Behind his back the 70-year-old dismissed Field Marshal Gerd von Rundstedt referred to his Fuehrer as 'that Corporal', yet when Hitler beckoned he came. For his part, Hitler despised von Rundstedt and his kind of archetypal, Prussian representative of an élite military aristocracy he could never aspire to. Yet ever since he had been discharged from the military hospital in 1918 after being gassed at the front Hitler had been behoven to the army. It was there that he had found his home, the wanderer and misfit of the pre-1914 years had finally discovered his true niche, for in his own words he was in great joy when war came in August 1914 and had hurried to enlist. And when peace had broken out four years later he felt desolate. It was the Army however that continued to mother him, to give him a home and employment as one of its spies, even after he had donned civilian clothes again. And when he went into politics he of course needed them to back his hand, and this need was to continue throughout his twelve-year reign, for his 'second army' was never of a size to supplant the regular Army.

Hitler's attitude to von Rundstedt, as with others of his higher military staff, was a curious one, for on the one hand he perhaps envied them, as well as despising them. They could never become his true friends, like perhaps his Party comrades from the old days. On various occasions, commencing in the Russian campaign, he began the habit of dismissing his generals for their misdemeanours, often reinstating them later. If a general failed him in the field or flatly refused to agree then the Supreme *Feldherr* threw him out, this often following violent debate. But with von Rundstedt, perhaps because of his age and position there had been no rage or bullying, merely a polite dismissal notice. But by 1 September Hitler had recalled him. The whole business was cynical, for as much as Hitler disliked the man he was a realist and knew he needed the old man, the Fuehrer could adapt himself to any new situation given time, using guile and charm to enlist help when needed. And he needed von Rundstedt to act as a figurehead and inspirer of his armies as he planned a counter-offensive. In Germany's grave hour of need the dictator turned to the senior Field Marshal.

The meeting between the two might have been an uncomfortable one, yet Hitler was able to rise above any embarrassment in welcoming the much older man back into the fold. For his part von Rundstedt is said to have sat stiffly and erectly, his wrinkled face unmoving as his Fuehrer waxed eloquently in his usual manner when inspired:

'We shall yet master fate!' Hitler declared, attempting through his great will power to draw the old soldier into his own web of belief. Although impaired in some ways and obviously not in the best of health following the attempt on his life and years of quack medicine from his physician Dr Morell, Hitler could still emote strongly his ideas and hopes and cast a spell on most. Not that there was any question of von Rundstedt wavering, he was perhaps still influenced by the *Fahneneid*, the ancient soldier's oath passed down from the Teutonic knights which bound warriors to their Emperor. And he had served willingly as head of the Military Court of Honour to expel those fellow officers implicated in the attempted *coup d'etat* in July.

But first the front had to be stabilized: with the Allies on its western borders the Nazi government made a drastic comb-out of its remaining manpower to create Himmler's Home Army and a Replacement Army. Minister Goebbels produced scores of thousands from the home front, while many more were simply transferred from existing branches of the Wehrmacht no longer considered essential — the Navy and various branches of the Luftwaffe. A few weeks of hurried training produced new defence divisions.

Of immediate concern and surprise to the Allies was the recovery made at the front in the meantime. Hitler had called on his 'fire brigade' general, Field Marshal Model, the master of the defensive battle, a rough mannered soldier who complained bitterly of the great shortage of everything among his army in the west. Nevertheless, he stabilized the situation, placing Paul Hausser in command of Army Group G.

The Allies were in any case in trouble: Montgomery had not put in the necessary effort to take the vital port of Antwerp, those harbours further west were too far off or ruined by German demolitions. The supply problem exacerbated existing friction between Montgomery and his American allies; overall field command had now reverted to General Eisenhower by prior agreement.

The now well known controversy concerning Montgomery's advocacy of the 'single thrust' policy as against Eisenhower's broad front approach exemplified the lack of a really solid, definitive military doctrine in the Allied set-up. By now, the Americans had the preponderance of strength in the field and political wallop as Churchill and others had foreseen, the involvement of America to rescue Britain from the clutches of Hitler entailed the end of the Empire and the reduction of Britain to second status. This was reflected in the field so that despite his total lack of experience Eisenhower was placed in overall command of the huge Allied conglomerate of armies which did not sit well with Montgomery. Curiously, there is certain evidence that 'Ike' had some grasp of field command, with more commonsense than say, his General Bradley, but he was walking the usual political tightrope, trying to allow any of his generals to run with the ball as they may.

The fight for supplies and status among the generals finally ended in Monty's uncharacteristically bold thrust at Arnhem, a little Dutch town that had already seen SS troops in action in May 1940 and was now to be their unwilling host once more. An élite British unit, the 1st Airborne, was committed against what was believed to be weak German forces, in reality a recuperating 9th SS Hohenstaufen who with adequate armour were well able to defeat the British division in a battle that has gone down in history as both a disaster and a hallmark of British military tenacity. Bad planning resulted in the death and injury of thousands of very highly trained British paratroops and gliderborne infantry, plus the deaths of thousands of Dutch civilians and much suffering for the population later.

As to the conduct of the SS troops, every account shows that they had fought a 'clean' battle and showed much respect and chivalry towards their opponents, though there was at least one prisoner shot later. The SS units suffered many casualties as they tried to winkle out the red berets from among the houses and gardens of the town. Germans later referred to the intensity of the fighting while the British felt sure that victory would have been theirs in straight infantry combat; in other words, it was only the presence of the German armour that defeated them. And it was to Arnhem that Karl-Heinz Roberts was despatched to render his services during the interrogation of prisoners. Roberts had been loaned to the Waffen-SS command in the battle of Normandy, provided with a little Kubelwagen in order to flit from one sector to another, sometimes having difficulty owing to the state of the roads and air attacks. This is what he had to say of some prisoners he met:

'They were always in a state of some depression, but when they came to the outcome of the war they were in no doubt at all that they would win, and this sentiment I privately agreed with. I remember one tough Canadian Sergeant who smoked the Players cigarette I gave him. He was very talkative about the war and his family back home. The prisoners were on the one hand sad to lose their mates but glad to have survived, so it was often the case that they poured out their hearts to a friendly listener, and in this we learned a great deal.

'I was always given a little room with something to drink and cigarettes and perhaps even some food in order to assist in creating a friendly atmosphere. In one place I even had a radio with music playing. It all helped. I had never had training in such work, all that was needed was my knowledge of English and in some cases French when we had French Canadian prisoners. These men were *very tough and quite fearsome-looking and not at all co-operative and we learnt nothing from them.*

'I remember one little English Tommy, an ordinary chap whose home was in London. All he wanted, he said, was to get home again. He was worried about his family in the "buzz bomb business" (ie the V1 doodlebugs). He had plenty to grumble about he said, poor food, rotten officers who did not know what they were doing, the generals sitting in safety at the rear, and Monty, who he said was a "silly prick", so we found him rather amusing.

'In the American sector I had a lot of work and we had quite a few prisoners who were badly shaken but in fair shape I think. The paras were the best of the bunch and said nothing, but most of the doughboys talked quite a lot of home, wherever it was, and the general state of things in the war, how they missed their "moms" and "gals" and all the comforts of home etc. When I asked them what they thought of the Germans as soldiers they said "Oh — the best! They're too good for us but they'll lose because we've got plenty of everything and that's what counts!" This was all very true.

'Then the big retreat began and we returned to Brussels and then Germany, but I had apparently done well in my new job and was sent to the 9th Hohenstaufen who I had not actually been allocated to in France. I was sent to them just as things grew quieter in September, just as the Arnhem affair was ending, and there I took part in the interrogation of British paras and glider troops captured in that battle.

'I saw some of the terrible effects of war on a nice little Dutch town which was ruined. I also know that certain reprisals were taken afterwards against the population who had already suffered enough.

'The prisoners were absolutely exhausted, starving, thirsty, and in many cases wounded, and I felt very sympathetic to them. They had fought like demons and done all that could be expected of them and were only defeated by bad planning. I remember one Sergeant who was a cockney I think. He was very cheerful but downhearted that his hopes had been dashed and so many of his comrades lost. I asked him what he wanted most out of the war, and he said to go home in one piece.

'Another fellow who I believe was a glider pilot was a very good type and quite well educated. I asked him how he had come to join the airborne and he said from choice. It was the élite force of the British Army and he was proud to have been at Arnhem. I asked him if he thought his officers had let him down and he said no, not really. "We all make mistakes, including the Germans. What about Crete?"

'Then there was a tall officer with a leg wound who looked as if he had been through hell and I asked him how he saw the war. He said simply: "Nearly over, thank God!" I said to him, what do you think of the troops you've fought here? And he said, "They're good, but we would have beaten them easily if they'd been without armoured support".

'He was taken away grinning.

'Then there was a man who I believe had led the dash to the bridge at Arnhem. He had very little to say, but I could see the disappointment on his

face. There were a lot of private soldiers who had endured much. All in all they were in good heart and we respected them greatly. In fact I would say they were as good as our own best troops but it was a shame they were wasted.'

Hans Postenberg entered the Waffen-SS in June 1944:

'After my training I was sent to the 12th SS Hitlerjugend which had retreated across France back to Germany and was a mere shadow of its former self. Most of the lads had been killed or wounded in Normandy and those that survived were very shaken and in no state for further combat without a good rest and of course reinforcements.

'We were sent to a rest area where a lot more lads were awaited, but the Hitler Youth division never got back its old strength again. We received new tanks , mostly Panthers, and began training as a unit, but this was curtailed by the great battles which took place as the Allies broke into Germany. And then came the Ardennes offensive.'

Again the old Field Marshal played his part, however much he may have disagreed with Hitler's Ardennes plan, issuing an Order of the Day on 15 December:

'Soldiers of the Westfront! Your great hour has arrived. Large attacking armies have started against the Anglo-Americans. I do not have to tell you anything more than that. You feel it yourselves. WE GAMBLE EVERYTHING! You carry with you the holy obligation to give everything to achieve things beyond human possibilities for our Fatherland and our Fuehrer!'

For Operation Watch on the Rhine the Germans had managed to assemble three armies, one of these the 6th SS Panzer Army under Sepp Dietrich who once again had his old 1st SS Leibstandarte under his command, plus the reconstituted Das Reich, 9th SS Hohenstaufen and Hitler Youth Division. To Dietrich, Hitler entrusted the most important task of the offensive — the drive to Antwerp.

Postenberg:

'We were told that a very great blow would be struck at the Allies which would split them and throw them back into the sea. Our barrage was very fierce and we all went forward in vehicles through the ice and snow. Then we had to advance on foot and I saw many dead Amis and prisoners. Then we had our first battle.

'I was with a group of my comrades and we came under fire from two sides as we ran towards a crossroads. But when we took cover our officers urged us on, and as we leapt up the Ami machine-guns hit us and several of our friends were hit. But we raced on and were able to take the enemy in the flank and silence them. This was a short, hard fight and a loss for us as we lost so many

friends. But its was no time to lament for our big Tiger tanks came along and we had to climb aboard them and move on again. This was a very, very slow process as the traffic was all jammed up along the narrow roads and it was impossible to move across the countryside. But at last we made progress and covered a few miles and saw many American POWs. Then we had another fight and had to leap off the tanks and race forwards under fire. More men fell and we went into cover. Our officer was one of those killed so our NCO took his place and urged us forward again.

'We ran through a little wood with a good deal of noise going on and lost sight of the other units on our flanks as well as our tanks which had become engaged with some Ami artillery and pak guns. Our job was to deal with these guns, and this we were able to do by outflanking them, although the American infantry were in the area. Then the Americans withdrew and we advanced again. By then it was evening and dark and cold so we waited near a road for some hot food, but when it finally reached us it was cold. We had hardly started eating when an enemy artillery barrage came down and we dived for cover. Everything was lost in the undergrowth and we ran back the way we had come, taking shelter in some American dug-outs where we were very glad to find some food and cigarettes.

'The barrage lasted a long time, but then our NCOs took us out of the comfortable dug-outs and we advanced again. The respite had enabled the Amis to get more organized and although our tanks had advanced we had lost contact with them, as a result some of them were ambushed and lost. Others were stranded for lack of fuel, so all in all the grand offensive was not going too well. But we had not given up and advanced again to the road where we met some of our tanks and a general forward move began again. The American artillery was very active all this time and hindered us, but it was really the nature of the country which caused us problems as the tanks were confined to the one road of advance and this alone hindered us too as we were supposed to protect them from enemy infantry attack. The Ami Shermans proved no real threat as they too had been unable to deploy, the only way they could hurt our Tigers was from the flank.

'We had a few more days of this, with our being freezing and hungry much of the time and confused fighting during which we advanced very slowly as the ground was frozen over and we were always under artillery fire. Then the worst happened, the weather suddenly improved which meant that the tremendous Allied air power could take a hand in the battle again. This was a new experience for us newcomers and a very bad one. The jabos gave us no rest, we were chased everywhere and only safe when we could find some cover in woods, but even there we were at the mercy from airbursts from artillery, so we were caught between this and the fighter-bombers. We were forced to retreat in bad conditions until at last we were back where we had started from in Germany, having lost heavily, especially in tanks and other vehicles which were mostly lost in the Ardennes.'

Owing to the shortage of NCOs Hans Postenberg was promoted to Corporal and placed in charge of a group of new recruits, even though his own experience was limited to a few days of combat in the abortive offensive. By the collapse of May 1945 he comments, 'the Hitler Youth division had almost ceased to exist.'

The interpreter Karl-Heinz Roberts also had a part to play in the Ardennes affair:

'I had to assist in the interrogation of American prisoners. This was of no great importance really, but interesting. All prisoners captured in battle are gullible and open to suggestions and good treatment and often talk a good deal. But since the offensive failed it was all futile.

'I did however get a good insight into American mentality at the time.'

Karl-Heinz Roberts' war ended where it had begun, in Berlin, but he managed to escape the doomed city with some other troops before the Russian ring closed on them.

As the histories show, the efforts of the three German armies in the last great German offensive proved futile, and the clues to their failure are shown in the testimony of Hans Postenberg. It is interesting that having succeeded against the French in the Ardennes in 1940 they should have failed so completely by the same route in 1944. The only German group to achieve any promising success was the SS unit commanded by Joachim Peiper, the officer held responsible for the 'Malmedy Massacre'.

The gamble had cost the Germans around 120,000 casualties, plus 600 tanks and assault guns, while the loss of 1,600 planes spelt the end of the Luftwaffe.

It was Hitler's determination to give Dietrich's SS the glory of crossing the river Meuse and pushing on to Antwerp that resulted as the German Army Commander had predicted in a complete unbalancing of the whole offensive, for the SS divisions did not have the strength to carry out the tasks given them. As Dietrich said later:

'All I had to do was cross the river, capture Brussels, and then go on to take the port of Antwerp. The snow was waist deep and there wasn't room to deploy four tanks abreast, let alone six armoured divisions. It didn't get light until eight and was dark again at four, and my tanks can't fight at night. And all this at Christmas time.'

One German Army general, von Mellenthin, emphasized that no large-scale offensive including massed armour has any hope of success against an enemy in complete control of the air.

But, initially, the Germans had their successes, and there were those who gloried in it. An SS panzer Lieutenant recorded how his unit of 60 Panthers had pulled up beside a road and waited until a large American truck convoy filled with infantrymen had come along and run into their trap.

'A concentrated fire from 60 guns and 130 machine-guns, it was a glorious bloodbath, vengeance for our destroyed homeland. The snow must turn red with American blood.'

After this failure the 6th SS Panzer Army was refitted and switched to the Eastern Front to try and stem the Soviet advance in Hungary, the Wiking and Totenkopf divisions having had no success. Oddly, the greatest danger to the Reich at this time lay on the river Oder, yet Hitler chose to send his best troops to the Danube valley, which at the time added to fears in the West that Hitler was about to set up some kind of Wagnerian last stand in a redoubt, probably in the Alps.

Dietrich's troops went into the attack early in March 1945 and at first achieved some success, but were then pushed back on the defensive, and by the end of the month were in retreat. When the Leibstandarte fell back into Vienna Dietrich received the following signal from Hitler's HQ:

'The Fuehrer believes that the troops have not fought as the situation demanded, and orders that the SS divisions Adolf Hitler, Das Reich, Totenkopf and Hohenstaufen be stripped of their armbands.'

Dietrich threw the radio message down in anger, exclaiming to his fellow officers: 'There's your reward for all you've done over the past five years.' According to some reports, he then returned all his own decorations to his Fuehrer, the man to whom he had once been a 'constant companion' and vowed that he would rather shoot himself than carry out the order received.

Dietrich's SS forces and those of the Wehrmacht were driven back into Austria where, following Hitler's suicide at the end of April 1945 they surrendered to the Americans. Following the cease-fire of 8 May all those Waffen-SS troops in a position to surrendered to the Western Allies, while those still alive in the east were captured by the Soviet forces and like many thousands of Wehrmacht personnel were marched away to the USSR. Most would never see their homeland again, for the Soviets looked on all these prisoners virtually as criminals, the 'fascist beasts' who had invaded and ruined the homeland; only about 5,000 returned to Germany over the next years.

Many of the western volunteers had not survived, while men like Jutte Olafsen dared not return home for fear of persecution, some that did were arrested, tried and according to some reports, executed. But as the years passed the scars of war healed and amnesties were granted. When Jutte finally reached his home he found his father had died, but his mother and sister awaited him.

CHAPTER FIFTEEN

What then, will be the verdict of history on the 'Second Army' of Hitler? It is perhaps too early to say. Like that New Model Army of the great Protector in England in the 17th Century, the SS army was born of revolution, not quite as violent as in the civil kind perhaps, but certainly as a result of internal stresses. But, unlike that of Cromwell, this force earned its reputation largely on foreign fields of combat, and from the purely military point of view this proved to be second to none. However, the hopes of its creators to establish some great and honourable tradition of combat excellence were considerably dashed through the actions of a few. If it were not for this stigma, the short-lived army of the field SS might have gone down in history as a unique force in the annals of soldiering.

There are those who professionally or otherwise have been able to assess the Waffen-SS purely from the military stand-point, and in doing so they have always reported highly of them. One leading military writer gave it as his considered opinion that in equal combat the German soldier always came out on top; whenever an Allied force was met by a German one of equal strength it lost, or was at least stalled. Even the briefest consideration of the major war fronts lends weight to this belief, even though one can find exceptions as with most rules; individual actions where extraordinary bravery or some other circumstances helped win the day. In North Africa, Russia, and on the Western Front of 1944-45 the Allies won their campaigns by an overwhelming preponderance of men and material, including of course the 'human wave' tactics of the Soviets and the complete air mastery of the Allies.

Against this one finds a general public perception almost totally moulded by the surface skimming tactics of the popular media which ever since the 1930s have been presenting an image of black-suited SS thugs who invariably have been chosen by the mass entertainment industry to play the baddies of 'the Gestapo' in many a novelish piece of pap. The revelations of the SS-run concentration camps inevitably set the seal on this reputation and dragged into the general stigma the combat troops of the field SS, their own tragedy to be associated with a brutal and murderous regime and unfortunately aided by some within their own ranks who only added fuel to the accusations hurled at them. The myth of a murder force with a sinister reputation has after so many decades of propaganda become too firmly embedded to be dislodged by a work such as this.

But before examining how the Waffen-SS managed to acquire such a contribution to its own detriment let us hear what some of its creators have had to say over post-war years.

Paul Hausser:

'Looking back I see an experiment in the military field which held great promise. We succeeded in building a new kind of force which proved itself in many a battle. The morality of war is quite a different question. Our ideas were I believe ahead of their time, but not irrelevant in later years.

'It was always the case that no atrocities committed by the Soviets ever reached the light of day, we were always it seemed the culprits. This was something we could never get over, and a penalty borne for having been born of a political movement, even though to all intents and purposes we had relieved ourselves of the burden when war came. We should of course have rid ourselves of our gangster masters, but this never happened. It was never the case that we would have died for Hitler and his gang, although it must be said that their worst excesses were by and large unknown to us until it was too late, this because we tried to cut ourselves off from those people and remain embedded in the military side of things.

'We were certainly patriotic enough to die for Germany as would most soldiers for their country — but not for the Nazi Party, whatever oaths were taken. By 1943 the value of the Fuehrerprinzip *had worn a little and we had lost our faith in the leader of our nation. We were however honour bound to defend our country with all the strength and courage we could muster. The fact that we as military men had taken part in the brutal rape of other nations did not sit well with us. It had been rather different in the previous war, but the Nazi dreams of conquest entwined us in unnecessary wars we could not escape.*

'It may be said that we of all people were in a position to remove Hitler: this may be so in hindsight, and certainly I have no doubt that if we had known in 1943-44 of the true nature of things with regard to the concentration camps etc we would have taken action. Our troops allegiance was first and foremost to its commanders and to each other, not to Hitler. The oaths taken soon became quite meaningless, it is a matter of regret that ignorance and preoccupation with the battles prevented us from taking action.'

Felix Steiner:

'A great deal of misunderstanding and misconception came about as to the role of SS troops, and I refer not only to other countries but at home . . . it is true that oaths were taken, but this could not be avoided, as far as we the commanders were concerned the whole idea was to perform well militarily — I will say to perform superbly, for we had not gone to all that trouble just to be seen as another bunch of men in steel helmets. We had an ambition to fulfil.

'But the notion that our Waffen-SS troops were political troops is just not borne out by the facts. In no way were we prepared to see our creation used for the suppression of the German people, whatever Himmler and his gang might

have had. We used Himmler to gain our own ends, and once we had done this as far as we could we left him behind.

'*Himmler had certain forces of the Waffen-SS at his disposal for various duties, but they were not, despite anything said to the contrary, members of the regular combat formations of our force; they were police units, even though they wore Waffen-SS uniform. There were for example units of the Totenkopf division used in the Warsaw ghetto which was yet another blot on our reputation brought about by the Nazis, but they were not combat troops of the Waffen-SS, even though they were trained soldiers. It is a fact that the actions of a minority, sometimes under Waffen-SS command or Himmler's led to terrible incidents which were inexcusable. Yet, as has been recorded elsewhere it is not always possible to conduct war on the basis of chivalrous action, savagery does occur at times in the heat of the moment and it would be an unwise man who suggested that this only occurred on the German side. War is an ugly business, but since it remains part of the human make-up in this world at least some restraints should remain in place, at least as far as possible.*

'*In the Waffen-SS there were very few elements given to falling apart in battle, this occurred admittedly in certain isolated and well documented incidents, and it is hard to dissociate German troops from some of them. But, seen overall the self-discipline displayed by the Waffen-SS forces throughout the war was excellent. I will in no way excuse excesses, but I do infer that we were under great difficulties in some directions, circumstances came about which put us as commanders in an invidious position. I refer largely to the great use of civilians as* franc-tireurs *in the East which was contrary to the Geneva Convention. It was I suspect never fully realized by our opponents in the West just how savage was the war behind the lines in that region.*

'*Yes, we were the invaders, but as far as possible our operations under our political masters were carried out in a normal, conventional manner, we advanced and they retreated, but behind us in due course sprang up these growing groups who were armed and encouraged from Moscow. This was all very well from their point of view, but in a war when military operations are being conducted it is impossible for an army to allow the rear areas to be continually disrupted by guerilla activity. Our security was at stake, and in this I refer to the lives and safety of every individual in the German forces, women included.*

'*It was impossible to conduct such a war on strictly humane lines, for these people had no knowledge of such matters, they knew nothing of the Geneva Convention which in many cases the Soviet Union ignored as suited them. Our Finnish brothers-in-arms had had experience of the Soviets in 1939 and their inhumanity, but that kind of tale did not erupt into the overseas press then or later*. The Finns knew very well that they were up against a barbaric horde who in some instances used disgusting practices whenever it suited them.*

---

*Mention of Russian atrocities in Finland appeared in at least one hardback book in Britain in the 1950s. One practice was to tie a prisoner to a tree in the depths of winter and pour a bucket of water over him; the results can be imagined.

However, for our part we entered into that campaign without any preconceived notions of Nazi fanatics regarding "sub-humans" as some in the West seem to think, but as soldiers only interested in the job we were trained to do. It soon became evident to us through admittedly isolated incidents that there were those either in the Russian forces or secret police who had no scruples whatever about committing atrocities against our regular soldiers if they captured them. I will not say that this was general practice, it was not, but it did happen and such tales spread like wildfire. But, apart from the disgusting activities of the SD Einsatzgruppen and a few others who acted under specific orders from Himmler and Co. there was never any organized murder or atrocities under Waffen-SS command.

'At no time were the Waffen-SS forces engaged in anti-partisan operations, they were always at the front or refitting or resting, it was quite beneath our code to indulge in that kind of warfare. I will not say that we could not have done. We ourselves were at the mercy of such incursions behind our lines which caused us difficulties and, if serious, interfered with our operations at the front. It was inevitable that when savagery by the bandits occurred that more second line formations were brought in to try to deal with them, with varying degrees of success. These men were not of the highest calibre, but even so they were fairly normal individuals in the main who were confronted with atrocities and reacted accordingly. It really was a savage war and I thank God that our own men never became involved in that side of it.

'The indictment by the Allies at Nuremberg of the Waffen-SS as a whole as a "criminal organization" was a complete travesty of the facts. While it was right and proper that certain individuals who had overstepped the mark should be tried it was ludicrous to suggest that the many thousands of ordinary lads who had simply fought as soldiers at the front could be criminals. It soon became obvious to us after 1945 that various sets of double standards and conveniences were being applied by the victorious Allies, and this did nothing to alleviate the bitterness of the Waffen-SS men.

'Then there was the absurdity of having Soviet judges on a panel trying Germans for war crimes etc when even bigger criminals were in their own government. Then as we expected, the Allies (in the West) began to see the true face of Soviet communism, so they turned to the ex-Waffen-SS men and those who had served in the Wehrmacht and police for assistance in building up a new "front" against Stalin. So the whole process was put into reverse, embarrassing as it was for them, so that it became necessary to keep it rather secret. This process was well known to the Reds in the eastern part of my country, but they too had made sure that those of my kind who had gone over to them received due reward. The communists were never in the least bit choosy in matters of convenience.

'Finally, let it be said that many thousands of young Germans fought and died for their country, not because of some fanatical, blind faith in their Fuehrer, but simply through patriotism. It would be naive of me to suggest that they did not in many cases have faith in Hitler, they did, but then they did not know "the nature of the beast". By the time they learnt it was too late.'

In fact, the communists in East Germany actually published a 'blue book' containing voluminous names of ex-Wehrmacht, police and SS men serving in the West German administration and armed forces etc, in English, and distributed it in the West.

'The difficulty of always being tied to Hitler cost us dear', Steiner concludes, 'we should have cut loose from him at an early stage, but this proved impossible. It did not take us long to see which way the wind was blowing once war came. We were in a sense quite exposed, for while we had got our wish and produced the kind of army we wanted, we failed to be free of the political end of things, and this continued right to the end. I believe we were rather naive in imagining we could create the kind of army we had in mind without shaking off the Hitler gang.'

Naive indeed in view of the fact that all armies are usually subject to the whims of their political masters and often seen as an extension of their will.

Georg Keppler has stated that he and his colleagues really did see their creation as a 'new model army', but were never really allowed to develop their theories because of the way events turned out:

'In other words, we had no control over our destinies, just like other soldiers. We were forced into the Eastern war which was the greatest disaster in German history. It was there that so many terrible deeds occurred which had nothing to do with our concepts of war in general. I realize that when military men practise their profession lives are lost as a result, but the act of war is part of human make-up and brings out both the worst and best in men. In our case we had an ideal in mind and to a considerable extent succeeded in realizing it, but it was marred by a few whose deeds were reprehensible, and this has sullied our name ever since.'

These men were unable to alter the past, but felt it their duty to try and put the record straight. Too late, men like Keppler and his fellow generals of the Waffen-SS saw that they had so tried to bury their heads in the conduct of the war that they would be held partly responsible for excesses in all parts, for the top culprits were dead or missing. Keppler admits that:

'Of course we knew there were unpleasant things going on behind the front in more than one direction. I refer to both the anti-partisan operations and the activities of Himmler's police. However, we did not know of the extermination squads'.

Keppler has said that he first heard of them during 1944, after they had retreated from Soviet territory:

'By then it was too late and we were heavily engaged in trying to keep the Russians out of Germany'.

183

Theodor Eicke, referred to in some works as 'the butcher' was known to Keppler and his fellows as an ex-army artilleryman who proved to be a good commander in the field and with whom they had no problems whatsoever. The allegations that Eicke 'butchered' his men, involving them in needless casualties was Keppler claims, 'unfounded'.

It has long been the habit of historians, authors and others who have published works of this nature to point the finger of accusation at the Germans while ignoring misdemeanours of their own side. This is not only unjust, it does not serve the cause of truth which is all too often not only the first casualty in war but in peace also. The question of atrocities in World War II and who did what to whom is not at all the simple matter usually presented, especially by those who have chosen to prepare books on the SS. It is not a commendable attitude to be selective in this thing, any more than it would be to ignore the misdeeds of the Waffen-SS. It is a simple matter to simply refer to published works and copy out the usual list of known atrocities and include them in a military history. By this means a small collection of 'cases' has long been established and presented over and over again, they reside too in the files of every newspaper office and are so well known that one hardly needs to refer to the text to reel off the indictments.

However, to be fair, most attention to the Waffen-SS force has been given by a 'past generation' of writers who took up their pens at a time when ignorance was perhaps justified, since then certain new facts have come to light, and some will point out that the few 'misdemeanours' listed by Allied forces in these pages do not alter the fact of SS atrocities. Of course they do not, the attempt here is only to try and show there is a broader truth.

But on another tack, one otherwise worthy historian has admitted the high level of combat achievement on the part of the Waffen-SS, but insists that because of their Nazi fanaticism they were ever ready to commit crimes. This is very debateable.

Certainly Germans and many in the younger generations who view the bombing of Dresden for example as a British and American atrocity*, but then to widen the parameters of just what comprises an 'atrocity' would mean including the American fire raids on Japanese towns and cities and of course the use of atomic bombs on Nagasaki and Hiroshima. Still in the air war, there is a good case for condemning American bombing policy including the 'defoliation' programme in Vietnam. But then extending this debate to that war inevitably means including the actions of American infantry, the so-called 'Mai Lai Massacre' and other operations in which the only purpose seems to have been to achieve an adequate 'body count'. It will be remembered that pressure on the military not by them resulted in the presentation of a solitary junior officer as scapegoat and this man escaped virtually scot-free.

---

*Although it has been stated that war industries existed in that city.

The list is virtually endless, for wherever humans on this planet conduct war, sooner or later acts are committed that go beyond the 'accepted norms' of aggressive behaviour. It was not new in World War II, not new in the 1930s or before when for example the French were imposing their colonial rule in various parts of the Middle East such as in Syria and Algeria etc. Torture and the taking of hostages for subsequent execution was all part of the usual life and descended to its lowest perhaps in the Algerian war of liberation or whatever the protagonists preferred to call it after World War II. The French also of course had their 'problems' in what used to be known as French Indo-China, later called Vietnam, which culminated in an ignominious defeat for them as it did later for the Americans.

The colonial powers may have introduced certain 'civilizing' benefits and administrations to their territories, but these were always enforced by military power. The few thousand British civil servants who apparently ruled 300 million Indians were adequately backed up by soldiers, not all that many, but then the Indian continent was sorely divided within itself by sectarian differences so the occupiers seldom had any real problems. Yet, our enemy in World War II was able to produce evidence of British atrocities in that land as part of their usual barrage of propaganda, with much the same programme in hand in Britain, both sides of course having little regard for facts or truth but only in influencing their own and other peoples. The Nazis of course had long seized on the fact of the British having invented the 'concentration camp', and although some mention of these hell holes in South Africa has appeared on television, the mass of Britons has no knowledge of them whatever, whereas the terrible deeds of the Germans and of course the SS are part of our normal education. For those still ignorant of the facts, in their fight against the Dutch Boer settlers in the so-called Boer War around the start of the century the British Command found it expedient to round up the Boer families into camps, presumably in an attempt to deny the male fighters use of the farms for food supplies. But since most of the men were away in fighting units those locked away in these enclosures were mostly women and children and it is alleged that thousands died of starvation and neglect. The facts are not common knowledge nor too readily available for the simple reason that such dark events are swept under the carpet and hardly the subject taught in our schools. Exactly the same tenets have applied with regard to certain events in World War II, as the victors we were in a position to arraign those we decided guilty while making sure that all mention of Allied misdemeanours remained concealed. As one writer has pointed out, decades later it is time for the British to confront certain truths and myths and see themselves in a clearer light; we cannot hope to advance as human beings if we continue to apply hypocrisy and double standards. There have been encouraging signs in more recent years that this process has begun, this work is hopefully a contribution in this direction.

The misdeeds of a few in the Waffen-SS have to be seen in the overall context of the war and the foregoing, and here we can narrow down the debate to acts committed on land which go beyond the norms of even 'combat' behaviour. And before examining the well-established atrocities of the Waffen-SS a few deeds which have come to the notice of this author over the years and if these are any indication, then they were more widespread. It should be mentioned that having been brought up in a society where humanity and 'fair play' received such emphasis even in wartime (the old adage of the British regarding war as a game of cricket) I for one naturally believed all the bad things said of our enemy while assuming that our own side were as white as white if not whiter. Unfortunately, this wild belief has been rather dissipated with education.

A well-known researcher once told me of a German pilot shot down in the Battle of Britain being killed by an irate farmer with a pitchfork, thus (if it is true) pre-dating the attacking on Allied aircrew by German civilians (as *terrorflieger*) at a later date. Beatings of prisoners occurred, Luftwaffe airmen were sometimes given a pounding rather than a cup of tea and a cigarette. One Me109 pilot who descended by parachute near Chadwell Heath in the Greater London area on approximately 30 August 1940 was set upon by Local Defence Volunteers who minutes before had been trying to kill one or both parachutists coming down after a dogfight — the other happened to be an RAF pilot but the shooting by the LDVs on that occasion missed the mark.

Another German pilot who landed by parachute in the Thames mud during the worst air raid of May 10 1941 was also given a beating by Home Guards before being taken away. It is naive to suppose that civilians and half-civilians who have been bombed and seen their homes destroyed and kith and kin killed and injured will feel too charitable to the perpetrators should they land in their midst. It is alleged (in print) that one German aircrewman landing by parachute in Wapping in London's East End in the Blitz was killed by an irate mob.

These tales of course never appeared in British accounts of that period but had to wait several decades before becoming known. No matter what stories were told during the war, somehow they did not spread far and certainly never appeared in print if they were detrimental to our 'cause'. It is the same with the land war, ugly facts would never be permitted to surface in any publication and thus become common knowledge — if they concerned one's own side. It was a very different matter concerning our enemy, for Hitler realized long before he came to power the great potential of propaganda and how the Allies and especially the British with their jingoistic, all-powerful press barons were able to win over their nation and much of the world into believing the very worst of the hated Hun, the baby-killing *Boche* became one of the biggest myths of the 'Great War' and the German Army became hated for its alleged atrocities in France and Belgium. Yet, when the two sides were on a few extraordinary occasions able to actually meet between the trenches, the combat troops who suffered the most, they at once became pals and could only be induced to return to their holes to restart the killing match by their officers, especially the British.

The British government enlisted the help of the press barons in World War I and over the next four years these gentlemen made sure that the public were fed a constant diet of hate-filled propaganda that often bordered on the ludicrous, but was certainly a great influence over the masses. People in modern society inevitably tend to believe most if not all they are told by their national media, and in earlier days of the two world wars folk were less cynical than they are today. Our enemy the Huns were a bunch of cowardly, stupid, murdering thieves under an insane war-mongering 'Kaiser Bill'. Very much the same procedure was adopted in World War II that had apparently worked very well in the earlier conflict. Churchill started the ball rolling at an early stage when, as First Lord of the Admiralty, he stipulated that German submarines must be referred to as 'U-boats', for this was a stigma first applied in the earlier war when the dastardly, cowardly Huns had played unfair by lurking beneath the seas to prey on our merchant shipping. Naturally, the Royal Navy possessed 'submarines' — not 'U-boats'.

Again, when these same Huns had meekly surrendered their Grand Fleet of warships at Scapa Flow and to preserve their honour eventually scuttled every one of them the chagrin of the British was expressed through its press which screamed its hate-filled headlines of Boche treachery and cowardice. And as some German sailors escaped their sinking ships in lifeboats they were fired on by British machine-guns; the graves of those killed can still be seen in the Orkneys. Were the culprits prosecuted?

The catalogue of German 'frightfulness' was resumed long before World War II when the bombing of Guernica took place by Heinkels during the Spanish Civil War. Atrocities of the aerial kind were not new by any means, though German aircrews who struck non-military targets in Britain during the 'Great War' without intent could hardly be termed criminals, though such acts were a godsend to the peers of propaganda. The Guernica affair, although dwarfed by far worse incidents and raids has rumbled on ever since, though a reasonable explanation of how it happened has appeared in print. Similarly, the bombing of Rotterdam is also dredged up as an example of Nazi beastliness, though after very many years the original claim of '30,000 dead' has been reduced to some 800, even though one supposedly reputable historian writing in a popular part-history in the 1970s saw fit to quote the original figure. Once again, there does not seem to have been any intention on the part of the Germans to strike at civilians, but can the same be said of Allied air attacks later? Certainly not.

Attacks on field hospitals and ships clearly marked with the red cross seem to have been carried out by both sides in the later war, it is impossible to prove whether intentional or not, though there were those who saw wounded men as capable of recovery and returning to battle later, thus making them 'legitimate' targets.

On the battlefield it was customary for troops on both sides to shoot down tank crews attempting to escape from their disabled and often blazing vehicles. It was usually more convenient and far less dangerous to kill them than try to rescue them.

The business of 'convenience' in the heat of battle has often meant the wiping out of enemy soldiers, sometimes wounded and trying to surrender, and it is seen and argued as explainable, understandable, and even permissible, depending entirely on circumstances. The risking of one's own life and limb under fire to take prisoners or assist wounded can be seen as unjustifiable, and in the first case the enemy troops must be disabled to prevent their escape.

Inconvenience or hatred was apparently sometimes applied by Allied soldiers to enemy soldiers on occasion, and examples have come to light in recent years of apparent atrocities (for surely they were that just as much as were the better known examples from the German side). These stories emerge via the not widely read memoirs of ex-soldiers, usually ex-privates or NCOs who recount every incident they can recall. Such as one American whose buddy was detailed to escort two German prisoners to the rear. The soldier returned to his friends within a very few minutes, grinning, obviously not having gone further than the nearest hillock or copse. No questions were asked, but the two Germans certainly never arrived at the American POW cage. Then there is another example published in an excellent book on the Caen battle of summer 1944: a German prisoner had got rather tipsy on liquor, though whether he was in this state before capture or has celebrated his escape from the war with a British Tommy is not clear. The happy German is being wheeled along in a wheelbarrow by a cheerful Briton carrying a Sten gun. The Jerry is taken out of sight, there is a short burst of fire and the Tommy returns alone, grinning. Again, no questions are asked, it is just one of those things.

There were always circumstances arising in battlefield situations where it seemed far more expedient to get rid of prisoners than perhaps escort them through a danger zone with shells and bullets flying. After all, if a soldier trained to kill is 'on heat' in the sense of having killed already and in a trigger-happy state because of the stress and the well roused killer instinct, then to squeeze the trigger once more and get rid of the inconvenience is the simplest thing. Quite often, there is no one else around, and two or more bodies will not even be noticed in an area littered with corpses.

The military, being trained to kill and hardened in battle, do not become shocked by such things as do civilians later when stories are published of what seem to be horrible events in war. Soldiers become inured to death and killing which is why what are perhaps atrocities to civilians are overlooked or not taken too seriously by military men. In other words, 'so they're dead. So what? We'll all probably be sooner or later, so why worry? In any case, they're only Jerries (or krauts, or British Tommies etc)'. Killing becomes quite automatic with trained infantrymen, in a battle they do not have time for niceties, or questions or enquiries, and they see no need. They may or may not hate the enemy, it is irrelevant really, he is there so he must be stopped or killed — it's them or us, and the soldier will do all he can from sheer self-preservation to make sure he survives and not the enemy.

There is also the attitude taken by some in battle, that today's prisoner may conceivably become tomorrow's opponent once again, prisoners can escape to fight again if opportunity presents itself. 'Lets get rid of them now and be done with it, after all, we'll only have to guard them and feed them etc. They'll only be a damn nuisance'. This is sometimes the attitude of men in war.

Every nation has its share of hard men and sadists, a glance through any daily newspaper confirms that and it would be a foolish person who tries to pretend that there are no men in British society incapable of committing atrocities in war.

So then, to the specific question of the conduct of Waffen-SS soldiers at war and the small crop of well known almost anecdotal accounts of their crimes which our ex-enemies are as well aware of as we are. The whole point of this exercise is to see these events in their proper context, terrible though they were, they were far from being isolated examples of wrong-doing in war and not only possible in a German army dominated by Hitler.

The first known incident occurred during the Polish campaign when men of the SS Leibstandarte are said to have employed Jewish prisoners to build or repair a bridge. When the work was completed the prisoners were herded into a synagogue and shot. It is said that perhaps fifty or more Jews were involved and it has been assumed that they were civilians. A subsequent enquiry by the German Army command got nowhere as it was stalled off by Himmler, so assumedly the guilty men went unpunished. Details are lacking concerning this event, perhaps because it did not involve Allied troops. Obviously, it reflected on the 'honour' of the SS that seems to have been so heavily subscribed to by officers during training, and certainly on Sepp Dietrich. Georg Keppler said when this incident was mentioned that he doubted if Dietrich would have been too perturbed over the death of a few Jews. This must certainly be true, Dietrich would not be likely to have turned on any of his own men for such a crime, but one is bound to ask, was this the same 'premier' élite SS unit we have heard so much about through the testimony of others?

Next, incidents occurred during the battle of France in May 1940, all within a few days, and these are those that are fairly well documented up to a point, but certainly the whole story is not known and is never likely to be because of the loss or non-existence of key documents and the demise of witnesses.

On 28 May, over 80 British troops, mostly of the Warwickshire Regiment, were killed by men of the same SS Leibstandarte who then moved on in the general advance. The bodies of the dead Tommies were discovered by German Army officers.

An enquiry put in hand by the German Army command got nowhere, for the SS regiment had long gone and no accounting by their commander Sepp Dietrich seems to have taken place. What was the reason for this slaughter of prisoners who by their wounds had obviously been killed after capture? The only explanation seems to lie in a previous action in which the Leibstandarte had suffered casualties in a fierce battle with British troops in which Sepp Dietrich was almost killed and forced to take cover in a ditch for some hours. The SS men, perhaps stricken by the loss of comrades in the battle and fearing their commander lost, sought revenge in the killing of prisoners after the British were forced to retreat. Dietrich made no known mention of this event, not surprisingly. The next known illegal killings by that unit was that of villagers in northern Italy later in the war.

But the day before the killings at Wormhoudt by the LAH the Totenkopf had themselves been in action against prisoners, 95 men of the Norfolk Regiment being killed near the village of Le Cornet Malo. Once again it was left to men of the German Army to discover the bodies and institute enquiries which as usual led nowhere. These incidents remained generally unknown in Britain, only being publicly disclosed after the war through the published revelations of a solitary surviving British private, and known as the 'Le Paradis Massacre'. By then the responsible Waffen-SS officer had been tracked down, tried and hanged by the British. It has been said that in his defence this officer, Fritz Knoechlein, excused the action on the grounds of British war crimes. Of him Sepp Deitrich later said that he was 'never allowed to advance himself', but this is not apparently the case, for one historian has mentioned that Knoechlein had gone on to gain the rank of Lt-Colonel, win the Knight's Cross and command a foreign volunteer unit in the East.

But is there in fact more to these ugly incidents than has come to light, and if so is anything to be gained by dredging into them? Is it not high time to forgive and forget? Some will say yes, others will take a contrary view. The fact is that the 'Nazis' will not go away, the term crops up all too frequently and the misdeeds of the SS and by implication the Waffen-SS are dragged up at every possible opportunity, the gentlemen of the press are incorrigible in combing over certain essential subjects and will never let go.

By the same token, there are those in Germany who will not cease in reminding the outside world and particularly the British of the ruination of German cities by Allied bombing in the war, while conveniently forgetting that *that* kind of warfare was inaugurated by the Luftwaffe.

To the true historian there can only be one object in view, and that is to try and establish facts and report them objectively, even if the subject is ugly, emotive and controversial. Against this one must set the view that there are times when no useful purpose can be served; in this particular exercise the aim is only to strike a fair balance.

How seriously can we take the old allegation made by long-passed Waffen-SS men that the British 'played dirty' in France in 1940? Were such men simply trying to excuse the misdeeds of their own men?

For example, General Eicke, in command of Totenkopf, a field commander for the first time with most of his troops new to combat, asserted to his superiors in the field (ie — the German Army command), that his men had only committed reprisals because of the dirty tricks played on them in battle by the British. One of these was alleged to have been the displaying of a captured swastika flag by enemy soldiers on one of their positions, which led to the SS troops believing it was in their hands. But once these SS soldiers passed by that point they were mown down from behind by the Tommies and suffered heavy casualties. Then there was the charge that the British used dum-dum bullets, contrary to the Geneva Convention. Such a bullet does not penetrate the body but squashes on impact, making a ghastly wound that is harder to treat. Although one writer has quoted a case of a Britisher in the period loading his pistol with such ammunition, any suggestion that the Tommies used such bullets as a whole is ludicrous.

The only certain facts to emerge of the above is that the Totenkopf SS did suffer heavily, but then so did other German units when they came up against the hard-fighting British. Secondly of course, this SS unit or part of it did execute British prisoners in those days. It would appear that some of the unit's men, specifically Fritz Knoechlein, lost their sense of discipline and decency, went to pieces and took revenge on helpless prisoners. Counter allegations did not save such men from execution or prison if and when they were arrested after the war by the British; but then, as mentioned elsewhere, as soon as the Cold War against the Soviets hotted up a little the process of soft-pedalling the SS began.

It was also in May 1940 however that another incident appears to have taken place in which the roles were reversed: that is to say, German prisoners of the British were shot. It is probably impossible to find any mention of this in available historical records, for the simple reason that the British can be as deceitful as anyone and self-protective in the right circumstances. The incident appears to have first come to light via an exaggerated and inaccurate account published in the 1980s which alleged that a certain British infantry unit fell to pieces in France and shot a considerable number of SS prisoners.

In fact, the number of Germans killed was probably between twenty and thirty, and not SS, their captors a similar number of Tommies who under fire and without officers panicked, perhaps three or four led by an NCO shooting down their prisoners before running away from the German tanks and infantry on their heels. When British survivors reached England after Dunkirk word assumedly leaked out concerning the incident, for the men of the unit were interrogated by a Major who assured them his only interest was to establish the truth for the record and that no charges would be brought. And nor were they, witnesses told what they had seen and were instructed to forget about it. No court was convened and the matter swept under the carpet. Today it is virtually impossible to trace any surviving Britishers who know or will admit of such an incident. Even if there are some, they will never speak of it for the simple reason of pride in their regiment and seeing no point in it.

Why did those three or four Tommies crack? For the same reason that any other humans can under great stress. Worn out, starving, in panic and fear after suffering several devastating Stuka attacks. It is perfectly possible that the dive bombers destroyed the evidence, churning up the little wood with their bombs so that when an armoured car platoon of Rommel's 7th Panzer Division arrived to round up British stragglers they found a mess including torn-up bodies among the tree debris and cratered earth. In other words, there was nothing to show the German troops that any atrocity had taken place. It can be said therefore that there is no apparent connection between the above episode and the incidents involving SS troops elsewhere. Word of these is said to have spread through the ranks of the German Army soldiers in France and 'did not sit well with us' as one ex-Sergeant-Major put it, though adding that in his war experience such incidents were rare and the SS troops were always very tough in battle and put on a very good show.

However, despite the trial and execution of the SS officer on the spot after the war, the affair in France involving the SS will not go away. For a recent book has highlighted a further aspect that has been rumbling for years and this was recently the subject of a two-page spread in a national newspaper. Fifty-three years on there are those including the paper concerned who feel that one Wilhelm Mohnke should be put on trial since he is alleged to be the commander responsible for issuing 'no prisoners' orders not only in 1940 but later also, specifically concerning the killing of Canadian prisoners in Normandy and Americans later. Why Mohnke was not prosecuted sooner is not clear but to try an old man of eighty-five so long after the event seems pointless, and the business holds further ramifications. For this man is said to have pointed the finger at the British as instigating SS actions in 1940, quoting the incident described above which he most certainly picked up from the book *Dunkirk**.

It is worth mentioning that the newspaper concerned recently ran a sustained campaign against the pursuing of any enquiry into alleged British atrocities in the Falklands, pulling in as many big guns as possible to support it, military men, politicians and legal experts in the main agreeing that there was no point in pursuing the affair for a variety of reasons, including this kind of comment – Let's forgive and forget – it's time to build bridges – what is the point? – these things happen in war –

---

*Nicholas Harman, Hodder and Stoughton 1980.

it's too long after the event, etc etc. Only a very small minority thought the investigation should go ahead. The originator of the tale was downgraded as of unwholesome character.

While not afraid to criticize the government, the newspaper concerned has always been known as right wing, so far as such labels are accurate. It has in common with other popular newspapers seized on the SS as good copy on every conceivable occasion with an eye – as one journalist has put it – to the story rather than the truth. To follow up its assembling of heavyweight comments given by big names, it switched to allegations of atrocities carried out by the Argentinians themselves. Plainly, the paper found any enquiry into the conduct of some British troops undesirable. The other fact which emerged quite clearly was the opinion of many people consulted – that ugly events occur on the battlefield, it is to be expected, and that it was not the military men stirring up muddy waters.

To turn back to the Second World War and the Far East. Such was the state of outrage among all Americans following the attack on Pearl Harbor that it became customary when, on rare occasions Japanese soldiers were deprived of their weapons through wounding and trying to surrender, for them to be mercilessly cut down by American troops. One Marine has said that he and his buddies looked on them as 'vermin' and acted accordingly; in other words rather as the SS troops have been alleged to view the Eastern Europeans; the *untermensch* or sub-humans of the Slav races. And an ex-Major of Scottish origin who once commanded a unit of the Indian Army described to this author an incident during his war career. He and his men had come across a Japanese bivouac one evening and found all the enemy soldiers asleep; I asked him what happened next, and he replied:

'Oh, we killed them all.'

There had been no question of taking prisoners, it just was not convenient.

So now back to the Western Theatre where in the high summer of 1944 the cream of the Canadian infantrymen who had volunteered to join the great crusade against Hitler finally got their long-felt wish to fight in the little lanes and green fields of Normandy. It was here that the next atrocity involving Waffen-SS troops occurred.

The event in question did not really come to light until after the war when court proceedings were briefly and inadequately reported in the British press in a post-war era when the war-weary people of Britain and certainly Germany had perhaps heard enough. The later appearance of a book by two Canadian survivors did not of course reach the wider public or gain any great publicity. Their story was basically of the fighting against the SS troops and of being taken prisoner, of being lined up and searched in the normal fashion. But then came some small altercation as possessions were removed, then a burst of fire as not one but a whole row of Canadians were shot down by their SS captors. As was normal in such cases the surviving commanding officer was later held responsible, his men having been killed or vanished, so in this case it was Kurt Meyer, and his later testimony makes interesting reading and once more brings up the point, who was the guilty party who first killed prisoners?

'Very soon after we arrived in the battle zone an ugly incident occurred which sparked off a worse one. In the great heat of battle and what was to follow it was impossible to hold an inquest, and in any case most if not all the participants were killed, wounded, or went missing in a short time. I was not present in the particular sector where the incidents took place, but it was my division, so after the war I was held responsible and tried for the affair. I will give the facts as far as I was able to ascertain them at the time.

'A group of Canadian infantry had managed to infiltrate our positions and were opposed by some of our own young grenadiers who were then captured. But in a further bout of intense fighting somehow the SS lads were shot, it is impossible to say exactly how it came about, I cannot swear that they were killed to prevent their escape in the heat of battle or otherwise. But when found later by our own troops who recaptured the area in a counter attack they were without weapons and seemed to have died in dubious circumstances; the notion was soon rife that they had been murdered.

'It is a fact that blood runs very hot in battle and savagery occurs. Just after that a line-up of largely Canadian prisoners were gunned down by the very man who had found the bodies of his comrades. This was inexcusable, and as soon as I heard of the incident I ordered the officer on the spot to report to me. But the men were then involved in a very heavy bombing raid and ground action and nothing came of it. The officer concerned was, I believe, killed and things reduced to such chaos by the bombing that it became futile to try and get to the bottom of it. There were hundreds of bodies, both ours and Allied, some killed in the bombing, others in the incoming artillery barrages. I'm afraid that in such circumstances it is not time to be setting up courts of enquiry.

'The men who shot down the Allied prisoners were in a great state of upset because they felt that some of their comrades had been murdered by the Canadians, that was the general position. Terrible things happen in war, but that kind of action by either side is inexcusable. But I must say that the strain put on those young boys was enormous, far, far worse than anything on the Eastern Front. It is and was a wonder to me that they did not crack up and run away sooner. As it was, they largely kept their nerve and stayed to the last. Not one of these units deserted their posts, they fought and died or were captured where they were, or else were finally allowed to withdraw. Withdrawal would have been the sensible option. I had no desire to see all those young men killed, but we were under higher orders to hold at all costs and I'm afraid the price paid was very high. However, I believe we made the enemy pay heavily for every yard gained, it certainly cost them a great number of lives and countless tanks.'

There is little more to be said on that affair, it was just one more tragedy of war.

The final incident is the well-known 'Malmedy Massacre' which occurred during the Battle of the Bulge, the German offensive in the Ardennes in December 1944 when a number of American prisoners were allegedly murdered by SS troops.

Since the figure of those Americans killed seems to vary between accounts and was the subject of much dispute later, let us say that at least 71 prisoners were shot down by men belonging to the battlegroup commanded by Obersturmbannfuehrer (Jochen) Peiper, although Peiper himself was not at the scene. Of this fact there is no doubt, the murdered Americans were later found by other American troops and the facts had swiftly been relayed up the command chain through at least one American survivor who related how the SS men used pistols and machine-guns to shoot into a large batch of prisoners drawn up in eight tight rows, not to await transport to take them to the rear, but for execution. The Germans then went among the dead, dying and wounded to finish them off with pistols and showed calm enjoyment in the process. Before the shooting began one SS man had pressed his pistol to the heads of several Americans, telling them that they were to be shot in revenge for the bombing of German cities.

Before the war ended the Americans had already begun the hunt for those guilty, and in May 1946 Sepp Dietrich (as General commanding 6th SS Panzer Army), Fritz Kraemer, CO of the 1st SS Panzerkorps, and Joachim Peiper as CO of the battlegroup concerned, were arraigned, charged with giving an illegal order regarding the treatment of prisoners, it being made known that a 'no prisoners' order had emanated from the higher levels. Some American witnesses related that their own experience of Peiper had been that he treated his prisoners honourably, in other words the massacre at Malmedy was not his doing.

The case seemed fairly straightforward, the officers named plus 69 of their subordinates were found guilty, but then the problems began. For a start it was admitted by the prosecution that illegal methods had been used to extract confessions, hoods, false witnesses and mock trials. It would later be alleged in even more sensational and somewhat theatrical proceedings that the SS men had suffered other indignities including beatings. Nevertheless, all 73 defendants were found guilty, 43 being sentenced to death, including Peiper; Sepp Deitrich and 21 others were sentenced to life imprisonment, with other terms ranging from 10 to 20 years being given to the rest of the defendants, and the men were transferred to Landsberg, the very prison where Hitler had served his short term in 1924.

Then began by the usual American process of justice a series of 'review boards' at the end of which the convictions of 13 of the accused were disallowed and the death sentences reduced from 43 to 13. These reviews had taken three years, by which time the Cold War had begun and views began to change. Then the chief American defending officer returned to civilian life to begin a campaign on behalf of the accused and managed to enlist the support of the soon to become notorious Senator Joseph McCarthy who used the case to promote his own career and in further hearings in Germany turned the whole episode into a farce. By the end of this charade there were those who began to wonder if the murders had ever occurred, so denigrated were the witnesses and so prolific the charges of ill treatment of the SS defendants who must have been bemused by the way the Americans conducted justice. It began to look as if the accusers were the men on trial, and the liberated German press and religious leaders were sufficiently stirred to join in the campaign for clemency. The pressure on the commander of the US Occupation Zone General Clay became so great that by 1955 Sepp Dietrich was paroled, and by Christmas 1956 the last of the Landsberg prisoners Joachim Peiper was released. Of course, as is now known, by that time it had become expedient to win support against the Soviets among former enemies.

But it was not the end for some who felt justice had been thwarted. Peiper, clearly guiltless in the Ardennes affair, had perhaps unwisely gone to live in France with his family, and twenty years later his location was disclosed by the communist paper *L'Humanite*. The way to his home in a French village was inscribed in large white letters painted on the roadway, and two weeks later he and his home were destroyed by fire bombs. His executioners were probably Frenchmen who saw his men as implicated in the shooting of civilians in December 1944.

By a strange twist, the German government now took a hand and prosecuted Sepp Dietrich for the shooting of Ernst Roehm in June 1934, perhaps feeling the need to show their new allies that former Nazis would be confronted if suspected of crimes. Dietrich was sentenced to eighteen months' imprisonment at Munich on 14 May 1957.

The whole question of Waffen-SS culpability in war crimes overrides their performance as combat troops in the Second World War. This writer once became briefly embroiled by mail with a certain Member of Parliament of famous name; the man concerned informing me by the use of a term then current that the German force could in no way be seen as a 'Brigade of Guards' on the British model. Still in politics in the same role and unlikely to ever rise further, the fellow is given to emotional opinions, but given his position one would be very naive indeed to expect other than the customary stance in such a matter. One sees that the position of many in this thing has long been coloured by highly publicized facts concerning 'the SS' as a whole, sincerely held by decent people whose only knowledge of the subject has come via the popular media.

The assertion that the Waffen-SS should in no way be compared with the Brigade of Guards is an interesting one, and presumably meant to imply that the German force had neither the soldierly honour nor parade ground smartness of the British Guards. This is a theme not to be taken up at length here, but some points need to be mentioned.

To the public in general the British Foot Guards are those units who parade in red tunics and bearskins, most notably in ceremonials honouring the monarch and their own long traditions. In this respect they put on a public show as 'asphalt soldiers' which far overrides the fact of their combat capabilities. Obviously, a comparison with the short-lived Waffen-SS is hardly appropriate, the German force did not exist long enough to establish any traditions on the British model whose story stretches back centuries. There are only two possible points of comparison – that of parade ground turnout and combat ability. The 'show' rig of the SS troops may not have been too colourful, but the turnout and discipline of the original SS formations was of a high order. It has to be said that in one respect at least in some continental honour guard and élite formations such as the German, Polish and Russian the use of soldiers of uniform height creates a better impression, to ignore this basic invites a ragged appearance. As regards the other facet, no one with any knowledge of the German SS troops can deny that their battlefield record in combat was excellent.

But it would be difficult to absolve any army completely of all charges in, for example, the treatment of prisoners of war, and what once seemed a simple subject regarding the Second World War is rather more complicated. It would be an error to lay the blame for atrocities towards POWs at the door of the Waffen-SS alone. Judging by published accounts the care of enemy prisoners taken by the German Army sometimes fell short of reasonable, varying from failure to provide sustenance to beatings and shooting. German captors on the battlefield seemed to vary widely in their attitudes from compassion to indifference, while on rare occasions orders were passed down from on high inviting ill treatment or worse. Neither were the German land forces the only part of the Wehrmacht guilty of questionable conduct, as the following extract from orders issued by Admiral Carls before the battle of the Barents Sea 30 December 1944 seems to indicate:

'There is to be no time wasted in rescuing enemy crews. It would be of value only to take a few captains and other prisoners with a view to interrogation. The rescue of enemy survivors by enemy forces is not desirable."

As a British historian commented, the implications of the last sentence can hardly be misinterpreted.

But brutality breeds brutality. American soldiers, incensed perhaps by the discovery of wagon-loads of dead Jews and others (who had probably died of typhus), wiped out a considerable batch of combat SS troops trying to surrender near Dachau.

Then, according to published evidence, there was an organized attempt to starve German prisoners in some American compounds on the continent, this one assumes as reprisal for concentration camp horrors.

Also late in the war, probably September 1944, a mixed bag of German POWs were crammed into a small lion cage in Antwerp Zoo, a picture taken and eventually published. But another photograph taken later and unpublished shows the same men dead.

In the same war many Allied soldiers regarded their own military policemen as 'bastards', and not simply because of their maintenance of petty regulations and discipline. Things went on in British and American military penal establishments that were a blot and disgrace to these armies of democracy. In Britain conscientious objectors (COs) were subjected to degrading and brutal treatment at the hands of regimental police:

> '. . . the treatment given to us in the last few days. It is quite on the level of what you can read of in Nazi concentration camps – and it happened here in England.'

Veterans of that war and others may recall tales of brutality in British Army detention camps (the 'glasshouse'): the staff were given *carte blanche* and running for hours without pause in full kit was a standard punishment until one inmate collapsed and died which led to 'questions in the House' and restrictions on such practices. In a worse case a tubercular soldier unable to fulfil drill was kicked to death by two MPs who escaped punishment by posting to a unit overseas. The film called *The Hill* was based on fact, the notorious British detention centre in Egypt.

More recently, the British media have seized on alleged atrocities by British troops in Malaya in the 'Emergency' of 1948 onward, and the killing of Argentine POWs in the Falklands in 1982.

The time when it seemed expedient to point the finger of accusation in one direction only has long gone.

APPENDIX ONE

Ranks of the Waffen-SS

SS	Nearest Allied equivalent
SS-Schutze, Kanonier, Pionier	Private, Rifleman, Gunner, Sapper
SS-Oberschutze	Private 1st class
SS-Sturmmann	Lance Corporal
SS-Rottenfuehrer	Corporal
SS-Unterscharfuehrer	Sergeant (junior grade)
SS-Scharfuehrer	Sergeant
SS-Oberscharfuehrer	Staff Sergeant
SS-Hauptscharfuehrer	Sergeant-Major
SS-Sturmscharfuehrer	Warrant Officer
SS-Standartenjunker	Officer Cadet (Junior Ensign)
SS-Standartenoberjunker	Officer Cadet (Ensign)
SS-Untersturmfuehrer	2nd Lieutenant
SS-Obersturmfuehrer	Lieutenant
SS-Hauptsturmfuehrer	Captain
SS-Sturmbannfuehrer	Major
SS-Obersturmbannfuehrer	Lt-Colonel
SS-Standartenfuehrer	Colonel
SS-Oberfuehrer	Brigadier
SS-Brigadefuehrer & Generalmajor der Waffen-SS	Major-General
SS-Gruppenfuehrer & Generalleutnant der Waffen-SS	Lt-General
SS-Obergruppenfuehrer & General der Waffen-SS	General
SS-Oberstgruppenfuehrer & Generaloberst der Waffen-SS	Field Marshall (actually Colonel-General in the German Army)

Note: The original SS equivalent of the German Army Private of Schutze was SS-Mann, both became Grenadier later.

APPENDIX TWO

SS Unit Organisation

These names accorded to units formed the basis for the rank table, although in the Waffen-SS normal Army usage was adhered to (ie, company, regiment, corps etc). The term 'Trupp' was later dropped.

Schar	squad	Scharfuehrer	squad leader
Trupp	section	Truppfuehrer	section leader
Sturm	company	Sturmfuehrer	company commander
Sturmbann	battalion	Sturmbannfuehrer	battalion commander
Standarte	regiment	Standartenfuehrer	regimental commander
Brigade	brigade	Brigadefuehrer	brigade commander
Gruppe	division	Gruppenfuehrer	divisional commander
Obergruppe	corps	Obergruppenfuehrer	corps commander

The number of men actually comprising SS units was flexible: thus a squad could consist of 8–10 men, a Sturm (company) from 70–120, three Sturme making a Sturmbann (battalion) numbering 250–600 men while a Standarte or regiment could number from 1–4000 troops. Though establishments were set up for and within the component parts of an SS division the actual numbers varied very considerably from one to another, for no known reason, and were not fixed as in other armies. For example, while the Leibstandarte could number around 10,000 men, Das Reich boasted almost twice as many.

APPENDIX THREE

Component Organisation of the Waffen-SS

It would take many pages to provide a full description of the many parts of the total body of the Waffen-SS Army as it developed after 1936 and through the war, and the changing situation, especially after Germany's reverses began, had its effect on the structure, with less emphasis on some aspects and more on the purely combat side.

The following list of departments will suffice to indicate the scope of the Waffen-SS organisation:

Office for Political Education: responsible for propaganda and political education through verbal instruction and publications.

Office for Germanic Training: this body was set up to provide pre-military indoctrination training for foreign volunteers before they entered actual Waffen-SS units to begin recruit instruction. Whether it continued to function throughout the period to 1945 is unknown.

Office for Physical Training: this office was charged with responsibility for all physical training within the SS, this accomplished through instructors trained at the Central School. The department also promoted similar programmes for the Hitler Youth and foreign volunteers.

Higher Vocational Schools: these operated under the Education and Physical Training branch and promoted higher technical and educational instruction in a range of subjects including business and agriculture. This branch had originated in the non-military SS and its Waffen-SS equivalent was said to provide a lower standard of instruction and as the war progressed probably ceased to function.

Training Branch: this department was centred in the Kommandoamt of the Waffen-SS, the headquarters, and directed all military training throughout the force and was split into different sections, each dealing with a particular type of specialisation.

Inspectorates: ten of these units existed to supervise the various specialist facets of military training (artillery, panzer, etc).

Training Group: this department was responsible for the training of all officers and NCOs which it carried out through the Officer Training Office controlling the Junkerschulen (Bad Tolz, Braunschweig etc) and a separate office to oversee NCO training schools.

Special Service Schools: these provided specialised training courses such as those for mountain troops, cavalry, panzers, panzer-grenadiers but not infantry; the courses were further split into those for officers, NCOs and men, and Applicants and Reserve officers. The schools had their own demonstration units attached to them.

There were training schools for NCOs and separate courses for NCOs and these too were split into 'professional' and reserve sections. The schools trained both German and 'Germanic' personnel.

Specialist Training Schools: these were distinct from the 'Waffen' courses as they catered for technical personnel in driving, ordnance, motor transport and supply and even riding, veterinary, medical, radio etc.

Reinforcement Branch: this controlled all postings and movements of personnel from the Waffen-SS HQ in Berlin and was responsible for the sending into training of specialists as well as the normal movement of men to field units.

Main Department of Personnel: controlled the officer corps of the Waffen-SS, but all matters concerning the selection and sending into training of officers was handled by the Main Operational department, in other words, the former acted as a mere records office.

APPENDIX FOUR

Types of Waffen-SS Formation

During World War II the Waffen-SS developed formations along lines similar to the German Army but with some differences and often in greater strength.

SS Infantry Divisions: included a flak battalion and supply battalion.

SS Mountain Divisions: included a tank or assault gun company as well as the flak and supply echelons, its infantry components larger than those in the Army.

SS Panzer-Grenadier Divisions: were almost identical to those in the army but stronger, having 15 not 14 companies plus a machine-gun (flak), flak and supply battalions.

SS Panzer Divisions: contained panzer-grenadier infantry companies numbering 15 as against only 10 in German Army panzer divisions, its tank regiment was larger and it also contained: an engineer battalion, two bridging columns, plus flak, supply and a Werfer (mortar of multi-barrelled mortar) battalion.

SS Cavalry Divisions: consisted of two brigades plus a weak artillery unit and usual supporting echelons. Also included was a tank recovery and repair unit.

The salient points of the above are: every SS field division contained its own flak and supply battalions, every mountain division contained either a tank or an assault gun unit; every SS panzer division had its own Werfer projectile battalion. All were stronger in infantry than Army divisions.

In addition, the SS fielded specialist units such as:

Intelligence and Sabotage units: the SS-Jagdverbaende was formed in October 1944 from the old SS-Jagerbataillone and units of the Army's Brandenburg division taking over all functions of sabotage and secret operations such as those led by Otto Skorzeny and often including men of the SS-Fallschirmjager battalions.

Miscellaneous units: these comprised the SS-Wachbataillone or Guard Battalions used to protect important installations. SS-Bahnschutz were railway protection police and similar to the SS-Postschutz who took over security of the Reich mail services, a subsidiary being the SS motor service which provided transport for the above, all these personnel in the main simply former members of the State Postal Service under SS supervision.

SS-Begleitkommando: Hitler's personal escort battalion.

Begleitbattaillon Reichsfuehrer SS: Himmler's escort battalion.

SS-Flakabteiling B: the SS flak unit at Berchtesgaden.

SS-Standarte Kurt Eggers: the parent unit for the SS war correspondent teams, platoons which were attached to every SS division.

SS-Wehrgeologenbataillon: the SS military geologists, sometimes attached in small sized units to SS divisions as required.

SS-Rontgensturmbann: the SS X-ray battalion which supervised all SS X-ray technicians.

APPENDIX FIVE

SS Unit Nomenclature

The great expansion of the SS to include non-Reich German personnel meant the introduction of special distinguishing prefixes for the newly formed units. At first, the foreign volunteers emanated from north-western Europe and were considered sufficiently 'Germanic' to be called 'Freiwilligen SS units, hence 'Freiwilligen-Panzer-Grenadier-Division Nordland' or even 'Freiwilligen-Kavallerie-Division'. But once divisions and regiments containing a preponderance of non-Germanic personnel were formed such as those from the Slav states the term 'Waffen' was substituted, hence: 'Waffen-Grenadier-Division-SS', and into this category came some which proved notorious for various reasons, usually for unreliability or atrocities. Into the former came the 'Croatian No 1' 'Handschar', at first termed the Bosnian Herzegovinian Division which included both Moslems and Christians in its ranks and many from the Croatian National Army who were forced into the unit when recruitment lagged. In the other category fell the 'Russian No 1', so-called 'Waffen-Grenadier-Division' composed entirely of Russians including the notorious Kaminski Brigade and Sturmbrigade Rona who were responsible for the worst atrocities in Russia against partisans before being sent into Warsaw to combat the ghetto uprising in 1944. Their conduct was so bad that Kaminski and his officers were arrested, tried and shot by the Waffen-SS courts and the remains of the under-strength division dismissed from the SS roll and put into the army of the well-known Russian turncoat General Vlassov. The general and many of his men who survived the war were caught by the Soviets and executed as traitors.

APPENDIX SIX

SS Divisions

The expansion of the Waffen-SS in 1939–40 inaugurated a numbering system, but should not be taken to indicate that each and every unit listed was of divisional size. The final formations were either never activated or remained very small in size.

1 SS Panzer Division Leibstandarte Adolf Hitler
2 SS Panzer Division Das Reich
3 SS Panzer Division Totenkopf
4 SS Polizei Panzer-Grenadier Division
5 SS Panzer Division Wiking
6 SS Gebirgs (Mountain) Division Nord
7 SS Freiwilligen Gebirgs Division Prinz Eugen
8 SS Kavallerie Division Florian Geyer
9 SS Panzer Division Hohenstaufen
10 SS Panzer Division Frundsberg
11 SS Freiwillingen Panzer-Grenadier Division Nordland
12 SS Panzer Division Hitlerjugend
13 Waffen-Gebirgs Division SS Handschar
14 Waffen-Grenadier Division SS (Galizische Nr 1)
15 Waffen-Grenadier Division SS (Lettische Nr 1)
16 SS Panzer-Grenadier Division Reichsführer SS
17 SS Panzer-Grenadier Division Götz von Berlichingen
18 SS Freiwilligen Panzer-Grenadier Division Horst Wessel
19 Waffen-Grenadier Division SS (Lettische Nr 2)
20 Waffen-Grenadier Division SS (Estnische Nr 1)
21 Waffen-Gebirgs Division SS Skanderbeg (Albanische Nr 1)
22 Freiwilligen Kavallerie Division SS Maria Theresa
23 SS Freiwilligen Panzer-Grenadier Brigade Nederland (This designation formerly of the Waffen-Gebirgs Division Kama-Kroat Nr 2)
24 Waffen-Gebirgs (Karstjäger scouts) Division SS (Austrian-Italian)
25 Waffen-Grenadier Division SS Hunyadi (Ungar Nr 1)
26 Waffen-Grenadier Division SS (Ungar Nr 2)
27 SS Freiwilligen Grenadier Division Langemarck
28 SS Freiwilligen Grenadier Division Wallonien

29 Waffen-Grenadier Division SS (Russische Nr 1) (This designation given to the Italian Waffen-Grenadier Division Nr 1 in April 1945)
30 Waffen-Grenadier Division SS (Russische Nr 2)
31 SS Freiwilligen Panzer-Grenadier Division Böhmen-Mahren (Bohemia-Moravia)*
32 SS Panzer-Grenadier Division 30 Januar
33 Waffen-Kavallerie Division SS (Ungar Nr 3)
    (Wiped out in Budapest early 1945, the number given to the French SS Waffen-Grenadier Division Charlemagne Franz Nr 1)
34 Freiwilligen Grenadier Division Landstorm Nederland
35 SS Polizei Grenadier Division
36 Waffen-Grenadier Division SS (formerly the Dirlewanger Penal Brigade)
37 SS Freiwilligen Kavallerie Division Lützow
38 SS Panzer-Grenadier Division Nibelungen**

Miscellaneous Units:
1st Kosaken Kavallerie Division SS
2nd Kosaken Kavallerie Division SS
Ostturkischer Waffenverband SS
Kaukasischer Waffenverband SS
Serbisches SS Freiwilligenkorps
Indische Freiwilligenlegion SS
British Freecorps SS
Waffen Grenadierregiment SS (Ruman Nr 1)
Waffen Grenadierregiment SS (Ruman Nr 2)
Waffen Grenadierregiment SS Bulgar Nr 1)
Norwegisches SS Ski-Jäger Bataillon
Finnisches Freiwilligen Bataillon SS

Some one dozen further SS formations were designated and their names assigned but they were never activated.

---

* Formed from Waffen-SS training school personnel
** Formed from staff and students from the Bad Tolz school

APPENDIX SEVEN

Two Views

'The units of the Waffen-SS distinguished themselves by their discipline and excellent morale in battle, they proved themselves in attack and defence. Their *esprit de corps* resulted in outstandingly good comradeship . . . all members co-operated to produce a very high standard of reliability. Their readiness for action was excellent, and their superhuman bravery was also acknowledged by the enemy.

'The fact that Himmler to a certain extent had other objectives with the Waffen-SS is not the soldiers' fault.

'The fighting units of the army remember them and their fallen or wounded comrades gratefully, they were also fighting for Germany, they too suffered and were killed for it.'

Panzer General Hasso von Manteuffel

'The SS soldiers lived in another world . . . far removed from the ideologial verbiage of the SS . . . they won for themselves a select place in the annals of war.'

'The Waffen-SS became the personification of military steadfastness and aggressiveness . . . but has gone down as the most controversial troops ever . . . incriminated with many a war crime . . . at the end of the war the soldiers of the Waffen-SS found themselves divested of their military ranks, put on the same level with the murder forces of the SS guards of the concentration camps . . . (yet) they had become independent and free of all Black Corps mysticism.'

'The forcing on the Waffen-SS of camp guards and other lesser grade material, whose training contrasted with the military spirit, led to the force becoming susceptible to many kinds of inhuman warfare. It was the bitter struggle in Russia which finally broke the 'umbilical cord' connecting the Waffen-SS to Himmler.

'The emblems and memories of fallen comrades were woven to a mystical ribbon which kept the Waffen-SS together — to the bitter end.'

Heinz Hohne

BIBLIOGRAPHY

Beadle, Alan. *Waffen-SS Divisional Insignia*. Key Publications, 1971.

Carell, Paul. *Hitler's War on Russia*. George Harrap, 1964.

Degrelle, Leon. *Die Verlorene Legion*. Veritas Verlag, 1952.

Gilbert, Adrian . *Waffen-SS (An Illustrated History)*. Brompton, 1989.

Harman, Nicholas. *Dunkirk: The Necessary Myth*. Coronet, 1980.

Hastings, Max. *Das Reich*. Michael Joseph, 1981.

Hausser, Paul. *Waffen-SS im Einsatz*. Plesse Verlag, 1957.

Heiden, Konrad. *Der Fuehrer – Hitler's Rise to Power*. Gollanz, 1944.

Littlejohn, David. *The Patriotic Traitors*. Heinemann, 1972.

Meyer, Kurt. *Grenadiere*. Schild Verlag, 1957.

MacDonald, Charles B. *The Battle of the Bulge*. Weidenfeld & Nicholson, 1984.

Odegard-Dieter. *Foreign Volunteers of Hitler's Germany*. OD Enterprises, 1968.

Quarrie, Bruce. *Hitler's Teutonic Knights*. Patrick Stephens, 1986.

Quarrie, Bruce. *Waffen-SS in Russia*. Patrick Stephens, 1978.

Reider, Frederick. *The Order of the SS*. Foulsham, 1975.

Shirer, Wm. L. *The Rise & Fall of the Third Reich*. Secker & Warburg, 1959.

Stahl, Peter. *Die Waffen-SS*. Die Wehrmacht, 1969.

Stein, George H. *The Waffen-SS*. Oxford University Press, 1966.

Stoeber, Hans. *Die Eiserne Faust*. Vowinkel Verlag, 1966.

Sydnor, Charles W. *Soldiers of Destruction*. Princeton University Press, 1977.

Waffen-SS in Action. Squadron Signal, 1973.

Walther, Herbert. *Die Waffen-SS*. Ahnert Verlag, 1971.

Weidinger, Otto. *Das Reich* Vols. 1–2. Munin Verlag, 1967–9.

Wegner Bernd. *The Waffen-SS*. Blackwell, 1990.

Wilmot, Chester. *The Struggle for Europe*. Collins, 1952.

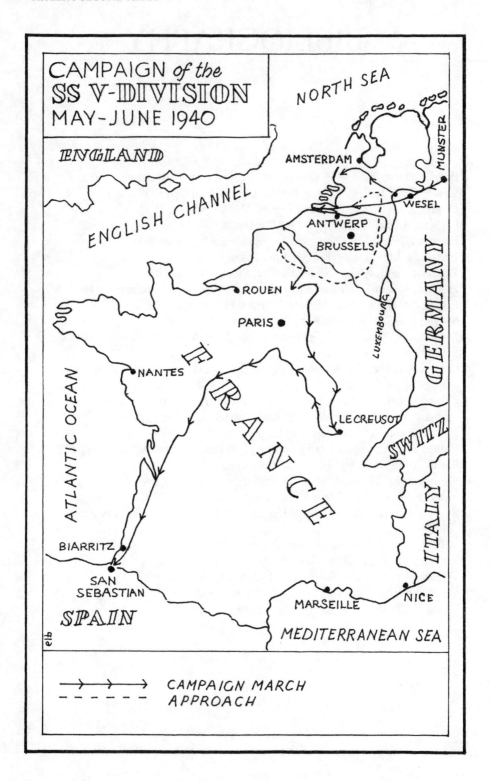

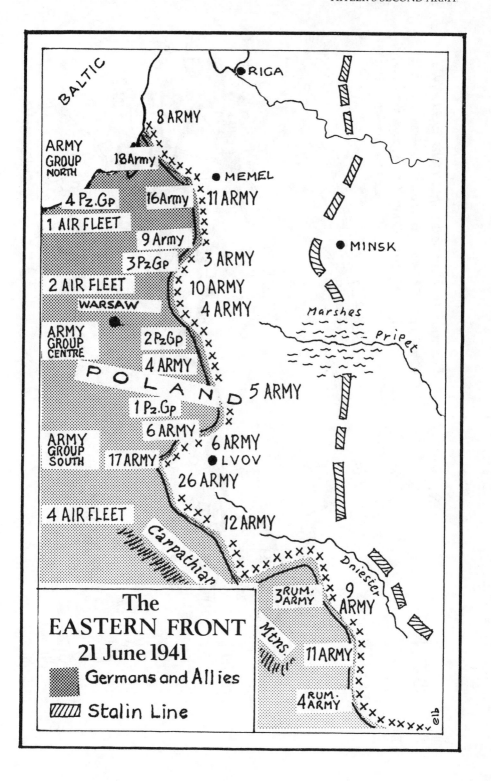

BALTIC

● RIGA

8 ARMY

ARMY
GROUP
NORTH

18 Army

● MEMEL

4 Pz.Gp   16 Army   11 ARMY

1 AIR FLEET

9 Army

3 Pz Gp   3 ARMY

2 AIR FLEET   10 ARMY

WARSAW   4 ARMY

● MINSK

Marshes   Pripet

ARMY
GROUP
CENTRE

2 Pz Gp

4 ARMY

P O L A N D   5 ARMY

1 Pz.Gp

6 ARMY

ARMY
GROUP
SOUTH   17 ARMY   6 ARMY

● LVOV

26 ARMY

4 AIR FLEET   12 ARMY

Carpathian

Dniester

3 RUM. ARMY   9 ARMY

The
EASTERN FRONT
21 June 1941
Germans and Allies
Stalin Line

Mtns.

11 ARMY

4 RUM. ARMY

elb

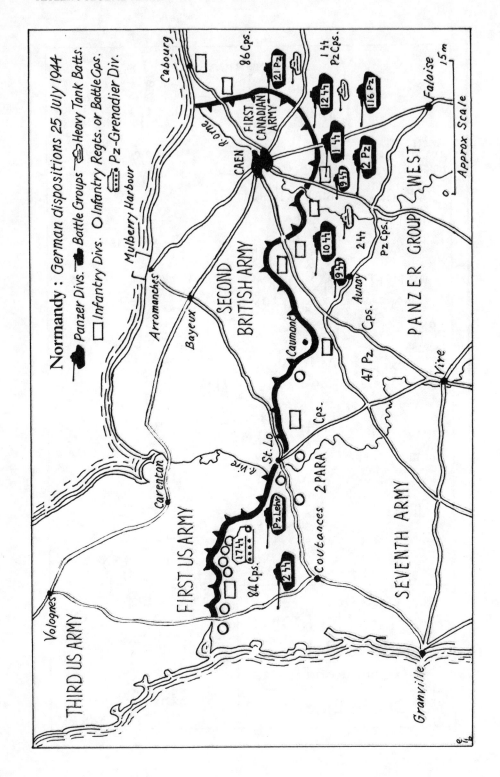

38 DIVISIONEN DER WAFFEN-SS

1. SS-Panzer-Division LSSAH

2. SS-Panzer-Division Das Reich

3. SS-Panzer-Division Totenkopf

4. SS-Pol.-Pz.-Gren.-Div. Polizei-Division

5. SS-Panzer-Division Wiking

6. SS-Gebirgs-Div. Nord

7. SS-Frw.-Geb.-Div. Prinz Eugen

8. SS-Kav.-Division Florian Geyer

9. SS-Panzer-Division Hohenstaufen

10. SS-Panzer-Division Frundsberg

11. SS-Frw.-Pz.-Gren.-Div. Nordland

12. SS-Panzer-Division Hitlerjugend

13. Waffen-Geb.-Div. der SS Handschar

14. Waffen-Gren.-Div. der SS (galizische Nr.1)

15. Waffen-Gren.-Div. der SS (lettische Nr.1)

16. SS-Pz.-Gren.-Div. RFSS

17. SS-Pz.-Gren.-Div. Götz von Berlichingen

18. SS-Frw.-Pz.-Gren.-Div. Horst Wessel

19. Waffen-Gren.-Div. der SS (lettische Nr.2)

20. Waffen-Gren.-Div. der SS (estnische Nr.1)

21. Waffen-Geb.-Div. der SS Skanderbeg

22. SS-Frw.-Kav.-Div. Maria Theresia (ungarische Nr.1)

23. SS-Frw.-Pz.-Gren.-Div. Nederland

24. Waffen-Geb.-Div. der SS Karstjäger

25. Waffen-Gren.-Div. SS Hunyadi (ungarische Nr.2)

26. Waffen-Gren.-Div. SS Gömbös (ungarische Nr.3)

27. SS-Frw.-Gren.-Div. Langemark (flämische Nr.1)

28. SS-Frw.-Pz.-Gren.-Div. Wallonie

29. Waffen-Gren.-Div. der SS Italien (italienische Nr.1)

30. Waffen-Gren.-Div. SS Weißruthenien (russische Nr.2)

31. SS-Frw. Gren. Div

SS-Frw.-Gren.-Div. Böhmen-Mähren

32. SS-Frw.-Gren.-Div. 30. Januar

33. Waffen-Gren.-Div. SS Charlemagne (französische Nr.1)

34. SS-Gren.-Division Landstorm Nederland

35. SS-Pol.-Gren.-Div. Polizei-Division (2)

36. Waffen-Gren.-Div. SS Dirlewanger

37. SS-Frw.-Kav.-Div. Lützow

38. SS-Pz.-Gren.-Div. Nibelungen

7 PANZER-DIVISIONEN • 8 PANZER-GRENADIER-DIVISIONEN • 3 KAVALLERIE-DIVISIONEN • 5 GEBIRGS-DIVISIONEN • 5 GRENADIER-DIVISIONEN • 10 WAFFEN-GRENADIER-DIVISIONEN

INDEX